Pop-Porn

Pop-Porn

Pornography in American Culture

Edited by
Ann C. Hall and Mardia J. Bishop

Westport, Connecticut
London

Library of Congress Cataloging-in-Publication Data

Pop-porn : pornography in American culture / edited by Ann C. Hall and Mardia J. Bishop.

   p. cm.

  Includes bibliographical references and index.

  ISBN 978-0-275-99920-9 (alk. paper)

  1. Pornography—United States.   2. Sex in mass media—United States.   I. Hall, Ann C., 1959–   II. Bishop, Mardia J., 1963–

HQ472.U6P68   2007

306.77—dc22   2007021028

British Library Cataloguing in Publication Data is available.

Library of Congress Catalog Card Number: 2007021028
ISBN: 978-0-275-99920-9

First published in 2007

Praeger Publishers, 88 Post Road West, Westport, CT 06881
An imprint of Greenwood Publishing Group, Inc.
www.praeger.com

Printed in the United States of America

The paper used in this book complies with the Permanent Paper Standard issued by the National Information Standards Organization (Z39.48-1984).

10 9 8 7 6 5 4 3 2 1

To our families and teachers

Contents

Introduction

ANN C. HALL
MARDIA J. BISHOP

In January 2001, George Bush was inaugurated president of the United States largely as a result of the "intern" incident of the previous Clinton administration. Bush's appeal, in the 2000 and 2004 elections, stemmed largely from his call to "family values," a new American morality, and an emphasis on the conservative Christian right, which many on that side argue established this country.[1] During that time, however, a strange phenomenon has occurred. In a nation committed to family values and morality, the consumption of pornography in popular culture has risen dramatically, perhaps more than in the history of the United States. What causes this phenomenon, this double standard, a national policy of morality versus the private citizens' voracious appetite for the prurient? This collection of essays attempts to offer some answers.

While many discussions have attempted to define pornography and distinguish it from "art," "erotica," or prime time televisions offerings, we will not attempt to do so in the scope of this introduction. Rather, we will allow each essay to offer its own definition, explicitly or implicitly, for as is frequently the case in the courts, on the television and computer screen, or the bookshelves of local libraries, porn,—ironically like beauty—is defined by the beholder. Instead, the collection examines how pornographic materials have become more prevalent in American culture, particularly George Bush's America, which defines morality as heterosexual monogamy only. Some essays examine how we use pornographic material. Others examine where it appears, and still others examine the effects of this material on our culture or question its ability to affect us in any way. All in all, the collection offers a comprehensive look at pornography in the 2000s in America under George Bush.

The incredible growth in the porn industry has been followed by a renewed interest in the study of porn. After a flurry of publications in the nineties, there was a dearth of work on pornography. In the early 2000s, however, some notable work began appearing which addressed our current porn saturated culture. Ariel Levy in *Female Chauvinist Pigs* examines what she defines as "raunch culture," arguing that women's participation in pornography as creators and consumers is not a source of empowerment, as posited by porn enthusiasts, but simply another way in which women are objectified, in this case, by other women.[2] Pamela Paul in *Pornified* demonstrates that excessive exposure to porn, particularly on the Internet, has detrimental effects on the porn consumers and the people in their lives.[3] Brian McNair's *Striptease Culture* examines the increased sexualization of culture and argues that it is beneficial for democracy in capitalist cultures because it encourages inclusion. He also argues that the fewer rules a society adopts regarding porn, the more rights and respect women in those cultures have.[4]

In *Porn Studies*, Linda Williams argues against the moral/immoral dichotomy that pervades porn studies. By focusing on hard-core porn films in particular, she shows that this film genre, like other genres, has its own conventions, conventions which, if examined carefully, express power relations detrimental to women.[5] Finally, Joseph Slade's *Pornography and Sexual Representation* not only offers a comprehensive compilation of research materials on porn, but it also examines pornography from "middle ground," neither endorsing the right's tendency to censor nor the left's tendency to view pornography as progressive.[6] Clearly, porn studies are still grappling with issues that have historically defined the field of study, as well as addressing and including the new media which makes porn much more accessible.

What makes this collection different from these other studies is its breadth of genres—film, radio, internet, print material, fashion, and hygiene are all represented here. This collection examines porn in our daily life, in our schools, in our homes, in our libraries—porn, as the commercial goes, in the fabric of our lives. Further, not all contributors share a negative view of pornography. Some see it as serving an important function. Others see it as a natural outcome of the capitalist system, and still others see it as a means of expression like any other means of expression. This diversity of opinions is not only entertaining and interesting, but it reflects our culture's contradictory views of pornography. Further, it illustrates, very clearly, how complicated the issue of porn is.

Katherine Kinnick's extensive overview of the increase of the consumption and availability of pornography begins the collection. Her encyclopedic overview of porn in the various forms of media, from print sources to fashion to film to music to the Internet, clearly establishes the ubiquity of the porno-graphic in our American culture. Through example after example, it is clear that pornography is mainstreamed. For Kinnick, what this means is that the American population is exposed to a "consistent representation of women and human sexuality that is molded by codes and conventions of pornogra-phy—codes developed around the exploitation, objectification and domina-tion of women." Like Andrea Dworkin before her, Kinnick concludes that the proliferation of pornography must be stopped by sixties-style activism. Certainly individuals have power, but there is greater power in numbers. She inspires readers to mobilize and put pressure upon the corporations creating the images.

Judith Roof's "Panda Porn, Children, Google, and Other Fantasies" chal-lenges the assumption that seeing pornographic imagery leads to porno-graphic or sexual behavior. Beginning with an arresting discussion of the manner in which the great Chinese Pandas in captivity are encouraged to mate by watching "Panda Porn," Roof demonstrates that seeing does not al-ways result in either believing or doing. She notes that in our culture, "images of sex present a three-pronged sociocultural threat." They provide informa-tion which leads to behavior which is enhanced by the visual and which results in an "irresistible and inevitable" imitation. The essay challenges these assumptions, and discusses the idealization of the Child in American culture, the preeminent victim of porn, according to anti-porn activists, and, accord-ing to Roof, the excuse for censorship. Keeping children away from porn on the Internet is the focus of the Google discussion, which highlights the very complex and frequently faulty definitions of porn that our culture employs.

Mardia Bishop's "The Making of a Pre-Pubescent Porn Star: Contemporary Fashion for Elementary School Girls" presents a differing view of the Ameri-can child. Her essay compellingly demonstrates how porn fashion infiltrates fashion for elementary school girls. Using contemporary body image theory, she discusses the psychological, physical, and economic effects that a porn fashion ideal has on little girls. Ultimately, she argues that profit value of the "sexy little girl" overrides the emotional health of the American girl for U.S. clothing manufacturers and perhaps society as a whole.

In another look at fashion, Hannah B. Harvey and Karen Robinson in "Hot Bodies on Campus: The Performance of Porn Chic" discuss porn in action through the porn-inspired fashions of college-aged women. Harvey and Rob-inson argue that by dressing suggestively, like a "porn star," college women are performing porn. Using performance theory and interviews with college-aged women, they examine this phenomenon on a Southern college campus. They note, for example, "pornography is not an inherent quality of any outfit, but the narrative frame and matrix of gazes surrounding and supporting a particular perception of bodies and artifacts."

Thomas Fahy's "*One Night in Paris* (Hilton): Wealth, Celebrity, and the Politics of Humiliation" examines America's obsession with celebrities, in this case Paris Hilton, the bad-girl heiress of the party circuit. Simply, Fahy asks, "why does she receive so much public attention?" Of course, there is her wealth and outrageous lifestyle, but there is also a desire to see her humiliated and denigrated, as in the amateur porn video, *One Night In Paris*, that appeared on the Internet one month before the premiere of *The Simple Life*, a show that films Paris and co-star Nicole Richie trying to work at "regular," simple jobs such as farming. According to Fahy, both the television series and the amateur porn film feed into America's love-hate relationship with wealth and fame. For those who do not have fortune and fame, one way to feel superior to those who do is through ridicule and pornographic objectification.

"*Fear Factor:* Pornography, Reality Television, and Red State America" by Jesse Kavadlo establishes the relationship between pornography and reality-based television. He notes that the 2000s "will be remembered as popular culture's decade of reality TV. But in the beginning, of course, there was pornography." The essay goes on to demonstrate that even television shows that are not explicitly pornographic share elements with pornography. Further, these shows exist within a conservative political culture that redefines reality on an "as needed basis." Kavadlo notes, "America is not living in reality but reality TV," a reality that enacts the "raw market forces of capitalism," showing that "people will do anything for money." And, finally, that the American and Iraqi people, like porn stars, are ultimately disposable.

Ann C. Hall's "Freak Shows in Jesus Land: Howard Stern and George Bush's America" illustrates the way in which Howard Stern uses pornography to liberal political ends. She also examines the very nature of the radio media which affords Stern a unique way to communicate his personal brand of porn. By investigating the difficulties Stern had with the Federal Communications Commission before his move to Sirius, the essay illustrates that pornography may be one of the only ways to break through the wall of conservative propaganda in a capitalist system, a system notorious for its ability to deactivate dissension.

"Toys Are Us: Contemporary Feminisms and the Consumption of Sexuality" by Dawn Heinecken examines pornography on a much more practical and personal level in the form of sex toys and their advertising campaigns. By examining the promotional material of two shops, Babeland and Smitten Kitten, she shows that the marketing reflects America's contradictory attitudes towards porn. On the one hand, the ads empower women, offering them sex toys that put them in charge of their own orgasm and sexuality. On the other, the marketing emphasizes traditional female roles such as a nurturing stance towards the environment, offering non-toxic latex products, for example, or demonstrating how kind and supportive the companies are to their employees.

Susann Cokal also gets up close and personal in "Clean Porn: The Visual Aesthetics of Hygiene, Hot Sex, and Hair Removal." Her essay examines the recent increase in pubic hair styling among American women. By examining the history of the representation of the pudendum, she demonstrates that this current trend is a natural outgrowth of American Puritanism, cleanliness being next to godliness. That is, women may be having their genital hair cut for sexual purposes, but the sexual overtones are minimized by this clinical phenomenon which also supports America's quest for hyper-hygiene.

Sue Banks's essay takes us out of the home and into the public libraries. "Your Privacy's Showing: Pornography at Your Local Library" examines the reports of library patrons who view porn, as well as those who raise claims that libraries encourage porn. Perhaps more than any other essay in the collection, Banks's work vividly illustrates the paradoxical nature of porn in American culture. By their very mission, libraries honor and defend expression, the pursuit of knowledge and learning, no matter what the cost. Consequently, public libraries are at the heart of the culture wars regarding pornography in contemporary America.

As we hope this collection illustrates, the question of porn in American culture is a complicated one. Without even examining the various definitions of pornography, there is still a great deal to be done. What do we do with pornographic material? How do we use it? What is it doing to us, if anything? All these questions are raised, and some of them are answered, but what is clear from this collection is that pornography in America is here to stay, and interpreting its significance will continue to foster discussions by scholars in the future. We hope that this collection helps to inspire further discussion and examination.

—————— 1 ——————

Pushing the Envelope: The Role of the Mass Media in the Mainstreaming of Pornography

KATHERINE N. KINNICK

TV will not rest until it's shown us everything. With every year, as the shock of the new becomes the yawn of the old, television shows us more and more, like a rising tide.

—*Fenton Bailey, producer of HBO's Shock Video*[1]

Every day, Americans are inundated with a mind-boggling collage of images and messages from the mass media. With greater access than ever before, we are tuned in, plugged up, and rarely able to escape the media's reach, even if we wanted to. Media historians and textbooks characterizing the current media frontier inevitably focus on technological advancements and the media adoption patterns of the "digital generation." Recently, however, some media scholars and critics began voicing a different take on American media in the 2000s: The new millennium is shaping up as a decade of sleaze. The forces driving the mainstreaming of porn are manifold, from the profit motive to the competitive rise of cable television, from fuzzy governmental regulations to public desensitization to sexually explicit content. What is clear is that the line between pop culture and porn culture is blurring, as the sexual themes, language, and production techniques that have made porn a multi-billion dollar industry are increasingly, and intentionally, cropping up in mainstream music, movies, TV and video games.

It's been called "pimp culture,"[2] "raunch culture,"[3] and "everyday porn."[4] While not porn itself (this is debatable to some), it is overtly sexual media content that is unprecedented in its explicitness, accessibility and pervasiveness. Janet Jackson's now infamous breast-baring "wardrobe malfunction" during the 2004 Superbowl launched a renewed focus on defining and regulating media indecency and community standards. But it is just one example among many in the media landscape of the new millennium. Porn has infiltrated television, advertising, video games, movies and mainstream magazines.

On television, we witnessed pop princess Britney Spears French-kissing Madonna at the 2003 MTV music video awards. The women of *Sex and the City* (1998–2004) discussed their sexual escapades, including S&M, anal sex, and erotic urination, and created a hit series. The 2003 Fox Television network mating game *Married in America* featured contestants cavorting with strippers and topless prostitutes, and licking whipped cream from each other's bodies. Most recently, the E! Television network debuted *The Girls Next Door*, a "reality show" that follows Playboy playmates living at the Playboy mansion and "documents" their exploits, including soft-core photo shoots.

In advertising, "sex sells" has morphed to new levels of explicitness, epitomized by a 2005 Carl's Jr./Hardee's ad featuring Paris Hilton in a soft-porn-styled carwash commercial. Clad in a barely-there swimsuit and stilettos, Hilton lathers herself and writhes against the car in scenes that borrow filmic techniques from porn conventions, including the "money shot" with the hose exploding with water from between her legs.[5] Similarly, magazine ads for teen-targeted Skechers shoes deployed pop singer Christina Aguilera in porn clichés as a garter belt-clad nurse with a phallic hypodermic needle; as a cop in short shorts with handcuffs and a suspect bent over the hood of a car, and, as a plaid-skirted schoolgirl and over-sexed teacher. Beer commercials gave us female mud wrestlers who seemed to be enjoying the twosome. Hour-long infomercials for the video series, *Girls Gone Wild*, tease viewers into subscribing to the series with "amateur" style video clips of college-aged women baring their breasts, lifting their skirts, kissing each other and simulating sexual acts.

Television networks' own promos for upcoming programs are among the most sexually explicit ads on television, a point noted by parents when these promos air during family-friendly programming. For example, ABC's promos for *The Bachelorette*'s "*Trista and Ryan's Bachelor and Bachelorette Party Special*" showed a topless stripper with digitally blurred breasts straddling Ryan. The promo aired twice during ABC's *A Charlie Brown Christmas* in December 2003, as reported in the *New York Daily News*.[6] Sexually-charged promos for *Desperate Housewives* aired during family-friendly *Extreme Home Makeover* and *Monday Night Football,* outraging parents watching with children.

Nowhere is the mainstreaming of pornography more evident than in music videos. Rap and hip hop music, in particular, rose to a level of objectification and misogyny that was deplored by *Essence* magazine in a multi-issue series during Spring 2005 called "Take Back the Music."[7] Women in rap videos are rarely presented in any role other than sexual objects, and are routinely referred to "in terms normally reserved for prostitutes and canines."[8] A 1997 study documented numerous instances of simulated intercourse, oral sex, masturbation and sexually suggestive dancing in rap videos, which had many more sexually explicit depictions and references than videos of other music genres.[9] The music video for rapper Nelly's 2004 single "Tip Drill" (slang for sex with a woman who has a good body but an unattractive face) made the commodification of women literal by depicting the rapper running a credit card through a woman's buttocks. That the line is blurring between music video and porn is evidenced by the fact that top-selling rappers have "branched out" to hosting triple-X-rated videos, including Snoop Dogg and Hustlaz, who had the top selling adult videos of 2001 and 2003, respectively, as well as 50 Cent, Lil' Jon and Ice-T.[10]

Video games also reflect the trend. In July 2004, an explicit porn video clip was discovered in the nation's top-selling video game, *Grand Theft Auto: San Andreas*. The *Grand Theft Auto* series has held the top spot among video games for much of the past five years. "M"-rated *Grand Theft Auto: Vice City* was the best selling video game of 2002. It allowed players to hire hookers, engage in sex in a rocking car, and then earn extra points by punching or killing the prostitutes and stealing their money back. According to the 2003 Gallup Annual Teen Survey, 75 percent of boys 17 and younger reported that they have played at least one of the games in the *Grand Theft Auto* series.[11] Across video game titles and genres, female characters are routinely sexualized with exaggerated (and in some cases bouncing) breasts, tiny waists and long legs, in skintight or skimpy clothing.

Movies have left parents wondering whether there has been ratings "inflation." Would what qualifies for a PG-13 rating today have been rated R several years ago? Would those rated R today have been rated X? Experts say yes. R-rated theatrical films have "upped the ante . . . by increasing the sexual tease factor for the essential teen market, and film producers increased the level of explicitness of foreplay and intercourse in movies tailored for adults."[12]

Magazine content in mainstream men's, women's and teen magazines is increasingly sexually explicit. Cover teasers routinely mention orgasm and sexual techniques. A recent study of magazines targeting teen girls found an average of more than 80 column inches of text per issue on sexual topics.[13]

Of course, *real* pornography is just a click away on home computers, and it seeks us out through unsolicited pop-up ads and spam e-mails. The widespread adoption of the home computer and Internet during the past decade has exploded the accessibility and profitability of the porn industry. "Porn has always been there, but it's always been in a lower volume [until the computer]," according to Michael Bradley, a psychologist and author specializing in adolescence. In recent years, he says, "It's been like a tidal wave that has swept over kids."[14] Child-protection filters have been shown to be ineffective.[15]

What the media examples above share in common is a consistent representation of women and human sexuality that is molded by the codes and conventions of pornography—codes developed around the exploitation, objectification, and domination of women. Pop culture and porn culture have become part of the same seamless continuum. As these images become pervasive in popular culture, they become normalized, unremarkable, and increasingly, accepted.

The vocabulary and "tools" of porn culture have spilled over into common usage, product marketing, and plastic surgery. MTV's popular car makeover show is called *Pimp My Ride*. Britney Spears and Kevin Federline's wedding party, including their parents, donned robes custom embroidered with "pimp" and "slut" on the back to party post-wedding rehearsal. Suburban fitness clubs offer soccer moms striptease exercise classes, and the stripper pole is now a hot piece of exercise equipment. Midriff and thong fashion have taken over the middle school crowd; Brazilian bikini waxes their mothers'. Plastic surgeons in the U.S. are experiencing a boom in demand for breast implants and vaginoplasty. As featured on the plastic surgery reality show *Dr. 90210*, the latter is designed to provide an "acceptable" appearance to post-childbirth women by trimming the labia to reduce their size and strategically injecting fat in areas that need "plumping."

The anecdotal examples noted here are supported by empirical studies that indicate the use of overt sexual content across all forms of media has increased dramatically in recent years, including in television,[16] video games,[17] music,[18] and advertising.[19] According to the longest-running systematic study of sexual content in television programming, the Kaiser Family Foundation's biennial *Sex on TV* study, the amount of sex on television nearly doubled from 1998 to 2005, due to both an increase in the number of shows that include sexual content as well as an increase in the number of sexual scenes within those shows.[20] Nearly eight in ten prime-time shows on broadcast networks now include sexual content. In those shows, the number of sexual scenes per hour has increased, from an average of 3.2 in 1998 to 5 in 2005. The rate is higher in the top 20 shows among teens, with an average of 6.7 scenes per hour. Similarly, Reichert and Carpenter found that magazine ads became significantly more explicit from 1983 to 2003, with the proportion of suggestively clothed female models doubling during this time period, while the attire of male models remained stable.[21] While 63 percent of MTV videos contained sexual imagery in 1992,[22] eleven years later, a study of music lyrics in the *Billboard* top songs of 2003 found 100 percent of rap and 80 percent of top hip hop songs referred to intercourse or oral sex.[23] These studies confirm that sexual content is pervasive in American media, and that it impacts media consumers' sexual knowledge, attitudes, and behaviors.[24]

HOW DID WE GET HERE?

How did we get here from the days when *I Love Lucy* couldn't use the word "pregnant," Rob and Laura Petrie slept in separate beds on *The Dick Van Dyke Show*, and Elvis was filmed from the waist up on *The Ed Sullivan Show*? The sleazification of today's media is a result of the confluence of a number of contributing factors, including historical media trends, the meteoric growth and profitability of the porn industry, ambiguous indecency standards, and Americans' continuing reluctance to criticize artistic speech.

A Quick and Dirty History of Media Sex

Pushing the boundaries of acceptability to gain public attention is nothing new. As Sivulka points out, at the turn of the last century, the Woodbury Soap Company's slogan, "the skin you love to touch," was considered a racy message.[25] In the 1920s, following several scandals involving Hollywood stars, public outcry against perceived immorality in Hollywood led some cities to pass bans on the exhibition of questionable films. To protect itself against potential government regulation, the movie industry formed the Production Code Administration in 1934. The Production Code provided a specific list of forbidden content, including "scenes of passion," nudity, and suggestive dances, and required that "the sanctity of the institution of marriage and the home be upheld at all times."[26] All films were required to obtain a certificate of approval from the PCA before being released. While the PCA appeared to be a noble gesture of corporate responsibility, it also hastened the dissolution of local movie licensing boards, and thus unfettered distribution of films. Through the Code, systematic industry self-censorship took place until the late 1950s. By this time, the competitive threats of television, racier foreign films, and a 1952 Supreme Court ruling (*Joseph Burstyn, Inc. v. Wilson*) that gave motion pictures First Amendment protection for the first time since 1915, led studios to defy the Code and release their films without approval. As self-censorship became increasingly unpopular among movie studios, it was selectively enforced and then abandoned. The Production Code was replaced in 1968 with the voluntary, age-based ratings system in use today, which allows greater leeway for sexual content.

The issue for television in the 1960s wasn't sex, but violence. The Surgeon General's Scientific Advisory Committee on Television and Social Behavior framed television violence as a threat to public health. Its report, released in 1972, chastised the television networks for increasingly violent programming and concluded that television violence is harmful to children. The networks responded by trading violence for sex. "Jiggle shows," notably *Charlie's Angels* and *Three's Company*, a sitcom whose humor was based almost exclusively on sexual innuendo, soon followed, as did prime-time trysts on soap operas like *Dallas* and *Dynasty*, and the late-night comedy *Soap*, which pushed the envelope further with irreverent references to promiscuity, homosexuality and impotence. By the late 1970s, the frequency of sexual content on television had exploded, with one study finding a ten-fold increase in sexual innuendos and a 25-fold increase in references to sexual intercourse between the mid-1970s and 1980.[27]

Out of Sync: A New Model Needed to Explain Media Sex

The "pendulum" metaphor is frequently used to describe the historical swings from conservatism to liberalism in American politics and culture. It has also been applied to media content. Increasing sexual explicitness in media is simply a sign of the times, and according to this metaphor, a reflection of the media moving in sync with an increasingly liberal society. The pendulum model, however, does not explain how current raunch culture can coincide with what is widely regarded as an era of social conservatism, a time when family values have proven key to winning elections. If the pendulum model were true, then in conservative social climates, media content would also become more conservative. This has not happened, however, in the more than 30 years since the Surgeon General's report spurred a turn to greater sexual explicitness in media. Rather than the pendulum model, a more accurate metaphor for the media's obsession with sexual content is the action of the surf: constantly pounding the sand, incrementally, yet unrelentingly eroding the shoreline.

The surf-pounding-sand model is supported by the experience of the 1980s. During the conservative Reagan era, even as the AIDS epidemic raged, sexual explicitness on television continued to increase, while mentions of safe sex and STDs were rare.[28] Madonna flaunted what McNair calls "porno-chic" in music videos and a sexually explicit book.[29] Films featuring the porn industry, notably *Boogie Nights*, legitimized the industry. Hollywood had discovered that reaching teenaged males was critical to box office success. The "juvenilization" of film (a term coined by director Peter Bogdanovich)[30] that resulted, meant less complex plots and more sex, nudity, violent action and special effects. Teen favorites of the 1980s, including *Porky's* and *Fast Times at Ridgmont High*, included more sex than many adult-targeted R-rated films, with as many as 15 instances of simulated sexual intercourse in each film.[31] The trend continues to be evident in the way films are promoted today. "The objective of nearly every trailer is to get teenage boys' butts into seats . . . And that means going for as much violence and sex as you can jam into 2 1/2 minutes."[32]

In other 1980s developments, rap music, with themes of sex, violence and anti-authoritarianism, emerged as a controversial new music genre. Porn films, once accessible only in adult theaters, quickly transitioned to the new and booming home video rental market. Some objections to media content were raised during this period, notably criticism of explicit music lyrics launched by Tipper Gore, wife of then Vice-President Al Gore. The efforts of her Parents Music Resource Center ultimately led to parental advisory labels and industry self-regulation. But Gore herself was frequently pilloried in the media as a prude and a censor. Sexually explicit and misogynistic music lyrics burgeoned unabated. The rap group 2 Live Crew earned the distinction of becoming the first music group to have its lyrics in *As Nasty As They Wanna Be* declared obscene by the courts in 1990. Far from mirroring the political pendulum's swing to the right in the 1980s, media sex was on an unstoppable roll, impervious to the political climate.

The march toward ever-increasing sexual explicitness has continued through the 1990s to today. Cable television, unhindered by broadcast networks' mandate to "serve the public interest," began to take a bite out of network viewership in the 1990s. The networks, in response, pushed the envelope further to try to maintain market share against cable's edgier programming, which included unedited movies and Fox's sexually-charged, over-the-top sitcom, *Married . . . with Children*. Streitmatter contends that the entertainment media were not solely responsible for moving sexual content to center stage. Mainstream journalism has also jumped on the bandwagon, he argues.[33] The Monica Lewinsky/Bill Clinton scandal provided reason for the most stalwart news organizations to venture to new frontiers of sexual explicitness: discussing oral sex and semen stains was no longer taboo, but front-page news. The pattern continues today, as respected media figures and news outlets choose to spotlight and legitimize porn-culture topics. Barbara Walters, for example, chose Paris Hilton, still recovering from her sex-tape scandal, as one of her Ten Most Fascinating People of 2004. *Oprah* featured the stripper pole as the latest "must have" piece of exercise equipment. In *People* magazine's celebrity-spotting reports, strip clubs are mentioned as destinations of choice for Hollywood's in-crowd, including under-age actress Lindsay Lohan.

The legacy of this history is that today, sex-themed entertainment media are joined by news and current events programming in elevating porn culture to new levels of visibility and acceptability. For the most part, the increase in overtly sexual content has been gradual and incremental, enabling it to remain largely under the radar screen, but ubiquitous enough to build a tolerance among the public, until an event like the Janet Jackson miscue perforates the public consciousness. Whether in movies, television, music or magazines, when one media outlet shows it can raise its sexual explicitness quotient and gain market share without triggering a backlash, others follow and often up the ante. "Sleaze simply seems to mutate into more sleaze," says advertising columnist Barbara Lippert.[34] For example, she says, the success of *Maxim* magazine, launched in 1997 to target 18- to 34-year-old men with sexually provocative editorial content and advertising, led other men's magazines to feature more sexually explicit editorial and advertising content as well.

Chasing "Obscene" Profits

As the pornography industry has evolved from a world of seedy adult video stores and skin magazines to DVD, pay-per-view, and global Internet websites, the financial success of the porn industry has multiplied exponentially. Pornography is estimated to be a $20 billion a year industry in the U.S. alone,[35] more than double the Hollywood box office take for mainstream movies, which totaled $8.9 billion in 2005.[36] Not surprisingly, mainstream media corporations have taken notice. Not only are porn producers reaping the profits, but major corporations are happy to get a piece of the action, including cable and satellite providers and hotel chains that provide porn programming. *Forbes* magazine notes that Internet porn companies are now listed on the NASDAQ stock exchange.[37] The success of porn is built on digital technology, which has made porn cheaper, faster, and easier to produce, more widely available, and more profitable than ever before. New delivery systems provide a disinhibiting anonymity that makes porn considerably more enticing: people who never would have been caught dead entering an adult theater now can order pay-per-view or download porn from the Internet in the privacy of their homes. In addition, the advent of digital cameras and home webcams "democratized" the ability of amateurs to produce porn for mass audiences, making everyone a potential porn producer as well as consumer.[38]

Eager to boost their own bottom lines, mainstream media producers are increasingly borrowing the themes, filmic techniques and personnel of the porn industry. Britney Spears and Michael Jackson, among others, have hired porn directors for their video projects.[39] The documentary film *Dreamworlds II*, a staple of college gender and media courses, catalogs the thematic and filmic techniques of porn that are ubiquitous in music videos, including filming "from the male gaze:" panning the body, shooting up skirts and down cleavage, framing the action in the triangle formed by a woman standing with spread legs, and close-ups focusing only on body parts.[40] Themes borrowed from porn include shower scenes, schoolgirl themes that depict grown women as childlike, one man with multiple women, and the nymphomaniac who is always willing, always ready, and depressed when men aren't available. Andsager and Roe argue that music video content has evolved through a kind of social Darwinism, in which "survival of the sexiest" is the new standard for commercial success.[41] This all but ensures that artists will increasingly use sex and violence to be noticed.

It is ironic that porn-inspired media imagery of women is proliferating at a time when women have reached new heights of power in the workplace, in politics and, arguably, in family dynamics. This pattern is no coincidence, say some scholars, who suggest that the upswing in trivializing images of women directly parallels a subconscious backlash against women's power. Kilbourne, for example, has argued that the media's increasingly unachievable ideal of female thinness is a symbolic representation of "cutting women down to size" while at the same time the ideal male image has become increasingly buff, cut and powerful.[42] According to this view, the porn version of women proliferates because it reaffirms, rather than threatens, men's dominance in society.

Ambiguous Legal Definitions Enable the Proliferation of Sleaze

Unlike the comparatively clear-cut prohibitions once provided by the Hollywood Production Code, ambiguous legal definitions of the constructs of pornography, obscenity and indecency—still unresolved by the courts—have themselves contributed to the proliferation of media sleaze. The difficulty in defining what is pornographic is highlighted by Supreme Court Justice Stuart Potter's oft-quoted 1964 admission that, even though he could not define pornography, "he knew it when he saw it."[43] A 1986 report from the Attorney General's Commission on Pornography further muddied the waters by declaring that "not all pornography is legally obscene."[44] With the exception of child pornography, the only media content that is not protected as free speech under the First Amendment is that which is determined to be obscene. And therein lies the rub. Current obscenity standards rely on a three-point test laid out in *Miller v. California* in 1973:

- Whether the average person, applying contemporary community standards, would find that the work, taken as a whole, appeals to the prurient interest.
- Whether the work depicts or describes, in a patently offensive way, sexual conduct specifically defined by the applicable state law.
- Whether the work, taken as a whole, lacks serious literary, artistic, political or scientific value.

The subjective nature of these guidelines has made their practical application somewhat like nailing Jell-O to a wall. The issue is even more problematic for Web-based material which may be viewed by anyone anywhere, as courts have ruled that web producers can't be responsible for discerning "community standards" anywhere in the nation.

The Federal Communications Commission's indecency standards, applicable only for broadcast media, present similar challenges. The FCC may limit the broadcast over the public airwaves of sexual content that is determined to be "indecent," but not necessarily obscene. FCC indecency regulations prohibit the airing of content between 6 a.m. and 10 p.m. that depicts or describes sexual or excretory activities or organs in a patently offensive manner, when measured by contemporary community standards. Again, difficulties in interpreting these indecency standards make prosecution and conviction difficult.[45] The FCC has been criticized for sporadic and nonaggressive enforcement of its own standards. For example, the first FCC fine for indecent programming in the history of television was not levied until 2004, against a California station, and to date the FCC has never revoked a television station's license for indecency.

Industry Rating Systems Haven't Kept Up

Adding to the factors that have contributed to the mainstreaming of sexual content are the current voluntary parental advisory systems employed in music, video games, movies and television industries. The ratings systems were developed and are operated by industry trade associations whose members have a vested interest in avoiding "adults only" ratings. This creates an inevitable conflict between industry interests and the public interest, one that leads to very few instances of media being given "adults only" labels. For example, despite the content noted previously in the *Grand Theft Auto* series, only when an actual porn clip was revealed in *Grand Theft Auto: San Andreas* was the video game's rating changed from "Mature" to "Adults Only."[46]

"Every year we claim that video games continue to push the envelope on sex, violence and inappropriate language," say the authors of the Tenth Annual MediaWise Video Game Report Card, published by the National Institute on Media and the Family. The organization used data generated by PSVratings, a content-based ratings system measuring levels of profanity, sex and violence, to compare six M-rated games from the late 1990s to six from 2004. The authors also note, "The results couldn't paint a more clear picture of what we have said all along; the ratings aren't reflecting the changes in game content."[47] According to the study, in the nineties only 16 percent of M-rated games contained any profanity at all, and just 33 percent contained sexual content. By 2004, all of the M-rated games contained both profanity and sexual content. "Kids are six times more likely to see nude or partially nude figures in M-rated video games today than they were in the late 1990s. But the ratings haven't changed."[48]

Criticizing "Artists" is Politically Incorrect

If Americans are unhappy with media content, why aren't they speaking out? According to Robert Peters, president of media watchdog group Morality in Media, those who defend pornography "point to the proliferation of porn as proof that either everyone is viewing it or that people no longer deem [it] unacceptable."[49] While everyone may not find it acceptable, everyone, it seems, has a reason to keep silent. Few celebrities seem willing to criticize raunch culture—and in so doing, their own industries. Those who do, like comedian Bill Cosby, often face an intense backlash. For elected officials, criticizing pop culture inevitably means being positioned as a censor, something downright un-American. For women, criticizing sexist content may mean being labeled a "feminist," which has taken on a pejorative tone equivalent to "man-hater." Pornography and related subjects are avoided as divisive issues for feminist organizations, which saw their ranks split years ago into pro-porn and anti-porn camps, diluting the women's movement's power.[50] For some black women, public criticism of the profanity and misogyny of rap and hip-hop is equivalent to betraying black men. Older Americans may be oblivious to messages on stations they don't tune into, and young families are just too busy.

Some Americans may simply be unaware that the First Amendment does not give carte blanche to media. Based on the volume of sexual content that we already see, it would be reasonable that the average American simply doesn't know there are indecency standards, or what they curtail. Others have adopted a widespread philosophy of ethical relativism, an anything-goes approach that validates every expression as legitimate: "If someone wants to buy that, watch that, listen to that, it must be okay." "He's entitled to his opinion." "Who am I to judge?" No one feels qualified to be a moral arbiter, so no one speaks.

WHAT IS THE PROBLEM?

Media industries would have us believe that concern about sexual content in media is much ado about nothing. Common counterarguments tend to emphasize individual freedom and an assumption of lack of harm:

- Concern about sex in media is a symptom of a sexually repressed culture that needs to loosen up, and become more like its European counterparts.
- Soft-core imagery of sexy women isn't exploiting women, it's celebrating them.
- Sexual content may have some prosocial effects, including educating society about issues like sexual addiction and sexually transmitted diseases, and promoting greater understanding of gay and lesbian sexuality.[51]
- If Americans want to fill their heads with media sleaze, they have the right to do so.
- If children have access to this imagery, it's parents' fault, not the media's.

What is missing from these arguments are the important concepts of "the common good" and ethical responsibility of corporations and society. More importantly, they ignore more than 30 years of empirical evidence, including compelling recent studies of teenagers, that overwhelmingly support the case for harmful effects to both individuals and society.

Sexual Objectification Hurts Women

The dominant story that today's media tells about women is that women are sex objects—defined and valued by their body parts. It is a representation of women focusing on a narrow aspect of female sexuality, which is largely depicted in stereotypes based on male fantasy, rather than focusing on women's intellect, accomplishments, and abilities. Cultivation theory suggests that the media's influence on beliefs and attitudes is cultivated slowly over time, through years of exposure to similar themes that are consistent and reinforcing.[52] This cultivates views of sexuality and gender roles that are more similar to the media's version of reality than reality itself. Evidence shows that the effect is most pronounced in heavy television viewers, who rely on television as their window on the world. Even when other variables, such as education and income are controlled, heavy television viewers hold more stereotypic beliefs and attitudes about appropriate gender roles for women,[53] overestimate the prevalence of extramarital affairs and other sexual behaviors, and are less likely to support a qualified female candidate for president.[54] Cultivation theory suggests that the continued presentation of women as sex objects contributes to the maintenance of beliefs that trivialize women and limit their power in society.

Viewing sexually objectifying media content appears to prime men to focus on women's sexuality even in non-sexual settings. A number of experimental studies of the effects of viewing such content show that men who later interacted with women were more likely to focus on the women's physical appearance and disregard other attributes, such as what the women said.[55] The men also held increased expectations for women's sexual attractiveness and sexual permissiveness, and displayed greater dominance when interacting with women.[56] Exposure to even soft-core pornography that is demeaning to women has been shown to foster both attitudes condoning sexual aggression and actual sexual aggression in experimental studies.[57] As mainstream media content becomes increasingly indistinguishable from soft-core porn, it is not a huge leap to anticipate similar findings. A 1995 study of misogynistic rap music, for example, found participants who listened to the rap music exhibited greater sexual aggressiveness to a female research associate than subjects who listened to neutral rap music.[58]

In a nation and a time when women have more power than ever before, why do we tolerate exploitative images of women, and why do we still have epidemic rates of crimes against women, including date rape, stalking, and domestic violence? Why do so many women report sexual harassment at work, where women still make 75 cents for every dollar earned by men, and where so few have climbed to the highest rungs of corporate and political power? Could it be that there is something about the way that we're socializing our citizens to think about women that is contributing to these problems?

Socializing Children with Sleaze

The debate about sex-saturated media rages loudest around issues concerning children and teens, including their access to sexual content in media, and the effects of media consumption on their sexual knowledge, attitudes and behaviors. One reason for concern is that American youth spend so much time with media: an average of 6.5 hours per day.[59] The typical daily media diet of 8- to 18-year-olds includes:

- 4 hours watching TV, videos, and DVDs;
- 2 hours a day listening to radio, CDs, tapes, or MP3 players, with older teens listening more;
- 1 hour using a computer for recreation, most often, games and instant messaging;
- 50 minutes a day playing video games—boys play longer, an average of an hour and a half;
- 43 minutes a day reading magazines, newspapers, or books not required for school.[60]

Some of these media activities are done simultaneously, such as reading while listening to the radio or television.[61] In addition, studies consistently show that black and Hispanic youth are heavier consumers of television, movies, video games and radio, exceeding the averages above.[62] "The sheer amount of time young people spend using media . . . makes it plain that the potential of media to impact virtually every aspect of young people's lives cannot be ignored."[63]

The spread of media technologies from the family room to children's bedrooms also means that many children routinely use media in isolation, without adult supervision.

- Among 8- to 18-year-olds, in 2005, two-thirds had a television in their bedrooms, and half had a VCR or DVD player in their bedrooms.[64] As early as 1999, 30 percent of youth reported receiving cable or satellite channels in their bedrooms.[65] By 2003, even 26 percent of children under age two had a television in their bedrooms.[66]
- By 2005, 50 percent of U.S. children had a video game system in their bedrooms.[67] It is noteworthy that only two percent of middle and high school students reported playing video games with their parents.[68]
- Nearly a third of 8- to 18-year-olds had a computer in their bedrooms in 2005.[69]
- Portable technologies mean that music and media follow children out of the house, with portable CD players, MP3 players (owned by 65 percent of 8- to 18 year olds), hand held video game players (owned by 55 percent) and portable DVD players.[70]

Not only are children and teens heavy media consumers, but the media channels they prefer often include more overt sexual messages than others. Kunkel et al. found that television programs viewed most frequently by teens have "unusually high" sexual content, more than prime time in general. Eighty-three percent of these programs had sexual behavior or verbal references, including 20 percent that contained explicit or implicit depictions of intercourse.[71] The most popular television network among teenage girls is MTV, where reality shows like *Real World* and up to half of music videos portray sexual themes.[72] Even in music videos where lyrics are not overtly sexual, visuals are often added that create an eroticism not present in the lyrics.[73] Beyond prime time, three to four million teens, particularly minority and low income teens, are estimated to be regular viewers of U.S. daytime soap operas,[74] the television genre most likely to portray sexual activity.[75]

Teens' movie, music and video game preferences are similarly sex-saturated. Leone summarizes studies which found that teens watched twice as many R-rated films than films of all other ratings, that R-rated films, on average, contain 14–21 sex acts, and that almost without exception, every R-rated film contains at least one nude scene.[76] Sixty-five percent of 8- to 18-year-olds listen to rap and hip-hop on a typical day.[77] In a 2005 national survey of 650 4th–12th grade youth, 86 percent of boys and 49 percent of girls say they have played M-rated video games.[78] Three-quarters of boys reported that M-rated games were included in their top five favorite games; 40 percent said an M-rated game was their favorite game. In another national study, two-thirds of 7th–12th graders say they have played the "M"-rated *Grand Theft Auto* game. Of these, 77 percent were boys.[79]

Particularly maddening to some parents is that some exposure of children to sexual media content is involuntary and impossible to prevent. From interstate billboards for strip clubs, to magazine cover teasers at the check-out line, to spam e-mails and network promos, even vigilant parents cannot protect their children all of the time. Involuntary exposure to online porn is among the disturbing possibilities. A nationwide survey of 10- to 17-year-olds in 1999–2000 yielded the now oft-quoted statistic that one in five children has been subjected to sexual solicitations while online, three-quarters of the time when searching the Internet, but a quarter of the time, through email or links imbedded in email or instant messages.[80] But mass media bear their share of blame for failing to protect children from involuntary exposure to adult material. A 2000 Federal Trade Commission report criticized the movie industry for adult-oriented movie trailers and promos on home videos that audiences may be exposed to involuntarily.[81]

Impact on Perceptions and Expectations about Sex

Because of its ubiquity, the media has replaced parents, peers, and schools as the leading sex "educator" in the United States.[82] But more than just a source of information, media plays an important role in adolescent sexual socialization. The stories the media tells about sex have been shown to influence perceptions about "normal" sexual patterns and practices,[83] including how sexual relationships evolve,[84] attitudes about casual sex,[85] and higher estimates of peers' sexual activities.[86] For example, adolescent viewers of daytime talk shows overestimated the frequency of teen sex, teen pregnancy and marital infidelity,[87] leading to the idea that "everybody's doing it." Researchers have found that college students' attitudes toward casual sex became more permissive after viewing shows that portrayed casual sex as routine and desirable, including *Ally McBeal, Dawson's Creek,* and *Friends.*[88] "Script theory" suggests that television's sexual scenarios provide "scripts" for young viewers that guide future behavior in sexual situations.[89] Regardless of their level of actual sexual experience, male college students who viewed more sexual content on television than those who did not expected a broader range of sexual activities with their partners. Heavy viewers of television with sexual content who were female, expected sex to occur sooner in a relationship than females who were not heavy viewers of sexual content.[90]

Of particular concern are messages from pop culture that equate young women's sexual objectification with sexual empowerment. "All the things that feminism once reviled—*Playboy*, strippers, wet t-shirt contests—all are currently being embraced by young women as supposed symbols of personal empowerment and liberation."[91] From the cover of *Cosmopolitan* to television reality shows, self-objectification is modeled to young women as the price to be paid to achieve a goal: to get the guy, to compete with other women, to win a challenge. Even highly successful women, like Ivy League-educated competitors on *The Apprentice* and Olympic athletes, feel they must prove their sexual desirability by stripping down in men's magazines. "Not one male Olympian has found it necessary to show us his penis in the pages of a magazine. Proving that you are hot, worthy of lust, and—necessarily—that you seek to provoke lust, is still exclusively women's work."[92]

Effects on Teens' Sexual Behavior

Several major studies since the 1990s have confirmed a causal relationship between exposure to sex on television and an acceleration of sexual activity leading to intercourse. An important 2006 study—one of the few to consider the impact of multiple media on pre-teens as young as 12—measured 12- to 14-year-olds' exposure to sexual content in television, movies, music, and magazines and found that exposure to sexual content accelerated sexual activity.[93] The authors found that the more sexual media a teen saw, the more likely he or she was to become sexually active over the next two years. Those who consumed the most sexual content were twice as likely to engage in intercourse than other teens. This confirms the findings of a national longitudinal survey of 1700 teens conducted in 2001–2002 that found that adolescents who were heavy viewers of sexual content initiated intercourse sooner and progressed more rapidly to intimate levels of sexual activity than light viewers.[94] When compared to light viewers of sexual content (10th percentile), heavy viewers (90th percentile) were twice as likely to begin to have sexual intercourse in the next 12 months. Whether the sexual content was verbal references or visual depictions made no difference in the acceleration of sexual activity. These findings ring true with parents and teens. In a national survey sponsored by the Kaiser Family Foundation, 83 percent of parents and nearly 75 percent of teens said that exposure to sex on television accelerates teens' involvement in sexual behaviors.[95]

The relationship between exposure to sexual content in media and sexual activity is bi-directional and mutually reinforcing. This means that not only does exposure to sexual content lead to increased involvement in sexual activity; but that adolescents who are sexually active are also more likely to seek out sexually laden media content.[96] This cycle is of particular concern given that the U.S. has one of the highest teen pregnancy rates of industrialized nations. In addition, there is evidence that young people are engaging in a range of sexual behaviors that were not common among teens of generations past. During the last decade, the proportion of teens and young adults engaging in oral sex has more than doubled.[97] While teen girls have always engaged in boy-chasing, porn culture has ratcheted up what girls feel they must do to win the guy: from dressing and dancing in an overtly provocative manner to engaging in sexual behaviors that are staples of male porn, including performing oral sex (which Levy found is rarely reciprocated),[98] and kissing other girls for the viewing pleasure of teenaged boys—a phenomenon labeled "bisexual chic" by news reports.[99]

HOW FAR CAN IT GO?

Is there a limit to what mainstream media will show us, or to what Americans will tolerate? The habituation effect says no. Experimental studies show that frequent exposure to sexual stimuli results in a gradual desensitization and decline in reaction. As viewers become habituated to sexual content, more titillating, "harder core" fare is needed to arouse and interest them.[100] The solution, for both the porn industry and mainstream media, has been to continually push the envelope, adding more explicit sex to maintain appeal.[101] Evidence suggests that over time, harder core content becomes increasingly acceptable, with viewers less likely to rate the material as offensive, pornographic or in need of restriction.[102] The powerful combination of human nature and the profit motive seem to ensure that, without externally imposed interventions, the momentum to show more explicit media content will continue.

Surveys show a majority of Americans support greater government intervention to enforce and control sex and violence on TV. They believe the FCC is doing a poor job, especially during prime time. A 2005 Pew Research Center survey found 75 percent of adults favored stricter government enforcement of television indecency rules, and a 2005 *Time* magazine poll found that 53 percent of Americans support stricter government controls of the amount of sex and violence on television.[103] In June 2006, as a result of public pressure from the Janet Jackson debacle, the maximum fine for violations of the broadcasting indecency law was raised from $32,500 to $325,000. The full impact of this change is yet to be seen.

Some government investigations do get results. In response to the Federal Trade Commission's 2000 report of industry practices that market violent entertainment to children, three movie studios announced that they would not run commercials for R-rated movies during television programs with an under-17 audience of more than 35 percent, or run ads in magazines and websites that attract a similar proportion of youth. Many pledged not to attach trailers for R-rated movies to PG-rated movies. Although a follow-up report showed general improvement,[104] violations included advertising R-rated movies on websites targeting young audiences, including gamespy.com and teenpeople.com.

California and Illinois have successfully enacted legislation to prohibit the sale and rental of M-rated video games to children.[105] However, across the country, getting retailers to *enforce* parental advisories is another matter. As part of its investigation of the marketing of adult material to minors, the FTC sponsored mystery shopper investigations of children's access to adult content. It found that retailers sold R-rated DVDs to 81 percent of unaccompanied 13- to 16-year-old teen shoppers. Similarly, 83 percent of teen shoppers were able to purchase explicit-content labeled music, including 69 percent of 13-year-olds. Sixty-nine percent of teen shoppers were able to by M-rated video games, including 56 percent of 13-year-olds.[106]

As noted previously, legal ambiguities often make legal approaches to regulation difficult. This has been particularly true with efforts to limit children's access to cyberporn. The Child Online Protection Act of 1998, which would make it a federal crime to a website to post materials "harmful to minors" unless accessibility is restricted to adults, was struck down by the courts in 2000, which said that it was impossible to apply local community standards to the Internet. The case remained mired in lower federal courts until March 2007 when the Act was ruled unconstitutional by a federal court judge in Philadelphia and a permanent injunction against its enforcement was issued.

Technological solutions to the access of minors to adult material have failed to live up to expectations. More than a decade after Congress initiated the current television program rating system and the V-chip became required on new televisions, they are widely regarded as ineffective.[107] The problem is not with the technology, but with parents who don't use it. A recent national survey reveals a widespread lack of parental involvement in children's media use:

- Half of all 8- to 18-year-olds say their families have no rules limiting television use.
- Only 6 percent of 8- to 18-year-olds reported that their parents used parental control technology, such as the V-Chip, to control what they could see on television.
- Only 5 percent of 15- to 18-year-olds say their parents have imposed

rules based on the video game ratings system about which video games they can play.

- Only 14 percent say their parents check the parental advisories on music.[108]

In another national survey, 50 percent of parents admitted that they weren't present the last time their child bought a video game, and, more than 60 percent of 4th–12th grade youth (and 78 percent of boys) reported owning their own M-rated games.[109] More surprising, according to industry data reported by the Federal Trade Commission,[110] nearly 40 percent of M-rated video games purchased in 2002 were given to children younger than 17, suggesting that parents either don't pay attention to package labels, don't understand what the M-rating means, or know what it means but provide the game to their children anyway. As sexual content in media becomes increasingly accessible and intrusive, and as children become more technologically proficient than their parents, it will only become more difficult for parents to monitor their children's media usage, for instance, what they download onto an I-Pod, the web sites they visit, and television they watch in their own rooms.

Although the focus on children in the discussion of increasingly sexual media content is important, it should not be the only focus. The socialization process is life-long, and media continues to play a role in influencing the beliefs, attitudes and behaviors of adults long after they leave their teenage years behind. While parents have a special responsibility to speak out against media content they find offensive to their families, other adults have reason to take up the charge as well. Yet when it comes to complaining in ways that count about media content, Americans tend to be a passive bunch. This passivity in speaking out against offensive media content is an enabling factor that helps to perpetuate the mainstreaming of pornography. A 2003 *TV Guide* survey of 1,015 adults found that Americans were more likely to change channels than to call a network to complain about offensive content. Only 8 percent reported that they had ever done so.[111]

STEMMING THE TIDE OR SWIMMING UPSTREAM?

The responsibility for slowing the tide of the mainstreaming of pornography should not rest solely on the shoulders of individual viewers. As corporate citizens, media outlets have a social and ethical responsibility to develop reasonable boundaries for sexual content in editorial and advertising content. The actions media can take can be relatively simple. For instance, Morality in Media, an interfaith action group, has suggested extending the ban on broadcast indecency from 10 p.m. until midnight.[112] The Parents Television Council (PTC) has advocated a return to the "family viewing hour," when programming before 9 p.m. could be considered safe for children. In 2001, the PTC asked Fox to move *Boston Public*, a high school-based drama that aired at 8 p.m., to 10 p.m. "If it's too much to ask that they take a program that shows high school kids giving oral sex in the hallway and ask them to put it on at 10, then we're really in trouble," said PTC President L. Brent Bozell III.[113] These suggestions have received little attention from broadcasters or cable networks.

If sex is here to stay, then media can demonstrate their social responsibility by making a greater effort to incorporate messages dealing with sexual risks and responsibilities when sex is portrayed. Studies of television show that prosocial messages can have a positive influence on viewer attitudes and behaviors about sexual health issues. When *Friends* featured an episode revolving around condom failure, for instance, a post-show telephone survey identified teens who had seen the show and found that 10 percent had talked with an adult about condom effectiveness because of the episode.[114] College freshmen who watched TV dramas that depicted characters experiencing regret after having casual sex expressed more negative attitudes toward premarital sex and more critical judgments of the moral character of the sexually active characters.[115] Despite these positive findings, media by and large are not providing prosocial messages. Even when television characters engaging in sexual activity are teens, fewer than one in four of these episodes included references to risks and responsibilities.[116]

When media are not responsive, consumers and activist groups resort to more extreme tactics. Complaints to the advertisers who sponsor objectionable programming, as well as boycotts of their products, have proven to be effective. Letter-writing campaigns and boycotts are frequently spearheaded by media watchdog groups and religious organizations. In recent years, The American Decency Association, a Christian activist group, sent weekly letters to advertisers on Howard Stern's radio show, quoting examples of Stern's raunch-filled, on air comments. According to the ADA's data, 90 percent of advertisers withdrew their advertising as a result of the campaign,[117] and the ADA took partial credit for Stern's move to satellite radio in 2006. Similarly, the blinder covers now in common use by retailers to obscure sexually explicit magazine covers in their check-out lanes are the result of a letter-writing campaign to the CEOs of national grocery chains by Morality in Media.[118]

Grassroots protests that can capture the attention of the news media have also achieved results. In October 2005, a Pittsburgh girls' group launched a "girlcott" against clothier Abercrombie & Fitch, after t-shirts appeared in the store that read, "Gentlemen Prefer Tig Old Bitties," and "Who Needs Brains When You Have These."[119] After the girls appeared on *The Today Show*, the store pulled the t-shirts off the shelves. The Internet now makes it easier for individuals who would like to complain about media to locate and join forces with organizations that can channel concern into mass action. In addition, consumers can find contact information needed to send complaints to media outlets, advertisers, the FCC and the FTC.

The mainstreaming of pornography is about the inundating of the American public with media content that is borderline pornographic, but not explicit enough (essentially showing frontal nudity or the sex act itself) to be ruled obscene. In this collage of media images, sex is distorted and commodified, and women are trivialized and objectified. If what we see in mass media is a litmus test for the state of gender relations and societal values, then the new millennium's test results are alarming. The scientific evidence provides a compelling argument that media sleaze is harmful on individual and societal levels, and that action to stem the tide is merited. As the line continues to blur between porn and pop culture, we can expect to see more debate about the conflicts between freedom of expression versus public morality, and individual responsibility versus corporate and government responsibility. And that would be in everyone's best interest.

2

Panda Porn, Children, Google, and Other Fantasies

JUDITH ROOF

Giant pandas are apparently a bit on the prudish side. Or it may be that they lack the drive and imagination to discover what humans believe are either the pleasures or the frantic instincts of mating. Not vigorous copulators in the wild, pandas are even more reluctant to take part in breeding activities in captivity. Of course, even in the most hospitable zoo, the circumstances haven't been exactly propitious for giant panda courtship. Pandas lack sufficient exercise. They rarely have other giant pandas as companions, and do not share in a multi-generational panda society. A choosey beast, giant pandas' blind dates give them no range of partners from which to select and no chance to find their stride in the prolonged mating rituals in which females in heat climb trees and let males fight it out below. The result is that very few captive males are capable of breeding naturally.

Because it is desirable to maintain substantial numbers of endangered species such as the giant panda, the answer has been to use artificial insemination, which has produced successful panda births. Wishing, however, to increase the numbers of captive breeding stock and to retain some memory of a panda breeding legacy, panda specialists have decided that pandas need to take more of the initiative themselves. One answer has been to show pandas movies of other pandas copulating. The strategy was first used in China in 2000 without appreciable results. Researchers tried the ploy again in 2002, this time showing groups of six-year-old male pandas (six being the age of panda sexual maturity) a video tape of giant pandas mating. Zoo official

27

Zhang Hemin commented that "Through this kind of sex education, we expect to arouse the sexual instincts of giant pandas, enhance their natural mating ability and raise their reproductive capacity."[1] As the theory goes, like chimpanzees that will imitate humans smoking cigarettes, pandas will imitate what they see other pandas doing and thus regain the panda culture of which captivity has deprived them.

Aside from issues of how animals consume mediated visual images, the panda ploy assumes an entire chain of interesting propositions about the relation between seeing sexual behaviors and imitating them borrowed from everyday assumptions about the human consumption of sexually explicit material. First, the strategy assumes that seeing pornography inevitably launches its viewers into a state of sexual excitement, if not spurring them to actual sexual activity with others (or vice versa). Second, it assumes that panda viewers identify with properly sexed panda positions and simply copy them. Third, breeding and sexuality in general are catalyzed by knowledge. A process which has long been thought to have been instinctive behavior has somehow, in the case of pandas, become an effect of nurture and enculturation. Instinct has disappeared and with it panda sex and panda cubs. A slice of virtual culture, it is thought, will refresh pandas' instinctual memory.

In human culture, images of sex present a three-pronged sociocultural threat. First, they provide knowledge about behaviors and presumed feelings. Second, knowledge of sexuality directly incites imitative behaviors and/or, worse, appropriate titillation. Knowledge leads to action leads to feelings. Third, visual models are irresistible and the inevitable mode of their consumption is imitation. The idea that viewers will imitate in some fashion what media presents is a time-honored one, sustaining campaigns for the control and censorship of media. And in the case that viewers do not literally reproduce the activities they see, then they will be at least incited to experience the feelings that accompany such activities. Viewing sexual activity destroys innocence, innocence being a supposed state of ignorance combined with a certain purity of feeling. Pandora's box being opened, previously innocent viewers will avail themselves of an entire range of lascivious feelings, which are themselves, in certain ways of thinking, the real evil, or in the case of pandas, the desired end. Unless we want offspring, innocents should neither know nor experience sexual feelings.

We might think that using panda porn as a strategy to encourage panda mating is merely informational, its exemplars instructional rather than stimulating. Pandas' reluctance to breed is a mechanical rather than an emotional issue, which can be resolved with a do-it-yourself video. No one is particularly worried about panda feelings—about the suddenly ruined innocence of panda virgins or traumatized young panda males with fears of inadequacy. In the wake of instructional videos, however, panda keepers report that the boys "show signs of excitement while watching film." Knowledge indeed leads to titillation for non-humans, and maybe, judging by the amount of media attention the ploy has garnered, for humans as well, who are treated to images of mating pandas on the internet.

From the perspective of the human, imitation is clearly a virtue in the realm of the non-human. Which is one reason why panda porn, though a newsworthy novelty, doesn't really pique our sense of decency or offend the hair trigger alarm of twenty-first century human morality. Unlike other animals such as dogs or horses, whose training occurs through complex systems of communication and reward, pandas, like the great apes, occupy a quasi-human space, like that of a child. Instructing the innocent panda in the ways of the flesh will hopefully result only in a brief exchange of fluids and sweet little baby pandas whose toy-like size makes them seem even more precious and innocent. As we imagine children do, chimpanzees and pandas imitate, where such imitations are understood to be almost devoid of feelings or understanding, being instead a set of empty gestures, the taking on of an action only vaguely associated with a position or circumstance. We don't expect pandas to fantasize, become perverted, or experience sexual enjoyment. Instead, we understand panda imitation to be a return to properly instinctive behavior where instinct itself is automatonic (though the boys get excited) rather than emotional or even sexy. Imitations represent a compromise, a stage of maturing in which children and animals (such as chimps in clothing) can try on the postures of adulthood without suffering or enjoying the knowledge and desire that mar it. Like our imaginary of the child as a pure site to preserve and protect, pandas are surrogate children onto whom we displace our nostalgia for ignorance and our desire to desire. While we want pandas to reach the fulfillments of adulthood, which we imagine to happen pretty dispassionately, we want children to remain the pure, ignorant, unsexual beings our own desires require them to be. Seeing copulating pandas is one thing for pandas; seeing humans copulate is another thing for the human child who must remain the site of projected purity in a culture which simultaneously seeks and denies sexual gratifications.

In stating this, I am not claiming that children do not consume images differently than adults or that if they see sexual material they necessarily understand it. I am suggesting, following the estimable work of James Kincaid, that our fantasy of the child is not about actual children at all, but is about preserving in their image a necessary but imaginary locus of purity and ignorance in relation to which our own desires can operate.[2] We project onto children our own salacious interpretations and responses, against which we then devise policies to protect children. These policies, which try mainly to restrict the knowledge believed to spark a cascade of undesirable effects, operate in contradictory ways. On the one hand, we have come to believe that children are not the same as adults. On the other hand, despite that difference, children's exposure to information must be restricted because we believe that children will simultaneously be psychically damaged by sudden exposure to material we imagine they will not understand and will probably misinterpret, and, that they will respond to that material the same way adults would—with curiosity, interest, and pleasure. We fear they will be prematurely titillated, which will inevitably lead to a life of tragic sexual dissipation. Or we fear that the purity they represent for adults will be marred forever, with consequences less about the child than about the culture which depends upon sustaining the site of innocence that is the Child.

Sexuality or a lack thereof, we imagine, constitutes a large part of the difference between children and adults, a tenacious idea Sigmund Freud shockingly debunked in *Three Essays on the Theory of Sexuality* in 1905.[3] Anyone who has ever been a child knows that such lack is not the case. It may be true that childhood sexuality does not respond in the same way to the same kinds of stimuli as adult sexuality, but it is difficult for us to know, since the only concepts and language we have about sexuality and desire refer to the experiences of adults. If we really wanted to monitor children's sexuality, we might worry more about their contacts with other children and their parents. But the question of children's sexuality is actually beside the point, since what actual children feel is irrelevant to the cultural fantasy that is the child. What that fantasy suggests we worry about is not the destruction of children's innocence through sexual knowledge and feelings, but our forced recognition that the site of innocence we believe to be the child will be abruptly and prematurely eliminated, an effect that forces adults to see how the imaginary Child operates in the management of their own desires.

This fantasy Child is the construction whose purity is preserved through the sets of contradictory policies by which we police representations. For example, the idea of the literal imitation of image content constitutes one contradictory set of ideas. It is generally accepted that children learn through imitation.[4] They do what they see others doing. The mechanism of this imitation is less well understood, as it is a complex, highly developed capability. Children do not always imitate what they see, imitate actions exactly nor indiscriminately, nor do they imitate everyone they are around. Often, they invent their own performances. We do know for example, that children of a certain age are likely to repeat swear words they hear. But in so doing are they adding to their vocabularies or are they more attracted by the affect that accompanies such expostulations? Does it matter who says the words? Why do they repeat those words and not others? Is it the number of syllables? "Fuck" might be a problem, but is "motherfucker" too long?

The notion that children indiscriminately imitate provides what appears to be a rational justification for our limitation of media content. Certain materials—adult nudity, swear words, graphic violence, the accidental revelation of a nipple—are restricted to broadcast times when it is assumed all good children are in bed. We demand that children should not see these things in the media, even though children may see them often in their own lives (nipples probably, but not specifically Janet Jackson's nipple). What young people see must be controlled because impressionable beings, such as pandas and human children, will respond to such sudden and unwelcome knowledge by attempting to do what they see. What, however, is the problem with their imitating? Will imitations, as with pandas, suddenly thrust them into parenthood? Or does the embarrassing occasion of their imitation sully the category of the innocent Child, and reveal perhaps that children have never really been that tabula rasa all along. When children begin to imitate what they see, which they sometimes do, not because they have somehow gotten hold of contraband images, but because they are children, their imitations both compromise the fantasmatic category of the Child, and bring the lives and behaviors of the parents into question. Since we cannot perceive children as having any kind of perverse will of their own, the destruction of the fantasy of the Child becomes quite openly the problem of the adult, not only in so far as the system of projections and displacements of desire is disrupted, but also in a more literal, family values, bad parenting sort of way.

The fears about childish imitation depend on another contradiction about how we believe representations themselves work. The venerable institution of the "young person," whose fragile sensibilities have sustained campaigns against the representation of everything from sex education to violent dismemberment since the nineteenth century, depends upon the assumption that representations are in themselves dangerously efficacious.[5] This is not merely a matter of a knowledge that might catalyze feelings which then may suggest emulations. This is representation as a direct inoculation, as a kind of instant transformation more akin to concepts of instinct than reason, more like stimulus/response than subjective process, more like pandas than human (or more like the odd notion that children are to pandas as pandas are to adults). If pandas, who are after all, mere beasts, respond to sex videos by having sex (though it seems to take a bit of repetition to get them to that point), then human children who are purer and smarter than pandas will be all that more suggestible.

Not only, does such Podsnappery presume, do words and images instantly convey ideas and actions, but sexual ideas themselves are particularly seductive, especially when visually rendered. Print culture is irresistible but takes work and imagination, which makes it safer for children who are not quite sufficiently sophisticated to enable complete efficacy. Visual culture is more irresistible because it is instantly consumed (it is believed), the alluring "realism" of moving pictures too much to fend off. So, on the one hand, we believe representations to be completely efficacious, stimulating imitations. On the other hand, it is quite clear that they aren't, or that for programmatic reasons only the bad ones are. Our negotiation of this contradiction is displaced into a set of fuzzy beliefs about the power of media itself.

If it were the case that children imitated representations the same way that they may imitate some behaviors of the people around them, such a fact would make any kind of visual representation a very powerful tool, capable of shaping behaviors and cultures in inestimable ways. And we believe such is the case, although we never reap the benefits of such instant learning. If media really were the infinitely imitable, we would have a spate of bad comedy, hoards of children dressing up as fuzzy animals, a frenzy of home repair, better vocabularies, and daily instances of people trying to be superheroes among other things, effects which have never been exactly forthcoming from the viewing audience. But the idea that any mind is a blank slate upon which media can efficaciously inscribe its contents misunderstands both minds and media. No mind is blank; all will pick and choose what attracts them, choices which are idiosyncratic and dependent on individual histories, circumstances, phobias, and pleasant associations. In addition, media itself is a complex phenomenon, hardly news one would think, but apparently forgotten in diatribes about family viewing.[6] Media is as much style and narrative as "content." Events in media are never easily isolated from either their story or their stylized contexts. Not all violence is the same violence, for example; the shape of narrative defines some violence as retributive or necessary (wars, for example, to which we seem to have no problem exposing children). Even youthful viewers do not quickly dismiss the medium itself. They know they are watching television; they know they are watching cartoons. They do not think that what they see is their immediate reality (they can look around). Children, even those who insist on maintaining their fantasies, know fantasy is fantasy.

Imitations of media do occur, but imitations of what and imitations how? Do children imitate their heroes or the power their heroes wield? The worlds they inhabit? The pleasures they enjoy? The imagined efficacy of media enables us to displace our fears about ruined childhood innocence from the Child to the medium. Instead of acknowledging that in their imitations, children may reveal desires and proclivities that suggest they are not so innocent after all, we blame media for their mental molestation. Although we may fear that our children are already perverts who are unhappy at home, we can displace this fear into campaigns against the demonic messages revealed in records being played backwards or the diction of hip-hop artists. The problem is not the media which takes the blame, but that in revealing desires at all, children cease to be the Child whose imagined innocence fuels our seductive fantasies of pornography and evil. Pandas, fortunately, do not pose the same problem, though their sexual reluctance is very much in keeping with our notion of them as big stuffed animals.

The imitations we imagine are incited by a very efficacious practice of visual representation are less imitations than identifications—a putting oneself in the place of the figure whose actions or manners attract one, or putting oneself in the fantasy world depicted, often a more pleasant place then one's own environment. Our typically unexamined assumption that pandas and children simply imitate what they see obscures a far more complicated process of identifications and subject formation. And even if we acknowledge that identification (i.e., the "role model") plays in the mix of media effectiveness, our unacknowledged understanding of identification is such that we believe that identifying reveals some native inclination towards the role adopted, some intrinsic attraction of same towards same, which suggests that the children who so identify already have formed desires and ideas of themselves.

This is indeed probably the case, but the problem is that we get it backwards. That children identify with people and roles is about what the child already is. We want to work that process backwards by thinking that the role seduces and shapes the child who is somehow innocent of choice. Hence by saturating the environment with only "good" roles, we think, we can control what kind of subjects children come to be. The point here is not that we should not surround children with positive role models (knowing that such a category is full of cultural biases and isn't equally good for every child—the gender dysphoric have a little difficulty), but that we need to acknowledge that subject formation is a complicated process that involves complex processing rather than the instantaneity of impression. Media is not as efficacious as we might like to think, especially when we can use it as the scapegoat for the everyday violence children see around them.

It may be that the contradictions around representational efficacy and imitation can be resolved if we limit the idea of efficacy only to the consumption of sexual material. Somehow, we believe, the sexual is more seductive than anything else. Unlike the vast universe of other offerings, which at best seem to stimulate only a certain amount of consumerism, sexual content, it is believed, gives viewers irresistible ideas and simultaneously lowers their inhibitions. The idea of the ultra-efficacy of the sexual, displaces the hovering fear that somehow the innocent "young person" may never have been so innocent after all. Why would children be so quickly and easily seduced by sexual imagery and not, say, ethical acts, questions of philosophy, or the proper use of power tools? Apart from the ensconced Manichaeism of various religious beliefs which equate sexuality with evil and evil with the irresistible (or with that which must constantly be resisted), why do we believe that sexual representations are more effective than any others? Such an assumption displaces adult guilt over what may be most interesting to them onto representation itself as the agent of seduction. The special status of the sexual is a cultural complex that provides titillation through prohibitions, and that assuages guilt in pleasure through a series of mediations such as secrecy, double entendre, jokes, and mystery. The fear that children may be far more direct in their consumption of sexual material not only undoes their cultural function as Child, but undoes the seductive eroticism of the ploys of indirectness that are intrinsic parts of titillation itself. Children's curiosity and half-formed theories about sex (and they all have such theories) betray the difference between actual children and the cultural icon of the Child so important to our formulations of the pornographic and the limitations of evil. Children imitating adult sex exposes this travesty.

In the case of what we assume to be the impressionable and imitative consciousness of adolescent pandas and adolescent children, the problem still is not so much behaviors, which we would like to believe are devoid of requisite feeling, but the feelings themselves. While the panda primal scene will stimulate the reproduction of other pandas, the human primal scene may efficaciously suggest both playing mommy and daddy and *feeling* like mommy and daddy. The roles are fine. Feeling sexual is not. We know children have sexual feelings and we do not want to know it, not only because it mars the cultural functioning of the figure of the Child, but also because acknowledging a child's sexual feelings may mean acknowledging that sexuality in general is more pervasive and complex than we might like to think and that adults, even "normal" adults, may respond sexually to children. The problem is not sexual feelings for children in so far as we may well have some sort of sexual feeling for everyone, nor that such feelings, even if acknowledged, need be acted upon. The problem is that the site of the child represents simultaneously both the greatest purity and greatest evil accomplished by those who let their feelings get the best of them. Singling out sexual feelings for children as the prohibited of all prohibitions, as the evil beyond which we cannot go, draws attention to those feelings, and in part produces the evil it wishes to suppress. Although pedophilia has been a constant possibility in cultures throughout history, and more accepted in some cultures than others (depending often on what a culture defines as a child and what functions that category has), the category of the pure Child, as Kincaid suggests, produces the category of the Sexual Predator as the correlative monster deluxe. The more innocent the Child, the more heinous its molester. The category of the Child produces and makes necessary the category of the Predator. It also sustains the category of the Pornographic against which it must be protected.

The other spoke in this causal representational wheel is the vagaries of identifications themselves, which when they appear to go awry, reveal how untrue the wheel might be. The chain of causality, which runs from knowledge to behavior to feeling, becomes unlinked at the point at which children's identifications run counter to what it may be assumed they should be. What if a boy wants to be mommy or a girl daddy? With the realm of the panda our assumptions about gender alignment are pretty safe. We wouldn't, for example, see some rogue female panda erroneously admire and try to emulate a huffing, rutting male or a shy male frantically climbing a tree. Panda keepers do show mating videos to both male and female pandas, although the focus is on the males and the purpose of such screenings differs for each gender. Because panda females are an especially reluctant bunch, showing female pandas such as the American captivity-bred Hua Mei sex videos is understood as educational. "She has not had the chance to observe the natural course of panda reproduction in the wild. So officials have shown her videos of mating pandas and taken her to see other pandas copulating."[7] Showing such videos to panda males is more like a stag party. Sex "education" is now de rigueur for captive males, as adolescents watch mating videos on a daily basis and get excited. As Zhang, director of the Chengdu Research Base of Giant Panda Breeding, observes, "It's the sounds of breeding that stimulate them. Pandas are just like human beings. They understand everything."[8] Panda porn, like human porn, is 98 percent sound, which raises an additional set of issues about the continued insistence on the power of the image. Perhaps the image is the education part. The sexually exciting sound track is pornographic. Perhaps we should just turn off television sound.

Human children, unlike pandas, are more flexible in their identificatory choices, but when they do choose to identify and emulate in a cross-gendered fashion, their choice reveals the extent to which they are already subjects consuming and processing rather than simply ingesting and mimicking representations. Cross-identifying children unravel our comfortable system of assumed normalcy as well as our notions that children have no desires. What we think of as gender misidentifications (even though for the child they might quite innocently be the right and most comfortable identifications) pervert the proper alignments of representation. Girls who imitate daddy shaving or boys who wear mommy's clothes do not simply imitate daily actions; they are revealing desires and identifications already in place, tabulas that aren't so rasa. By the time such behaviors appear, it is too late to consider the frantic uselessness of orthopedic role modeling (another, more desperately sought version of efficacious representation). Children are suddenly no longer the Child, especially in so far as gender identifying is an intrinsic part of the (hetero)sexual scenario about which we would like to keep them innocent. Our response, except among the very unthreatened and enlightened, is to wring our hands, force the boy into the football helmet and hand the girl her pompoms, assuming that correct dress will correct the mis-identification, and that such gaffs really are a simple matter of naive imitation. We do not worry so much when children misidentify with classed figures, and want to be a maid or a garbage man, because such jobs are themselves perceived to be childish. When children identify with doctors, we understand it as laudable ambition, though we should perhaps be aware of its more clinical aspects. But children who misidentify with genders are no longer the Child.

The not-so-covert gendering subtending our faith in (or fear of) the imagined success of representations is actually a necessary component of our idea of efficaciousness. Believing representation to be efficacious means that we believe that it is transparent, means what it says, has no slippage. Children having sexual feelings or misidentifying their genders are evidence of such slippage, evidence which is displaced into the sinful content of representation or the potential perversion of the child, when what the problem really is that representation isn't efficacious at all. Even the simplest television show is open to multiple and conflicting interpretations. The ways people consume media are widely varied and complex, depending on such immeasurable elements as narrative dynamics, subjective processes (and the processes of subjectivity), context (both of the representation and of its viewing), attention, identifications, repetition, memory, and the imitation of others' consumption.

The figure of the Child, then, must be preserved not to protect children or even to protect our own titillating system of prohibitions, but to protect our idea of representation itself, to prevent us from knowing or realizing the vast slippage that occurs every time we utter a word or watch a television show or a panda sex video. The Child guarantees a universe of frankness and sincerity by mooring a set of assumptions about how representations themselves operate purely and innocently. The Child, like the panda, guarantees that languages and images mean what they say. The Child protects us from the cynical knowledge that representations are neither fixed nor efficacious. Nothing means what it says and no one knows that better than children.

The creeping post-structuralism which challenges the efficacy of representation is not an accident here, but a symptom of the kind of binary alignments that attend the whole question of representation, prohibition, and sexuality. These alignments produce extremes, the kind of either/or that enables us to evade any profound consideration of child development or the functioning of media. Although the issue of representation appears to be a question of truth, it is really, in the end, a question about the relative stakes in concepts of representations themselves. To believe in the Child is to believe in the transparency and efficacy of representation—it means what it says and directly provokes behaviors and feelings. To believe in the efficacy of representation is to undertake a series of cultural controls around the availability and consumption of representations, including age requirements and censorship. To question the Child is to question representation (and vice versa, since questioning representation, as Kincaid has demonstrated, leads to the deconstruction of the Child). Representation never means what it says and always means both more and less than what it says, if it can ever be understood as communicating anything. To be cynical about the efficacy of representation is to resist cultural controls around representation such as censorship and even the conclusions of those more empirical disciplines such as sociology, media studies, and contemporary psychology, which depend upon representation's transparency. To believe that representation is neither transparent nor efficacious is not, however, to toss meaning away, but to admit the complexity of signification, a complexity that is mainly ignored, especially in matters of public policy. And why is this a problem?

GOOGLE

The fantasy of the Child moors our fantasy of efficacious representations, but it also alibis a not-so-fantasmatical set of statutes and other social controls. Much can be and is done in the name of the Child and the problem with this is not such policies' occasionally hysterical proponents, but that the fantasy Child has little to do with the capabilities and living conditions of actual children. Making laws to protect the pure and innocent that do not exist in such a form is like making laws to protect teddy bears—or pandas (whose very existence is threatened). Not only do such laws work to perpetuate a fantasy, they also provide the appearance that child welfare is at the center of the social program, while legislators chip away at family support programs such as welfare, access to education, and medical care; fail to take steps to rescue the environment; and wage wars, all of which adversely affect children's lives. In this context, the great energy expended to construct and sustain legislation ostensibly designed to protect the Child from the obscene is even more obviously symptomatic of something other than a generous culture looking to nurture its young.

The fantasy of the Child produces our fantasy of pornography as that which must be kept from the realm of the Child in order for both categories to continue to survive. What we currently consider to be pornographic consists generally in representations of explicit sexual activities designed to excite their consumers sexually. Historically, our notion of pornography is a rather recent category, arising, as Walter Kendrick has shown, about the same time as our fantasy of the Child.[9] The deeply impressionable "young person" of the nineteenth century became one of the pretexts for the censorship of material deemed to be pornographic because its subject matter would sully the absolute innocence of the young person. As tautological as this is, its causal circle is the only possible logic in the realm of cultural fantasy, which substitutes for some version of empirical "truth" about the nature of beings. Tautologies replace linear chains of causality when the phenomena at issue—such as representations and human development—are badly understood, oversimplified, highly complex, and even cybernetic. In other words, tautologies become the cultural rendering of the complexity of systems when there is no theory of complex systems generally available. The emergence of the tautology in which the Child defines the Pornographic which must be kept from the Child (and later, women) is a symptom of a culture that increasingly represses the complexities of its understandings of human development and representation itself.

The problem is that cultures, such as ours, tend to act on the basis of these fantasies and repressions instead of fashioning a culture premised on the best knowledge the culture has to offer. Ironically, perhaps, this is no more true than in relation to what is for most people the most advanced technical trend of our culture—the internet. The internet and World Wide Web are generally not censored under the protection of the First Amendment of the Constitution. In 1996, Congress passed the Communications Decency Act (CDA), which made criminal "the knowing transmission, by means of a telecommunications device, of 'obscene or indecent' communications to any recipient under 18 years of age" (47 *USCS* 223(a)), and "the knowing use of an interactive computer service to send to a specific person or persons under 18 years of age (47 *USCS* 223(d)(1)(A)), or to display in a manner available to a person under 18 years of age (47 *USCS* 223(d)(1)(B)), communications that, in context, depict or describe, in terms 'patently offensive' as measured by contemporary community standards, sexual or excretory activities or organs" (47 *USCS* 223(d)).

Like Atlas bearing the globe, the fantasy Child is still the bulging sinew of this first, as it turns out, unsuccessful venture at control and censorship of the internet. It is fairly clear in retrospect that this first attempt was, like Einstein's model of gravity, bending and warping a much larger fabric of intersecting interests, policies, changing mores, and issues of expression. Ranging from First Amendment rights to issues of property, child protection, privacy, and of course, sexuality, the interconnectedness of that nexus around the fantasy of the Child became even more glaringly visible on the internet, unrestrained by the various barriers and safeguards controlling print and broadcast media. On the surface, the CDA was attempting to nip a large source of pornography in the bud by imposing burdens on internet speech and access. On the surface—and by on the surface I mean in terms of the discourse around the ostensible need for the regulation and criminalization of internet expression—these provisions again ranged around the modern version of our fantasy Child: child protection.

The problem with the Internet, and the difficulty that stimulated this first legislative attempt at its control, is that although it can be expertly deployed by most young people, it has no locus for the imposition of community standards, the cover through which various belief systems and sensibilities prevent the public circulation of certain materials.[10] This lack of community enables the internet to display all kinds of pornography, although the unmentioned and possibly more acute source of concern about the internet is not its prurient content, but two more narrow possibilities it facilitates: an internet supply of child pornography and a means by which minors can be solicited for sexual acts, a possibility most recently illustrated by the acts of employees of Homeland Security. Although the Child still looms behind attempts to manage access to internet content, more draconian laws emerge in response to the Child's flip-side, the evil Predator whose diabolical fumblings are imagined to be facilitated by this uncontrollable machine.

Generally, statutes designed to "protect" attempt to remove the opportunity for bad choices. In other words, protection means trying not to permit a choice in the first place. The original CDA from 1996 protected children by preventing messages from being sent, or if sent, sent in such a way that children were unable to gain access to them. Its version of protection followed the maxim "Ignorance is bliss," assuming that children are ignorant in the first place, which if we remember our childhoods we know they are not, to varying degrees. Producing a law to protect ignorance produces the spectre of ignorance the law supposedly protects. This concept of protection by delimiting access is a venerable trope in American law (think of Prohibition), but it is precisely a trope in the sense that it is always figurative; that is, it is never really about the thing it seems to be about.

The CDA, above, appears to address the problem of minors receiving "obscene or indecent communications" including, oddly, images of excretion. Excretion provides the clue to how this statute operates. If the statute protected children against their finding images of sexual activity and thereby traumatically losing their innocence, then we might understand this as simply a moral enactment, not at all unusual in the United States where the separation between church and state has increasingly snuck back into national consciousness as if it had always been the fundamental case to begin with. But excretion brings in another set of considerations—that of taste. Certainly children know about excretion. They love it. It is the occasion for their best bad words. What does it mean that a federal statute wants to limit the circulation of images of excretion? What does the law imagine here?

What it imagines, of course, has nothing to do with protection from information or ideas, but rather protection from sexuality, not as an image, but as an enjoyment. Given the fact that children already enjoy illicit delight in defecation, a delight connected to their own sexual world recently experienced as anal, images of excretion can be harmful only in so far as they re-elicit that delight and re-elicit or produce what can only be the imagined sexual gratifications such images might provoke. The worst that can happen is that an unwitting child might think that talking about excrement is acceptable social fare, easily correctable like all such gaffs. Protection here really means a protection against adults having to have their image of the category of the innocent and empty child exploded by the actual child who delights in poop. Obviously, all adults know that children delight in these things and all adults know that children have sexual feelings, not because they have read Freud, but because they were children once. So the issue of protection here may well extend into another realm—that of adults' own histories as sexual children—to their own earliest sexual feelings. In the end this statute may well simply protect against adult embarrassment in the name of taste, aesthetics masquerading as morality or decency, and the niggling anxiety that such images are just too darn attractive, like roadkill or accidents. We don't want our children watching other people urinate, even though, of course, they already do, they just do it in the privacy of their own home.

And that may be the second and rather odd protection this statute affords—a continued sequestering of public and private. One problem the internet in general causes is a break-down in the imaginary line between public and private by importing the public domain of the internet into the private domain of the home. The internet is okay in doing this as long as it acts like a television or an encyclopedia, like another vector of public information managed at the convenience of the private. But the conceptual barrier of public and private is breached when the internet imports private material into the private sphere, or alternately, when it makes the private public in the first place, enabling us to import someone else's private or their privates into our private. This is different than obscenity is understood as a public phenomenon to be adjudicated by community standards. With the internet the entire morass comes into the home, where arguably public community standards should not necessarily hold sway. With the issue of privacy the argument brushes up against both privacy concerns and issues of parental responsibility and efficacy. At what point does the government, via the "community," begin to be able to tell others what they can think and see and what they can let their children think and see in their own homes? At what point do we enact legislation that backs up parental inability to control influences and information, or worse controls parents who do not believe in the fantasy of the Child, but who instead, like Judith Levine, believe that knowledge and openness are healthy?[11] What cost should society pay because parents are decreasingly able to parent? Or put another way, decreasingly able to control what their children may encounter. One might think, if this is the case, that such an inability would spur renewed dedication to information and education, enabling children to make good choices. But we go the other way and decide to limit what children (and all of the rest of us) can see at its source so that no child or parent has to make a choice or expend energy supervising.

The CDA was declared an unconstitutional abridgement of First Amendment rights, for several reasons, including the fact that it was not sufficiently restrictive; that is, it potentially outlawed too many kinds of protected speech. In a perseverant zealotry, Congress, thus, had to repair the overly broad scope of the CDA and quickly passed what is known as COPA, or the Child On-Line Protection Act. COPA provides the following:

(a) Requirement to restrict access
    (1) Prohibited conduct
    Whoever knowingly and with knowledge of the character of the material, in interstate or foreign commerce by means of the World Wide Web, makes any communication for commercial purposes that is available to any minor and that includes any material that is harmful to minors shall be fined not more than $50,000, imprisoned not more than 6 months, or both.

Key terms of COPA include:

(6) Material that is harmful to minors
    The term "material that is harmful to minors" means any communication, picture, image, graphic image file, article, recording, writing, or other matter of any kind that is *obscene* or that—
    (A) the average person, applying contemporary *community standards*, would find, *taking the material as a whole* and with respect to minors, is designed to appeal to, or is designed to pander to, the prurient interest;
    (B) depicts, describes, or represents, in a manner patently offensive with

respect to minors, an actual or simulated sexual act or sexual contact, an actual
or simulated normal or perverted sexual act, or a lewd exhibition of the genitals
or post-pubescent female breast; and

(C) taken as a whole, lacks serious literary, artistic, political, or scientific
value for minors.

(7) Minor

The term "minor" means any person under 17 years of age.

—Child On-Line Protection Act 47 *U.S.C.* § 231 et seq. (Emphases mine)

COPA recasts the terms of the CDA as a "Restriction of access by minors
to materials commercially distributed by means of World Wide Web that are
harmful to minors" (47 *USC* 231). "Obscene and indecent" from the CDA
are replaced by "harmful." "Under 18" is replaced by the term "minor," which
lowers the age to 17. Most of the changes reflected in the new statute attempt
to address portions of the CDA the court suggested were overly broad such
as, for example, limiting coverage to the World Wide Web instead of the
entire internet and targeting only "commercial" sites, two changes that employ the exact terminology of the Court's decision.

This terminology, itself, however, enacts yet another displacement of the
empty category of the Child and the nexus of representational efficacy again
doubly masked. The term "minor" lacquers a legalistic cast onto under-18's
evasive euphemism, neither term existing in the interest of any kind of clarity.
Instead the stake in protecting the fantasy Child becomes even more evident
as a mere pretext, because small children and teens are categories of beings
with different capabilities, responsibilities, and feelings. A teen is much different from a small child, and though more likely to seek out prurient material,
is also more likely to feel adult sexual feelings in response to it or even as
motivation for looking for it. Teens will have sexual feelings anyway despite
the governmental imposition of various forms of asceticism and abstinence,
which may be great as religious training for the Anchorites, but which don't
exactly serve as realistic protections in a culture full of communications devices, automobiles, and parental neglect. And as before, protections against
what? The feelings they already have? Through its attempted prohibitions,
COPA is conditioning teens to become full-time consumers of the pornographic.

The term "harmful" is even vaguer than the somewhat silly prohibitions
of the CDA against images of excretion. "Harmful" simply covers over the
broadness from CDA, this time employing the terms "prurient," "obscene,"
and "lewd" in representations without redeeming aesthetic value, all of which
are utterly in the eyes of the beholder. What it does do is preserve the notion
of "community standards," by importing the test from *Ginsberg v. New York*,
logical given the tradition of Constitutional law around the first Amendment.[12] Sex, the unquestioned and empty category of the Child, is a veiled
belief in textual efficacy once again.

As might be expected, this second venture was also challenged in Federal

Court, and was also held to be overly broad, which decision is currently under appeal by the government. At stake again is the frantic desire to "protect" the Child, which is no longer a child, but a "minor." Apart from rehearsing a century-and-a-half's justifications for such "protection," such as the supposedly inherent dangers of sexual knowledge, or the more threatening idea that children might enjoy sexual feelings, COPA adds several intriguing propositions to its version that completely undermine its alibi of custodial protection. The first is the legislators' attempt to inscribe a "community standards test" into the statute, suggesting that the World Wide Web is something that the "average person" can "take as a whole," even though the vast majority of adults have no idea how large it is. Since children are not the average people whose prejudices define local ideas of the pornographic, encoding the test is obviously aimed at the adults who would somehow stumble accidentally onto such material (those who look for it are unlikely to report it). One imagines a scenario in which a concerned parent standing behind his or her child as he or she surfs the Web, recoils in horror when the child accidentally keys into the LESBIAN CHICKS GO AT IT site. With the child beginning to ask what lesbian chicks are, the parent quickly covers the child's eyes and calls the local prosecutor. Search engines developed content "filters" precisely because most children do not surf the Web with their parents standing behind them. Although including the community standards test might be wise legislating, it points towards other motivations for the statute lurking behind the fantasy Child, such as censorship. And we modern Comstocks are still at it, weasling through the records of search engines to see who is accessing pornography and how often, all in the name of the Child.

Or, as is increasingly insisted, COPA provides protections against the masses of stalking sexual predators who have opportunistically deployed this new technology for their nefarious ends (to be heroically entrapped by crusading television news shows). If this is the case, one wonders why legislators took the time to exempt specifically images of pre-pubescent female breasts (6 (B)) above. Wouldn't those breasts be exactly what on-line pedophiles would be looking for? And isn't the problem with sexual predators (remember, the flip-side of the fantasy Child) that they use innocent chat rooms and other non-pornographic sites as ways to forge connections with their potential victims whose clandestine meetings with on-line dates can occur only with some degree of parental non-supervision? COPA certainly does try to make pornographic images of children a crime, but any protection is a secondary effect of censorship, not the focus of the statute itself which apparently permits images of nude little girls.

The problem with COPA is a fact of the contemporary disparity between children's surfing skill and the knowledge and skills of their parents. The Child may be innocent, but children are too smart, and not at all the innocents of our fantasy, which is why we need the statute. The threatened dissolution of the fantasy Child plays out on the face of legislative attempts to purify the Child. The problem occurs not because the World Wide Web is full of obscene web sites with candy, but that children are very good at finding such candy when they want to. And that is the protection the laws are really designed to provide: protecting the Child from the child, protecting our conservation of the fantasy of the Child from the behaviors of actual children, and protecting parents from the questions their curious children will undoubtedly ask which reveal that they are more sophisticated than our image of the fantasy Child can bear.

It is this last issue that has spurred the glut of subpoenas issuing from the Attorney General's office in a fact-finding mission to help the government's case supporting COPA.[13] If the government can show that a child—a mere child—can easily navigate the internet to obscene and pornographic sites, it might provide a basis to defend the claim that COPA is overly broad. The material these subpoenas request is important not only as a way for the government to show the ease of access to the prurience the World Wide Web provides, but might on a more basic level assault the very nexus I have been trying to map: the battle of epistemologies, the battle about the maintenance of representation itself as transparent and efficacious, and about things meaning what they say. Among other things, COPA works to guarantee the efficaciousness of World Wide Web representations by assuring us that they are there and that they are harmful. If harmful, they must be efficacious. And also, and as its protection, the gleaming fantasy of the Child as the pure space whose presence produces the most degraded and ecstatic feelings.

If children can navigate the internet, then isn't this proof that representation is in fact efficacious–that is, that there is some ability for some people to follow directions? But if children can surf the internet, if they are competent, how would they come upon prurient sites by accident? Many of us have encountered obscene sites by accident, looked around guiltily, hoping the government search engine subpoenas won't come up with our home addresses when we have accidentally tripped into the SEXKITTENPUSSY site while doing research on feline health. Anyone who has so fallen is immediately warned by the garish and tasteless design of the sites as well as their practical illegibility and utter silliness. The pure Child who accidentally wanders into MENAGEATROIS land while looking up the word "menagerie" may be fascinated, but whatever innocence they have is probably pretty safe. This kind of accident, which is the only kind of scenario possible in relation to our innocent Fantasy of the Child, is less the real fear here than those Web browsings that are not accidents. If children can surf, they won't come upon most prurient web sites simply by accident but because they want to come upon them. So much for the Child. The problem with the internet is not that it offers too much, but that it too easily reveals that our pure Child may well have motives, desires, and now the untrammeled ability to fulfill them unless the government steps in. Cast as the trauma of passive exposure, isn't the problem with the internet that it affords curious children the tools to find what they may well be looking for? What the law tries to protect is not children, but a culture which needs to sustain the fantasy of the Child in the face of the recognition that children may well be curious and pleasure-seeking skeptics who do not take our word for it and who are better than adults at finding what they want.

The search engine Google refused to comply with the government subpoenas. Commenting on Google's recalcitrance, Jack Samad, senior vice president for the National Coalition for Protection of Children and Families, said, "Young people are experiencing broken lives after being exposed to adult images and behaviors on the Internet."[14] Samad commented further, "I'm disappointed Google did not want to exercise its good corporate branding to secure protection of youth." On the other hand (or side), sex educators Hazel Beh and Milton Diamond remind us, "The debate regarding what to teach minors about sex is a political battle over defining American values." The fantasy of the child is the fantasy of pornography and both fantasies insulate us from our fear that things don't either mean or make us do what they say.

3

The Making of a Pre-Pubescent Porn Star: Contemporary Fashion for Elementary School Girls

MARDIA J. BISHOP

In the 1980s and early 1990s, Madonna was blamed for girls' pornographic fashion choices of black short skirts, black lacy stockings, and black corset-style tops. Based on media comments, it seems the Material Girl was wholly responsible for the consumption of pornographic clothing options by girls.[1] In the late 1990s and early 2000s, former Disney Mouseketeer, Britney Spears, carried on the tradition of becoming the role model for porn fashion, most notably ushering in the popularity of low-rise jeans and the bared midriff.[2] No doubt, some girls specifically dressed to emulate their role models of Madonna or Spears, but the emergence and popularity of pornographic styles in mainstream fashion is part of a larger cultural movement, which has seen pornography become ubiquitous in American popular culture. Much research has been done in several industries where the crossover is most apparent— the media, advertising, fashion. Yet, as argued by Susan Driver, "complex questions about how youth engage with the intensification of their sexual fields of vision as part of their daily routines watching TV, playing video games, enjoying films and music videos as desiring subjects and desired objects are often overlooked."[3] What is most overlooked is how the emergence of stereotypical pornographic clothing as fashionable or socially acceptable dress affects girls. Studies have addressed the influence of "stripper" or "porn star" fashion on teenagers and fashion in general,[4] but as for young girls, only studies on the sexualization of girls exist, not studies specifically on how fashion sexualizes the pre-teen-aged or elementary school-aged girl. By examining the popular clothing for girls ages 5–11, it is clear that porn fashion is not limited to grown women or teenagers. It is everywhere, and its effects are powerful and far-reaching.

My synopsis of what is currently popular for elementary school-aged girls is based on observations of clothing for sale at a typical suburban, middle-to upper-middle class shopping mall. The majority of the clothes described are from Macy's, a national, well-respected department store. Although photos of clothing in retailers' weekly advertisements and fashion magazines provide suggestions of clothes that are currently in style, I opted to browse the malls to find out what is really available and what choices are afforded young girls and their parents when they partake in that great American pastime, mall shopping.

In order to address contemporary fashion for elementary school-aged girls, which would be girls in kindergarten through fifth grade or aged 5–11, I had to look in two different departments due to the U.S. fashion world's sizing policies. In the U.S., there are several levels of sizing for women and girls. Women's sizes, which are sizes 2–16, are geared toward women in their mid-20s and older. Junior sizes, which are sizes 1–13, are primarily for teenagers (7th and 8th graders) to young women in their mid-20s. Kids sizes, which are sizes 7–16, are for girls aged 7–11, or 2nd to 5th grade. Girls' sizes, which are sizes 4–6x, are for girls aged 4–6 or kindergartners and 1st grade. There are also sizes stratified for toddlers (2T–4T), babies (0–24 months), and, of course, larger sizes for women who are bigger than a women's size 16, as well as larger sizes for kids within kids sizes. The descriptions of size and age ranges are typical ranges. How small or large the clothing is and what age it fits depends on the designer and sometimes the cut of the clothing. Some designers' size 10 would be similar to another's size 8 or another's size 12.

Currently, the majority of clothes on retailers' racks for girls aged 5–11 are styles that stem from the porn industry. As Valerie Steele points out, there is a relationship between clothing and sexuality. "Fashion is a symbolic system linked to the expression of sexuality—both sexual behavior (including erotic attraction) and gender identity."[5] According to Steele, clothing, materials, colors, and trends that are connected to sexual themes, and commonly used in the porn industry, include corsets, high-heeled shoes and boots, the materials of leather, rubber, fur, the colors of black and red, and the trend of wearing underwear as outerwear. Indeed, as described in the following, what is contemporary fashion for elementary school girls is straight from the porn industry, including the use of underwear as outerwear, the types of materials used, and shoe styles.

The most popular style of top currently available for purchase is a spaghetti-strap tank top or camisole, traditionally a garment worn underneath a blouse, but currently worn on its own. These tops are made from satin, silk, lace, and sequins—materials that have traditionally been associated with the porn industry or as erotic clothing. The camisoles are meant to fit tightly and are low-cut in the front and back. Another popular top is a corset-inspired one, which either is a shirt with corset stays in the back that can be tightened to emphasize body shape or an actual corset. Again, the corset is traditionally an undergarment, and when not worn as an undergarment it is associated with the porn industry or is considered fetish-wear.

Sometimes worn on top of the camisole is the shrug, which is a short sweater-type garment that ends just below the breast area and is tied in a knot underneath the breast area, forming a plunging "V" neckline. The most common shrug is loosely crocheted out of various types of yarn. Based on my observations, the shrugs on the mannequins in the girls' department seem to fall closer to the breast area, whereas the shrugs on the mannequins in the women's department fell to the waist. The result of such a length for girls is that their breast area was emphasized more than women's. Of course, most girls from aged 5–11 have not developed breasts. Consequently, their emerging and pre-emerging breasts are emphasized.[6]

Another trend in upper body wear is the conversation t-shirt, a t-shirt with a phrase written across the chest area. Hollister's, a store similar to Abercrombie and Fitch, sells junior sizes (for 12- to 25-year-olds). Since Hollister's sizes run smaller than a typical junior size, 9- to 11-year-olds tend to frequent the shop. Some phrases on t-shirts included: "The Love Doctor Is In," "Naughtier than I Look," "Life Is Better Blonde," "Catch Me and I'm Yours," "Your Boyfriend Says Hi," "Say Hello to My Little Friends," and "No Tan Lines on this Beach Bum." Limited Too, which sells clothing in sizes for 2nd–5th graders and is considered the "cool" place to shop among elementary school girls, had several conversation t-shirts, including one that said, "This Is What Cute Looks Like."

The most popular items available that are to be worn with the camisole top are either jeans or tiered skirts. Both items are low-cut, often beginning just above the pubic area, so that pelvic bones are exposed. The most popular jeans are distressed or torn in various ways. The tiered skirts are short skirts that appear to be made by attaching layers of ruffles together. Most skirts have three tiers. Based on the garments, it seems the skirts are to be worn as short and as low-cut as possible, earning them the nickname of "belts."[7]

Dressier fashions are just as porn-inspired as the casual wear of camisole tops and tiered skirts. An investigation of what is available at the mall in formal dresses for 5- to 11-year-olds brought forth clothing that seemed to imitate Frederick's of Hollywood lingerie. The formal wear section at Limited Too featured halter dresses, extended camisoles or "baby doll" dresses, and tight mini-dresses. Most of the dresses were made from a satiny-type material. Based on the clothing available, it seems girls are supposed to wear to their dressier occasions (weddings, bat mitzvahs) what is advertised in the Frederick's catalog as erotic lingerie for women.

Trendy footwear for elementary school girls consists of high-heeled boots with numerous buckles on them or high-heeled and platform shoes. Also prevalent are high-heeled sandals featuring thin straps. In fact, it was difficult to find low-heeled shoes in sizes to fit elementary school girls.

In contemporary fashion, in addition to wearing traditional "underwear" as "outerwear," special underwear is available to be worn with popular fashions. Limited Too sells low-rise underwear starting in a size 7 (basically for seven year olds) to be worn with low-cut jeans and skirts. The store also sells string bikini underwear. Abercrombie and Fitch, which markets to 7- to 14-year-olds, sells thong underwear to prepubescent girls, some with phrases, such as "Feeling Lucky," "Wink Wink," and "Eye Candy."[8] Thong underwear, of course, comes directly from the porn industry. Ariel Levy retells the story of thong underwear's creation to "cover" strippers so that New York wouldn't get a bad name during the 1939 World's Fair.[9]

For the upper body, padded bras featuring brand images of popular toys Bratz, Barbie, and Saddle Club are now available for girls as young as age six. The spokesperson for the distributor of the bras or "bralettes" claims, "The idea of padding is for girls to be discreet as they develop."[10] Although padding would hide girls' emerging breasts (until the emerging breasts pushed the padding out further) from the inquisitive, objectifying eyes of others, potentially saving girls from embarrassment and/or sexual comments, the presence of "breasts" on a usually flat-chested six-year-old will simply encourage more eyes to be on that budding chest area, overemphasizing the importance of a girl's physical attributes.

Based on my observations, the majority of clothing available for elementary school girls at the local suburban mall is from the porn industry, which I will call "porn" fashion.[11] While perusing the stores, the same questions kept arising—"Why is the majority of clothing available for girls "porn" fashion? Why does contemporary fashion for elementary school girls look too old and revealing for a 7-year-old? Why is there not much difference between what is available for a 7-year-old and a 33-year-old? How do girls feel about wearing "porn" fashion? The theoretical answers to these questions I will address later in this essay, but the fashion answers deal with the trickle-down effect of fashion; basically, clothing is designed for women's or junior's sizes, then is adapted for kids' and girls' sizes through cut, fabric, and color changes. In conducting my survey of contemporary fashion, I first looked at the junior department because, as noted by clothing buyer and fashion consultant Brynn Chamblee, "porn" fashion was designed originally for junior sizes. According to Chamblee, fashion is traditionally designed for women's sizes, and then adapted for the younger size ranges, but porn fashion is different in that clothing is designed for junior sizes and then adapted for the younger and older sizes.[12] Another difference that the fashion world has experienced with the advent of porn fashion is how far the fashion adaptations extend. Traditionally fashion adaptations stop at the girls' sizes level: that is, women, juniors, and kids sizes (for ages 7 and up) will look similar, but designers will have different styles for younger girls. With porn fashion, the trickle-down effect is seen all the way down to baby sizes. Children's Place, a low-to-medium priced children's clothing store, featured faux-leopard mini-skirts in size 6–9 months.[13] Macy's featured black lace camisoles, black lace shrugs and black lace tiered skirts in size 2T, typically the size geared toward two-year-olds.

With the existence of "porn" fashion clear, the next question is, how do the children respond or react to these fashions? Obviously, their age and level of understanding of sexuality prevent collecting data from elementary school children. Instead, it is helpful to discuss the matter with elementary school teachers, men and women on the front-lines of childhood, and men and women who are fairly objective. Consequently, I turned to elementary school teachers to try to get an understanding of why girls dress in "porn" fashion and how girls interpret any meanings behind their clothing choices, basically, "how do girls engage with the intensification of their sexualization"? In addition, I wanted to find out why parents allow their children to dress in "porn" fashion. (I opted not to interview parents because I concluded they could not be entirely objective. I would after all be asking them, to paraphrase a recent book title by Celia Rivenbark, "Why are you dressing your six-year-old like a skank?").[14] Moreover, the teachers provided a practical perspective on the relationship between porn fashion and girls and their school environment. I conducted a survey of K-5th grade teachers of a county in metropolitan Atlanta. The majority of teachers were white females. The schools of the county represented, however, were diverse in socioeconomics and ethnic backgrounds.

Teachers of kindergartners through 3rd graders overwhelmingly agreed that girls wore "porn" fashion[15] because the girls thought it made them look older. The teachers commented that the girls were trying to emulate media stars or older siblings, so looking older was important to them. In addition, girls at all levels of elementary school wear "porn" fashion "to look cool." Beginning in the fourth grade, however, teachers noted that girls wear "porn" fashion in order to "be noticed by the boys." The majority of teachers also agreed that most girls are too young to associate specific feelings to their clothes or how they make them feel. Although kindergarten teachers mentioned that their students attach meaning to their clothing if it features a favorite animal or cartoon character or if it came from someone special. Girls wear "porn" clothes because that is what older kids do, so the younger girls think they will look older. The fifth grade teachers agreed that even though fifth-grade girls start to wear clothes to attract boys, only occasionally do they "use their clothes in a true sexual way." So they are wearing "porn" fashion because it makes them look older and because it's "cool."

For the most part, children are allowed to choose their clothes. Teachers indicated that as early as first grade, children are allowed and encouraged to make their own fashion decisions. Parents/guardians pay for the clothes, so why do they pay for "porn" fashion? Most teachers indicated that parents do not want to say "No" to their children, that they want to avoid a fight with their children and clothing always causes fights, that many times parents buy their children's affection, and that parents prefer to be friends with their children instead of disciplinarians. Fifth-grade teachers commented that parents allow the clothing "so they [their children] will be accepted by their peers." A few mentioned that parents were trying to live vicariously through their children or saw their child's presumed attractiveness level as a reflection on them, so they wanted to make sure their child dressed "attractively." A few teachers commented that some parents didn't see anything wrong with the clothing. The overall response, however, was that parents recognize "porn" fashion as inappropriate, but allow their children to wear it because they want their child to see them as a friend or they allow their children to wear "porn" fashion so that they "will fit in."

Teachers, however, state that "girls are pushed ahead to an 'older' age before they are ready to accept the responsibility that comes with it." Several teachers commented that girls are forced into looking and acting like an older person when they aren't at a developmental stage to understand boundaries. Consequently, they are at risk psychologically and physically. Further, wearing "porn" fashion encourages rewards for appearance, rather than academics. Girls get attention for what they're wearing, not what they're accomplishing academically. "Porn" fashion "reduces girls' self-esteem because it encourages negative attention and it reduces self-respect because by wearing it, girls communicate very clearly that they will tolerate bad behavior."

From a practical perspective, the teachers identified concentration and safety issues as repercussions. Basically, girls wearing "porn" fashion distract hormonal 4th and 5th grade boys, as well as the other girls. The teachers commented that they felt that most girls are uncomfortable wearing the clothing because they are constantly tugging at straps and hems, pulling them either up or down. In addition, girls seemed uncomfortable wearing some of the tops because the tops emphasize developing breasts, which most girls do not want emphasized either because their breasts are too big or too small or their physical maturation process is something they are embarrassed about and want to keep private. As for safety issues, the teachers identified high heels and boots as unsafe to walk in, especially in physical education classes.

All in all, teachers were divided on the fashion trend. Half of the teachers thought that "porn" fashion was more harmful than other fashion trends because it makes girls grow up too fast, and puts them at emotional and physical risk. As one teacher put it, "A tie-dye t-shirt doesn't say 'slut.'" The other half either wasn't sure or mentioned other fashion trends that they felt were more harmful than "porn" fashion, such as mini-skirts in the 1960s. The majority of fashion trends mentioned were trends that in their time period were worn as political statements; that is, conscious demonstrations of revolt against current power structures, such as women going bra-less in the 1970s. Although many fashion trends start as conscious political statements, such as grunge-wear in the late 1980s or Goth-wear in the late 1990s, the revolutionary purpose soon becomes lost once the style becomes popular and main-stream. "Porn" fashion is different than most trends in that, although some would argue that the fashion empowers women by allowing them to show off their bodies, the start of the trend was not a conscious political statement, but an emulation of current celebrities.

The results of the survey indicated that most girls are too young to associ-ate specific feelings with their clothes or how their clothes make them feel, but instead wear "porn" fashion because it's "cool" or makes them look older. Despite the girls' positive feelings toward "porn" fashion, from the teachers' perspectives based on their observations of how girls moved and behaved when wearing the clothing, the girls were physically uncomfortable wearing the clothing either because of the fit or how much the clothing exposed.

Many teachers and parents, however, argue that it is just fashion, just clothing. It is not, however, only clothing. "Porn" fashion is part of our cur-rent "pornified" culture in which aspects of pornography have infiltrated con-temporary pop culture from fashion and toys to television and music. And in this "pornified" culture, gender and sexual stereotypes predominate. Pornog-raphy reduces girls "to one of two sexist stereotypes: 1) sexual objects to be taken up and put down and 2) sex-crazed and on the make."[16] Basically, pornography positions females as objects that are there to sexually please males. "Proving that you are hot, worthy of lust, and—necessarily—that you seek to provoke lust is still exclusively women's work."[17] And sexually pleas-ing males, according to the pornographic world and our pornified culture, requires physical attractiveness. Consequently, as Ariel Levy argues, in our pornifed culture girls' value is tied to their physical looks: basically, a girl has value if she dresses and looks like a porn star, thereby, making herself attrac-tive to boys.

Having girls' value tied to their physical looks is not new. As Naomi Wolf has argued, equating women's beauty with their worth is centuries' old. She explains the beauty myth as a story that claims:

> The quality called 'beauty' objectively and universally exists. Women [girls] must embody it and men [boys] must want to possess women who embody it. This embodiment is an imperative for women . . . because it is biological, sex-ual, and evolutionary: Strong men battle for beautiful women, and beautiful women are more reproductively successful. . . . since this system is based on sexual selection, it is inevitable and changeless.[18]

The myth, like most, is not true. Beauty is not universal, but is a culturally defined quality. As such, it is a reflection of and a political tool of the culture that defines it. By "assigning value to women in a vertical hierarchy according to a culturally imposed physical standard," women [girls] are forced to com-pete.[19]

Contemporary psychological body image theory presents the beauty myth in a slightly different way. As Thomas Cash argues, women who support traditional gender roles—which pornography reinforces—tend to be more invested in their appearance and internalize cultural standards of beauty more fully.[20] Women who internalize cultural standards of beauty "experience them as coming from their own desires" and "connect achievement of these standards with their sense of self-worth."[21] Consequently, women will try to achieve beauty standards. Whether articulated from a body image theoretical perspective or a materialist feminist one, the basic idea is that when women's worth is tied to their physical looks or their body, they have to do things to adhere to or achieve the current beauty ideal. The closer they adhere to the beauty standard, the more value they have.

Based on images prevalent in the media—television, movies, and magazine advertisements targeting girls, the current ideal for young girls and young women is an extremely thin body (such as Paris Hilton's or Jessica Simpson's), blond hair, large breasts, full lips, and sculpted cheekbones (such as Pamela Anderson's).[22] And the type of clothing worn by representatives of the beauty ideal is "porn" fashion. Recent research indicates that fifty percent of girls age 8–11 read "teen" and "tween" magazines at least occasionally, "with as many as 25 percent reading them twice a week."[23] In addition, in a year's time, children "spend more time watching television than in any activity other than sleeping."[24] Obviously, the majority of elementary school-aged girls are exposed to images of the current beauty ideal and research finds that media exposure does affect body image. In fact, one study of adolescent girls links exposure to magazine images that have high levels of eroticism, sex role stereotyping with weight and appearance concerns, and eating disorders.[25]

Once girls and women accept the cultural beauty standard, they feel the need to emulate it or adhere to it because their worth is tied to it. This pursuit of the beauty standard has major economic, physical, and psychological ramifications. From an economic standpoint, elementary school girls feel pressure to pursue the ideal by spending money. In our current economic system, girls are encouraged to shop because media and store messages suggest that if they have just the right outfit, just the right accessory, they will be deemed "hot/beautiful." For example, Cosmogirl!'s November 2005 cover suggested that girls could "look amazing tonight" if they bought products to make their skin clear, fix their hair, and bought "cool clothes under $30." Store displays demonstrate that part of being fashionable and "hot/beautiful" means buying the "right" accessories, including jewelry, handbags, hair decorations, lip gloss, even mirrors to carry in the handbag. Girls, aged 8–12, take the messages to heart, spending more than 15 billion of their own money a year, and influencing their parents to spend another 30 billion.[26]

Physically, in order to reach the extremely thin component of the ideal, girls need to reduce their caloric consumption and increase their exercise. Unfortunately, for some 3rd, 4th, and 5th graders, the thin ideal is difficult to reach because as they approach and go through puberty, they tend to gain weight, develop breasts, and widen at the hips. Yet girls still try to reach the thin ideal as research indicates that girls as young as age six claim to diet. In fact, in a recent survey 40 percent of 9- to 10-year-old girls claimed to be on a weight-loss diet.[27] Meanwhile, the beauty standard of large breasts, which is difficult to achieve when trying to be thin at the same time, poses problems for girls who haven't gone through puberty or are going through it. Options for increasing breast size include "stuffing" or padding a bra, the new "bra-lette," a padded bra for girls as young as age six, or plastic surgery. There are no statistics on plastic surgery on elementary school girls, but there are on teenagers, which show that the number of breast augmentations on 18-year-olds tripled from 2002 to 2003.[28] The most common high school graduation gift for girls in wealthy Atlanta suburbs is no longer a car, but a "boob job."[29] Girls' inability to reach the beauty ideal leads to body dissatisfaction. "Studies routinely find that about 40 percent of elementary school girls [including girls as young as six] . . . are dissatisfied with their size and want to be thinner."[30] Although this age group doesn't experience eating disorders at the level of junior high, high school, and college-aged women, this group experiences the start of dieting and enough body dissatisfaction that causes psychological issues.

As mentioned earlier, beauty standards are not universal, but culturally defined. Because the standards are usually difficult to achieve, such as fuller lips and large breasts, girls will feel inadequate when comparing themselves to the standards and shame when they are not able to meet the standards. Studies show that body dissatisfaction "predicts the onset of dieting over and above the effects of other risk factors, . . . the onset of purging behaviors," and low self-esteem.[31] Girls early on learn that they are supposed to be attractive; consequently, their experience of their body is one of body surveillance, and girls learn to view their bodies as objects to be watched in order to avoid negative judgment.[32] In the case of the current porn ideal, girls are taught to internalize the porn spectacle—that they are on display to sexually arouse others. So they invest time and energy in watching and evaluating how their bodies fit cultural standards. Research shows that a woman who "is high in body surveillance believes that how she looks is more important than how she feels. For young women, higher body surveillance is related to lower body satisfaction, more eating problems, and lower levels of some measures of psychological well-being, such as autonomy and self-acceptance."[33] Furthermore, girls experience the double standard of having their value attached to their appearance. On one hand they are deemed not valuable if they don't adhere to the beauty standard, but on the other, they are deemed stupid for pursuing such a standard (or in the case of "porn" fashion, they are considered "sluts"). Consequently, they experience low self-esteem for not reaching the standard, but low self-esteem for pursuing it.

The majority of body image research has been conducted on young women, usually college-aged. While the complete psychological ramifications of pursuing beauty standards aren't currently understood for elementary school girls, there is enough research that indicates that 40 percent are dissatisfied with their bodies and that older elementary school girls start to experience self-esteem issues and eating disorders. Obviously, elementary school girls are participating in body surveillance and based on their shopping bills, they are pursuing beauty standards.

The above discussion of and research on the ramifications of pursuing a beauty ideal is for pursuing any beauty ideal. However, the ramifications are even more severe in pursuing the current porn star ideal. First, the porn beauty ideal positions girls as sexual objects. Research shows that "treating girls as sexual objects . . . might focus girls on their bodies, encourage comparisons to the cultural ideal and to other girls, and ultimately result in body dissatisfaction and low body esteem."[34] At the elementary school level, "such objectification might take the form of peer teasing that resembles later sexual harassment. For example, boys might . . . flip up their [girls'] skirts, comment on their appearance, and call them ugly."[35] Fifth-grade teachers from my survey mentioned that boys tend to comment to girls on their bodies more when they are wearing "porn" fashion. "Boys have commented to girls when they wear tops that show their stomachs" about the girls' stomach sizes or when wearing low-cut tops, they have commented about the girls' breast sizes or bra choices.

Second, by overly sexualizing girls, "porn" fashion gives them a warped view of sexuality. Primarily, they are learning that it is their job to be sexually attractive or that their value is tied to being sexually attractive. Many times younger elementary school girls use terms, such as "hot" and "sexy," to describe their looks or their clothing, but they don't understand what the terms mean. Consequently, they are learning about sex through the fashion industry and the media, and both industries emphasize that it is the girl's job to look sexy for boys. Furthermore, girls are learning that sex is one-sided, that it is something they are to provide for the pleasure of boys, and, based on clothing advertisements, that there are certain poses or movements that compose the sexual act. The majority of research on pornography's effects on children addresses the effects of hardcore internet porn on children aged 13 and above. According to Judith Coche, a clinical psychologist and professor of psychiatry, "the effects of such ever-present pornography on kids who are still developing sexually—or who haven't even reached puberty—have yet to be fully understood."[36] But what is understood is that because children have difficulty separating fantasy from reality, pornography teaches them "what women supposedly look like, how they should act, and what they're supposed to do."[37] Of course "pornography isn't mere depictions of couples having consensual sex or respectful photography of naked men and women,"[38] but depictions of women being humiliated or raped or insatiable in their desire for sex. In addition, researchers are concerned that because of pornography, "Sex becomes something you do in a disconnected way—looking at a person without actually being with that person"[39] and that sex is viewed as something rela-tionship-free. As a result of pornography, children won't understand how to relate to people they are interested in on a human or personal level.

Third, "porn" fashion targets girls at a younger age than any other fashion trend has. Starting at the age of six months, girls can be dressed in sexual clothing and begin learning their role as sexual object. With "porn" fashion girls are being immersed and participating in the beauty myth earlier than ever. As articulated by teachers, the elementary school years are extremely important for children's academic growth as they're learning how to read, how to write, how to think. In this state of existence that is saturated with learning, they are conditioned to learn other things as well, such as how to be sexually attractive, how to shop, how to evaluate their bodies in terms of impossible standards, how to treat their appearance as more important than anything else, and how to feel inadequate because they're not "hot" enough. Ultimately, young girls are learning that what they look like is more impor-tant than how they feel and how they perform in any other way. Indeed, a study by Patricia Adler found that by late elementary school, girls understand their status comes from "success at grooming, clothes, and other appearance related variables."[40]

Finally, elementary school girls dress in "porn" fashion because it makes them look older. In turn, as indicated earlier, the major concern teachers had about "porn" fashion is that it "pushes girls ahead to an older age" before they are socially and psychologically ready. When girls dress to look older and want to act older, they will be treated as if they are older. Whether those treatments are expectations of sexual performance or expectations of adult-level responsibility, elementary school girls are not capable of them; conse-quently, they are at risk physically and psychologically.

So in knowing what "porn" fashion does to girls, why is it so popular in today's America, one that has seemingly become more conservative politically and religiously? As mentioned earlier, beauty is a culturally defined quality that is a reflection of and political tool of the culture that defines it. As such, the "porn" star beauty ideal serves today's conservative culture in that it rein-forces gender stereotypes and it makes money. First, the gender stereotypes represented in pornography, such as the female who is there to sexually serve the male, supports the conservative Christian view that women are to be submissive to and serve men. Furthermore, the beauty myth at work in to-day's culture encourages girls to equate their value with their adherence to the current beauty ideal so that they can land a husband, not to how smart they are, how much money they make, or how productive they are. Ulti-mately, "porn" fashion keeps girls in their place—a place where, due to their pursuit of the beauty ideal, they become physically, psychologically, and eco-nomically weaker than, or subservient to, men.

Second, "porn" fashion is a huge moneymaker. The porn industry itself has been the largest growing industry of the past ten years. Just the adult film segment made $10 billion in 2003.[41] The profit capabilities of porn certainly aren't lost on marketing professionals either. In today's "pornified" culture, sex sells more than ever. Sut Jally refers to the crossover of porn into other industries as part of the commodity-image system, which is a marketing strategy that frames sexy bodies to encourage fast voyeuristic forms of consumption.[42] And sexy little girl bodies are definitely part of this marketing strategy. Henry Giroux argues that although children are pushed to the margins of political power in society, they still become a central focus of adult fascination, desire, and authority. "Children are constructed primarily within the language of the market and the increasingly conservative politics of media culture; [and,] within current representational politics, children's bodies are increasingly being commodified and disciplined."[43] In the profit-driven world of advertising and fashion, the child's body becomes a "site of spectacle and objectification where youthful allure and sexual titillation are marketed and consumed by teens and adults."[44]

Not only are girls being used to sell things, they are being trained to buy early on. Marketers recognize the value of strategically targeting young girls—get them addicted to fashion now while their parents are paying and girls will remain consumers when they are older and spending their own money. Moreover, treat them as independent, hip spenders as ads do and they will spend even more. According to Adler's study, by late elementary school, girls recognize that status comes from their appearance, as well as their "affluence and its correlates of material possessions."[45]

"Porn" fashion sells and as long as it does, it will remain popular, despite the ramifications for little girls. As pointed out by Giroux, although conservatives define family values in part on an image of a pure and sexually innocent child, they refuse to acknowledge the "immense sexualization of children within consumer capitalism."[46] Ultimately, conservatives support market values over human value, and the market value of the sexualized little girl is too high not to use. So until some other fashion comes along that will make a lot of money at the expense of little girls, "porn" fashion is here to stay.

———— 4 ————

Hot Bodies on Campus:
The Performance of Porn Chic

HANNAH B. HARVEY
KAREN ROBINSON

Cleavage emerging from the second skin of a shiny nylon blend that ends just under the breasts; tight "skinny jeans" riding below the hip. the pierced belly takes center stage. As she turns and leans down to pick up her buckled bag, the curvilinear "whale-tail" of the thong crowned with a tattoo appears above her crack. Up the aisle she sashays in her strappy sandals with the four inch heels: a vision in satin, distressed denim, and lace. No, we're not watching a singles commercial on nighttime TV, *Sex and the City*, or *Girls Gone Wild;* nor are we in a Buckhead bar on a Friday night. We are in an auditorium classroom on a medium-sized liberal arts college campus at 10:45 a.m., and, as instructors, we're reminding everyone there is a quiz the day after tomorrow.

We admit to being a trifle shocked, certainly distracted, perhaps turned on, and not a little disturbed. What business does this sexualized, or to put it bluntly, pornographied attire[1] have on a college campus whose constituents are admittedly conservative in matters of politics and religion? Coming from a theatre and performance studies background, we are interested in fashion as a *performance* of a particular or multiple "look(s)" involving the interaction between clothing, body, performer and audience. The apparent intersections between everyday campus fashion and soft porn raise interesting questions about how college women experience and perform popular fashion in campus life.

In this essay, we ask: how is college fashion a performance at our home

57

university? Do college women perceive their or others' fashions as pornographic? What are the ramifications when we view contemporary campus fashion as aligned with the performance of pornography? And what is at stake—what identities are at risk, what power may be gained or lost—for intelligent and "fashionable" college women who inhabit that liminal space between fashion and pornography?

ANALYZING CULTURE: A PERFORMANCE STUDIES APPROACH

"All the world's a stage/and all the men and women merely players"[2] is a Bardic trope that lies at the heart of our theoretical and methodological approach. Often we juggle multiple roles in our daily lives. Performance Studies analyzes everyday life as performance by asking the following questions: what role(s) do we play in life—for example, the role of mother, husband, co-worker, or (in the case of this essay) female college student? Where do the performances take place? When, how, and why?[3] These performances present a means for understanding those conscious and often subconscious ways in which we enact the multiple layers of complex selfhood.

In our brief reflection on college women and their fashions, we understand their daily lives as embodied performances of the self. Thus, as we look at fashion as the *costume* for women's roles as college students, we ask: how and why are women clothing themselves, and for what aesthetic, personal, and political purposes? With what effects? What norms of behavior and roles in society do these costumes reinforce or subvert?

METHODOLOGY

For this study, we observed various women on campus performing fashion—interacting with peers, with us, and going about daily life. We also spoke informally with and emailed a series of fashion-related questions[4] to female students of various races, ages, sexual persuasions, and dressing habits. These women were our "conversational partners," and as we spoke in the halls, over emails, and in our offices with them, we each learned from the other what it means to perform fashion on a college campus.[5] Our questions for them were open-ended, and asked them to reflect on their own experiences with fashion. Due to the personal nature of the questions and this project, which deals so intimately with women's bodies and individuals' perceptions of their own bodies, we focused our conversations toward those students with whom we had established trust relationships, thus engendering rich and open responses.

We worked outwards from the biographies of these women and their responses, following Norman Denzin's model of validating each as a *universal singular*—unique in their own individual experiences yet also able to speak for the wider campus culture from which they come.[6] Rather than making generalizable claims, this study is a "thick description"[7] of students' experiences and our perceptions of campus. Consistent with ethnographic projects, we use the voices of the participants, thereby foregrounding their own comments, perspectives, and ways of seeing.[8] For additional context, we informally spoke with male students about their impressions of women's fashions on campus. While our interviews included transgender students, our discussion here focuses on heterosexual performances of fashion, acknowledging the gendered means by which women perform fashion.

KENNESAW STATE UNIVERSITY: CAMPUS AS SPACE/SCENE

Performance Studies investigates roles in context, by asking the following: what is the scene of the performance, and how does the location affect the performances enacted within it? Our context is a liberal arts university, located in the northwest region of Georgia, approximately 30 miles north of Atlanta. It is the third largest university in the state, with a current (as of Fall 2006) enrollment of 19,500 students. The campus enjoys a diverse population of traditional and non-traditional,[9] commuter and residential students and "more than 1600 international students from 130 countries."[10] Minority students comprise 20 percent of the population. Many of our students grew up in Cobb County (including Kennesaw and Marietta, GA), which is historically a politically and socially conservative region. As faculty in the Department of Theatre and Performance Studies, we teach theatre and performance studies curricula to majors as well as general education courses in theatre/performance appreciation to non-majors.

By its nature, the college campus is a highly charged public arena that encompasses the very idea of performance. In a given day, the students walk through and "hang out" in numerous discrete and widely differing locales— classrooms, libraries, food courts, computer labs, parking lots, patios, and sidewalks—each with its attendant audience. When a woman traverses the terrain, she is continually on display and aware that the multiple audiences she encounters are doubly attuned to her dressed female form *as spectacle*:

> My cover up hangs loosely from my body, and my skirt is worn from its lavish use. When I wear this complete outfit, I feel that my clothing embodies my personality. I see people look at me differently, like I know who I am and what I want out of life . . . When I walk I am floating, accepting compliments on my outfit from the people who notice me.
>
> KSU Junior

Clearly this awareness raises the stakes for careful clothing selection: it may be a college campus, but everywhere audiences are appraising appearances with watchful eyes. The women we questioned celebrated their clothing choices as means to project confidence, beauty, strength and femininity·

Overall this outfit makes me feel confident and beautiful. The jacket looks vintage, and paired with great jeans and boots with a fantastic heel, the look is stylish yet retro, sexy yet totally mature and confident. I feel strong in this outfit.

FASHION PERFORMANCE: ACHIEVING "THE LOOK"

Thus, while the primary role on a college campus is ostensibly that of "student" who is there to learn, many dressed female bodies on campus communicate that the performance of heterosexual identity frequently takes precedence: a significant number of college females are single, and the campus is a social space where young women (and men) may meet their future partners. Their appearances and performances must be "top notch" if they are to attract mates. First, there is the careful pre-performance preparation—as one KSU Senior described it: "Jeans, a black fitted shirt, and black pumps. . . . I usually accessorize with an elaborate black belt, and chandelier earrings. When I wear this outfit I will most certainly take the time to fix my hair and wear make-up." Then comes the performance itself: "Of course, I am the same person, but I find myself sitting with my legs crossed, and always reapplying my lips."

Fashion literally has the power to transform the presentation of the physical self: for our Senior, she is both "the same person" and one whose outfit directs certain performances out of its wearer: legs crossed in a feminine in-tucking of the body. The outfit orders the wearer to paint her body into existence, "always reapplying my lips," understanding lips not as given body parts but as accessories applied along with the outfit. The gesture of applying lipstick becomes part of the performance. Consider also, the performative potential of high heels: while lifting, toning and featuring ankles, calves, and thighs, they completely transform a woman's walk into an action that commands attention. Fashion performance, then, encompasses both clothing selection as well as careful choreography by which women "work" both body and clothing to create a certain "look:" feet pumping, butt swaying, breasts leading . . . Women not only wear fashions as immobile mannequins; they "Work it!" "Own it!" and "Sell it!" down the campus street where they are prey to diverse gazes checking, judging, and assessing their worth. Indeed, we found our students to be rigorous critics of their peers' fashion performances:

> To top it off, some girls wear heels. It is sooooo obvious when a girl cannot A) walk in heels the correct way, or B) stand wearing them any longer. It is actually quite embarrassing to watch a girl in pain because of her shoes. Another thing that bothers me is when make-up pretty much starts melting off. Makeup should look natural, especially when going to school.
>
> KSU Senior

> I don't enjoy the fact that young women on campus feel a need to wear extremely revealing clothes. If I didn't see them tug on the bottom of their very

short mini-skirts, or constantly adjust their low-cut tube tops and halter tops, or fiddle and play with their clothes nervously when asked to speak in class I probably wouldn't feel this way. But I don't like watching a young, beautiful woman put herself and her flesh on display when she is clearly not comfortable in that choice.

University of Virginia Graduate Student

As these comments demonstrate, the critical criteria range from disapproval about disclosure of flesh to practical concerns about the temporal reality of time and place (more than one woman we interviewed commented on early mornings and lack of time being factors in dressing down). Particularly telling is how attuned these students are to the dressed woman as a performer on display: their shared assumption is that if a woman chooses to wear these clothes in the first place, she ought to be able to "pull them off" with confidence and grace. If she cannot, she is regarded with derision; if she can, her performance is admired, and the whole woman is a success.

The film *The Devil Wears Prada*[11] offers an apt parallel. A recent college graduate, our "heroine" Andrea Sachs lands a coveted position in the fashion industry; as she is told *ad nauseum*: "a million girls would kill for this job." In her dumpy and lumpy sweater/skirt combos, clunky shoes, and size six body, not only is she an awkward misfit in the workplace—her cutting edge colleagues broadcast their disgust with curled lips and raised eyebrows—she is equally inept in her job performance. But Andrea catches on quickly and seeks out sartorial assistance from a fashion guru who loads her down with designer gems. An instantaneous Cinderella-esque transformation, and *voilà*: Andrea reappears the next morning in stunning garb with nothing less than thigh-high boots and a confident stride to seal the deal. She is physically *and* psychically transformed. Her colleagues now gaze at her with approving eyes. Moreover, trendy fashion displayed with flair produces superb job performance overnight.

Fashion performance identifies "looks" correlating to personality and ethnic types. Many fashion magazines offer the consumer ideas for a wide array of identities whether they be "dark glamour," "retro romantic," "girly grunge," or "updated prep."[12] Fashion may also serve as a mandatory marker of racial and ethnic makeup. There are palpable consequences to dressing outside of the given "look" of African-American or Caucasian dress. One student, a woman of color, noted:

> I feel that there is a cultural difference in the way people dress. Society seems to be influenced by the way they dress and expect others to dress by physical traits: race, sex, etc. I have observed this mainly in high school. For example, if you were a Black male you were expected to wear a hip-hop, baggy clothes kind of style. If a Black male were to stray from that style and were to wear something completely different then their pride in their race would be questioned and they would have comments thrown at them like "They're not really

black" or "They're trying to be White" or whatever race they identify that person's style with. People made these judgments without even talking to or getting to know that person.

"Pulling off" racial identity, then, is at least in part a fashion statement. As with Andrea's fictionalized example, where professional success or failure teetered on her fashion-ability, our respondent noted the real embodied risks of pulling off a racialized "look": "Ultimately it was like the group would 'punish' that person [who did not dress 'really black'] by not socializing with them and leaving them out of the group." Performing an idealized and visibly identifiable "look," then, has palpable effects and consequences.

Importantly, within fashion "choices" of the classy or preppy look, "sexy" in its various incarnations reigns supreme. As we discovered, today's popularized ideal for college women rides almost solely on what Paris Hilton, Heidi Klum, and several fashion-conscious students who regularly hang outside our offices, call "hot." It is also important to note that this hyper-sexualized fashion ideal transcends regional boundaries. Though our observations are of women at a southern university, the images to which these women turn for fashion inspirations are promulgated in nationwide and international advertising campaigns. Most American celebrity fashion icons (Paris Hilton, Carrie Bradshaw) emanate from Los Angeles and New York, rarely from Atlanta.[13] While the stereotypical woman of the American South unfortunately still resembles Daisy Duke of *The Dukes of Hazard*, the "real" Daisy—in new-release form, Jessica Simpson—lives in LA. Simply put: sexualized presentation of women's bodies is not "just a southern thing" (or, for that matter, "just a college thing").

CONTEMPORARY FASHION AND THE "HOT" BODY

Any performance embodies an objective or desired outcome, and many of today's feminine fashion goals are all too clear:

> Hotness has become our cultural currency, and a lot of people spend a lot of time and a lot of regular, green currency trying to acquire it. Hotness is not the same thing as beauty, which has been valued throughout history. Hot can mean popular. Hot can mean talked about. But when it pertains to women, hot means two things in particular: fuckable and salable. The literal job criteria for our role models, the stars of the sex industry.[14]

Sociologists, cultural historians, and feminists have been noting for several decades that contemporary fashion increasingly appropriates the iconography of pornography, sadomasochism and fetishism.[15] In *Fetish: Fashion, Sex, and Power*, Valerie Steele writes:

> Leather, rubber, "cruel shoes," tattoos, and body piercing—all the paraphernalia of fetishism have been increasingly incorporated into mainstream fashion.

The popular interest in subcultural style is not new, but there has recently been a qualitative change in the reception of sartorial sexuality. Today sexual "perversity" sells everything from films and fashions to chocolates and leather briefcases.[16]

Likewise, Naomi Wolf brought our attention to fashion advertising and its complicity with pornography in her vivid descriptions of "beauty" advertisements over a decade ago:

Beauty pornography looks like this: The perfected woman lies prone, pressing down her pelvis. Her back arches, her mouth is open, her eyes shut, her nipples erect; there is a line spray of moisture over her golden skin. The position is female superior; the stage of arousal, the plateau phase just preceding orgasm. On the next page, a version of her, mouth open, eyes shut is about to tongue the pink tip of a lipstick cylinder. On the page after, another version kneels in the sand on all fours, her buttocks in the air, her face pressed into a towel, mouth open, eyes shut. The reader is looking through an ordinary women's magazine.[17]

Although Wolf published this description in 1991, pornography and fashion today share icons of their industries more than ever: there are the ubiquitous and emphatic portrayals of "hot" bodies in seductive poses, whether they be those of celebrities or models in every media format imaginable: magazines, television, and of course the internet. One of the most notable and obvious of these icons is "that's hot" Paris Hilton, whose legendary fashion style and popularity among college age women is matched only by her popularity among internet pornography fans for her homemade sex tape. Or maybe these audiences are one and the same . . . ? Another cross-over between industries is the popular *Girls Gone Wild*, where college women on spring and summer vacation bare all and "make out" with each other in tight t-shirts for the camera's hungry eye. In *Sex and the City*, Carrie Bradshaw teaches us that good shoes can lead to (or follow, or be used in) good sex; Hillary Duff shows us that stylish clothing can transform her from pre-teen cutie to voluptuous vixen in a Disney magical moment; and Heidi Klum straddles a chair porn-style as she models Victoria's Secret underwear on fliers sent to thousands of households.

The ever-present influence exercised by designers and the media is not new news. Neither is the complicity of the populace, and the oft-repeated phrase reminds us of the truism: "Women are slaves to fashion." Fashion promoters relentlessly photograph admired celebrities embracing the hot fashion trends, and admirers desirously emulate their "looks"—looks that uncannily resemble soft pornography photos we found on the Internet. Consider, for example, the following two images:

1. A tanned and topless young woman lies on the beach, back to the sand; her long, wet hair drapes over her nipple. Her soaked white jeans stick to her glossy skin. Back arched, knees up, arms askew, she looks to the

    camera with mouth half-open. This is the first in a sequence of four images, culminating in a muscular man mounting this woman.

2. A topless young woman stands, and her left hand pushes aside a loose fold of red diaphanous fabric hanging beside her. A strand of black lace wraps around her neck and falls just over the nipples. Her right hand tugs (up or down?) at frayed, tight jeans, a black string bikini peeking out. She looks to the camera with moist lips parted.

Which is the soft-core porn image, and which the fashion advertisement? Given the similarities in content and style of presentation, the ambiguous identities of these two images highlights the notion that "fashion" or "porn" is a fabricated distinction made *nominally* between these types of images. And there's much at stake in these names. Interestingly enough, when we asked permission to use the fashion image in this essay, a company lawyer emphatically stated that the company would not want to be associated with anything dealing with pornography, reinforcing the importance of *naming* for at least one of these two industries. For those readers still perplexed: the first image is of a Calvin Klein model;[18] the second is of porn star Sora Aoi.[19]

    Admittedly, the advertisements are more blatant and perhaps more self-conscious portrayals than those of our students—but the parallels are undeniable. Consider first, contemporary clothing and its relationship to the body, in itself a pornographic performance of sorts: *partial* disclosure of flesh and *potential* disclosure of *more* flesh are key. Garments today flirt loudly with ever-shifting body boundaries. (Thus, we hear the popular term "flirty skirt" as if the *clothing* is doing the flirting, not the woman. And yet, if she dons the skirt, perhaps she can't help but bring her behavior into alignment.) Calculated "clothing tactics" in the fashion industry towards this end are neatly categorized by Dennis Hall as "the practice of turning underwear into outerwear"; plunging necklines, bare midriffs, skirts slit to the thigh, extremely short skirts, etc.; "diaphany" or transparency of fabrics; and "liquefaction" (inspired by a Robert Herrick poem), a second skin approach[20] (with interesting correlations to fetish fashion preferences for leather, rubber, and the like).[21] But where Hall argues in 2000 that extreme disclosure of flesh rarely makes it off the runways—although he allows it will appear in athletic wear—we attest, that in 2007 such preponderance of flesh has made its way into the everyday.

FASHIONABLE BODY PARTS: BREASTS, BOOTIES, AND BELLIES

Consider next, the body parts that are blatantly paraded and framed in both soft pornography and contemporary fashion: breasts, booties, and bellies playing peek-a-boo are enabled and enhanced by low-cut tops, low rider "skinny" jeans, thongs, piercings, and tattoos. Magazines currently preach that the properly (self-) policed body on campus wears an increasingly important fashion accessory: a nice bottom, popularly entitled in colloquial conversations and Internet soft porn sites as the "booty." *Cosmopolitan* recently cited Dr. Thomas L. Roberts III, a plastic surgeon in Spartanburg, South Carolina who had performed over 300 buttock augmentations: "Patients bring in magazine photos of people like Jennifer Lopez or Serena Williams and say 'I want one like this.'"[22]

Wanting "one" like another person—imitation is the sincerest form of flattery—means that these women have already dissected their bodies into "ones" and "anothers," splicing the body into sutured bits of flesh, flab, and muscle that the all-powerful Doctor can give them at the right price. The shift of erogenous zone[23] from Holmes's "breast boom"[24] to what these authors note as the "bum boom" we see today marks the well-shaped "behind" as fashion-forward.[25] For added fashion support, designer jeans with padded bums are now being offered in the marketplace.

Designed both to show off the contour of the new "bum" and offer accidentally-on-purpose exposure are the ubiquitous "low-rider" jeans. These jeans play peek-a-boo with a woman's posterior, falling down and showing the "whale tale" of a thong[26] and/or her "crack" as she moves through her daily routines. In front, these jeans direct the eye straight towards the waist and belly; and the hip-hugger cut offers an implied line leading straight to the crotch.

During our interviews we learned a colloquial term for the pooch of lower torso flesh excessively poofing out of low-rise jeans: "muffin top." The "muffin top"—ironically the most delicious part of the muffin, sold separately from its "muffin bottom" by some bakeries—names at least this part of the woman's body as edible, consumable, and like a purchasable treat in a store. *She* is a tart. Yet again, contemporary slang reveals parallels between a fashion feature and sexual objectification. Further colloquialisms abound, as several of our male *and female* KSU respondents informed us:

1. FUPA: fat upper pussy area; the front portion of the belly made visible by low-rise pants.
2. Tramp Stamp, or Ass Hat: a tattoo located on a woman's lower back just above the crack. One graduate student from another university described the term thusly: "If a girl's got a tramp stamp, you *know* she likes to fuck!"
3. Back Flap: rolls of back flesh pulled tight by a woman's bra, the contours of which are made visible by thin, tight, "made-to-layer" t-shirts.
4. Hip Tits: a.k.a. love handles, or a muffin top.

Each of these terms either overtly or covertly marks the female body as sexual object: for some, a "tramp stamp" literally imprints the body with desire—she *wants* to fuck. To the male gaze (adopted by both men and women in our interviews), tramp stamped women are "asking for it," harkening back to the oft-used rapists' excuse that scantily-clad women are "asking" to be raped. Moreover, each term relies on the choreography between flesh, fabric, and style, further illustrating the fact that "fashionable" clothing can never be discussed in isolation from the bodies it drapes, shapes, and produces.

Thus, when we observe college students participating in these "fashion performances" at school, we are faced with an uncomfortable impression: they are ostensibly performing soft porn as well. We are not alone: colleagues at other universities[27] and even our own students corroborated this observation. How intentional and deliberate are/were these porn fashion performances, we wondered? We sought clues about the ways that college women understood the difference (if any) between what they consider "fashion" and "porn" in relation to fashion advertisements, as these ads promote the materials through which women may produce their bodies as fashionable.

We sent our conversational partners several untitled photos, all of which were from fashion advertising campaigns, but which clearly promoted bare body parts as much, if not more than the clothing.

Photograph 1,[28] from a Sisley clothing campaign, features two women in heavy black eye make-up—one platinum blonde, one brunette. Both are tightly framed and naked from the waist up. The blonde, who stands behind and peeks out at us with one narrow eye, has ten polished nails evenly splayed over her partner's breasts. Her aureole rubs against the brunette's forearm. The brunette turns her head back towards the blonde, and their lips . . . almost touch. The brunette wears two fashion accessories: an asymmetrical chain necklace with one pearl, and a dangling earring.

Photograph 2,[29] also from a Sisley clothing campaign, features a blonde woman standing in a gilded, baroque rotunda. She leans into the camera; the position she occupies in the composition makes the white expanse of her voluminous breasts and long cleavage the focal point. Her arms tightly squeeze her upper torso. As if to mirror the seventeenth century-style space she inhabits, her breasts bulge over the narrow strip of a camisole or bra covering her nipples (or is it a spaghetti-strap sheath of a dress cinched with a belt?). We see very little of the rest of the garment, as the photograph cuts her off at the crotch.

Photograph 3,[30] a Dolce and Gabbana advertisement, features two women, clad in white lace corsets, mini-petticoats and thigh-high black leggings; they lie against each other in the hay, nose-to-nose, eyes half-shut, hands touching hair, and thighs intertwined.

Two questions accompanied the photos:

1. Are these photos from a fashion magazine or a soft-pornography magazine?
2. In which type of magazine (fashion/porn) does each photo "belong?" Whichever you choose, please explain why.

The student comments captured below reflect their struggle with clear distinctions, although bared breasts typically directed them towards the realm of soft porn and more "artsy" shots toward the world of fashion:

Photograph 1: One student commented, "I would have to say soft core porn—however, it looks strikingly like those Paris Hilton ads for Guess Marciano she did. The nipple, though, throws me off and makes me move away from fashion mag. [sic] into [the] porn arena." Another student: "I can imagine this photograph potentially being an ad for perfume or some other unseeable wearable (like liquor or hair or make up). But because the one woman's breast is completely visible, I would have to say it comes from a soft porn magazine. They aren't allowed to do that, are they?"

Photograph 2: "This looks like a fashion magazine picture, although I'm not really sure what is fashionable about it. No alarm in my head goes off about this picture at all—that there may be something inappropriate about it. Which tells me something may be wrong with my alarm."

Photograph 3: One respondent replied: "This picture is definitely from a fashion magazine. I am a little disturbed by its resemblance to [Photograph] one. But these women are so thin and dressed so extravagantly that I can't picture them anywhere but in a fashion magazine. Plus, the quality of the photography is much more artful." Another: "Definitely high fashion. . . . Even as I write that [a fashion shot is more "artsy and sophisticated"] the absurdity of calling high fashion ads sophisticated comes clear to me. I mean all I have to do is just look at our dead dolls in the hay . . . to laugh at that statement!"

It is difficult to place these images at any specific point along the continuum between the dressed body as "fashionable" and the eroticized body as "pornographic." The significance of these women's vacillating responses is two-fold: they balk at the visual evidence that fashion advertising is appropriating porn: "They can't do that, can they?" betrays a naïve trust that the industry wouldn't do that—and the industry plays into that trust. Furthermore, their responses demonstrate that no matter the *intention* of the wearers, the power to term their bodies as "fashion" or "porn" lies largely outside their control. Hence, for our fashion-conscious college women, the *perception* of their clothing choices as pornographic (or vice versa) *by the viewing audience* largely determines how their bodies are produced, understood, and used in campus culture. In many senses, with both pornography and fashion imagery, we're talking about the same sets of clothes; the same hungry, wanton glances from women to the camera's eye; the same seductive postures. It's the framing *as* fashion or *as* porn that distinguishes the two. Tattoo or tramp stamp? Midsection or muffin top? Pornography, like the designation "woman," is not an essence but a way of framing and viewing the (un)dressed body in performance. Pornography is not an inherent quality within an outfit, but the narrative frame and matrix of gazes surrounding and supporting a particular perception of bodies and artifacts. When we term a "fashion performance" as "performance of porn" we, too, are participating in that matrix.

PORN CHIC

While *we* may be dismayed by the alliance of fashion and pornography in some of our students' fashion performances, the fashion industry and popular culture clearly are not. Enter the term "porn chic." According to artist-scholar Nicola Bockelmann, porn chic "describes the infiltration of representations of pornography into mass culture, thereby becoming an accepted, even idealized, cultural element of the mainstream."[31] Considered in this light, "porn chic" illustrates how far society, and in our discussion, fashion, has come/gone in proudly adopting pornography into the mainstream.

Each word—fashion or porn—carries strongly felt denotations and connotations. By definition, the intention of pornography is to arouse sexual desire in others and presumably in the self. The common association is that pornographic intentions are "naughty" and, in America's Puritan-based culture, "nasty." Pornography is often associated with those of "low" moral stature. Its "sin" is lasting, and it's difficult to wash the stain (or stardom) of a pornographic past away. Pornography is a "dirty" practice, usually taking the form of women enticing men in exchange for money.[32]

Conversely, fashion is clean, respectable, and keeping responsibly up with contemporary culture: framing an image (and its associated brand name) as "fashion" elevates it above mere sexual fantasy into a "higher" realm of legitimized beauty. The understood intention of fashion is to feel pretty and look appealing (the implication is to look "sexy" though not always stated as such),[33] and is arguably a "good" intention. Calling a particular woman's outfit "fashionable" permits conservatives to wear what might otherwise be framed pornography. The association of an outfit with "fashion" inculcates the wearer into a different sort of community—not radical, condemned, and marginalized porn-folks, but socially appropriate and hip citizens of the times.

Calling an outfit "fashionable" also allows conservative Christian women to experience what might otherwise be considered a taboo (porn) by disapproving elders. The Christian-porn conundrum is interesting: while we did not inquire about the religious affiliation of our interview partners, many of our students at KSU openly confess to being conservative Christians. Why is there a predominance of pornographied dress on a (seemingly) religiously conservative campus? Are non-conservatives the only ones dressing this way? Or are conservative Christian women redefining what the book of *Psalms* means by: "Hear, O daughter, consider and incline your ear . . . the king [Christ] will desire your beauty. . . . The princess is decked in her chamber with gold-woven robes; in many-coloured robes she is led to the king; behind her the virgins, her companions, follow."[34]

If porn performance is taboo, then how could conservative Christian women "get away" with doing it? Richard Schechner contends every performance of the self is a dance between ritual and play. If the "chaste, pure" performance is the norm (or ritual), then sexualized fashion performances are an act of play: "play gives people a chance to temporarily experience the taboo, the excessive, and the risky. You may never be Oedipus or Electra, but you can perform them 'in play'."[35] Play simultaneously acknowledges the rules of ritual and allows a temporary escape from them. Fashion becomes a way for conservative Christians to hop outside the performance of "good girls" and play in fashion-land: a world of costumery and make-up (with its connotations of make-believe) somehow separate from the mundane world of everyday life.[36] As playtime, fashion performance offers a relatively safe and socially acceptable way for women to try on the taboo of porn.

Further, women may obliterate the perception of taboo altogether through fashion's new vocabulary. The term "porn chic" conflates and confuses the seemingly separate industries of porn and fashion, making publicly acceptable those costumed performances that might otherwise be fashion-policed as lowbrow smut. This label has enabled us to understand, reconcile, and condone fashion's "flirtation" with pornography as just that: harmless flirtation, not all-out debauchery.[37]

STRADDLING PORN-FASHION: RAMIFICATIONS

American consumer culture performs porn-fashion *on* the bodies of women, and women's bodies become a *worn* (used, tattered) stage as a result. The public eye is not only permitted but invited into women's pants through the language of porn chic fashions. Porn chic clothing forces women to perform a peek-a-boo display of their bodies, showing a little flesh here and there when bending over, reaching upwards, or even walking down the hall. Further, these women are encouraged to shape their bodies to resemble an unattainable fantasy ideal. This unattainable body ideal rests in part on the exoticized backs (literally, the backsides or bums) of black women. The effect is to reduce the complexity of women's embodied experience on the college campus to snipped and sutured slices of commodified body parts. Let us take each of these ramifications in turn.

The very term "porn chic" makes public the usually unspoken yet understood correlation between women, bodies, fashion, and sex. Women are commonly described as dressing sexy or sharp, or like whores or prudes, terms which carry both the baggage of moral judgment and the assumption of sexual insight through visual appraisal. Thus, the vocabulary through which we may understand women's fashion is often aligned with an invitational view into women's bedroom behavior: tramp stamp, FUPA, hip tits . . . ; we are always already scripted to think about women's fashion in sexualized terms— now even more blatantly with "porn chic." How we look at women's dressed bodies is often a question of how deeply we *think* we know how (and how often) her undressed body performs with other men and/or women.

Today's fashionable clothing leaves the college woman two main postures:

either I suck my body into these jeans and heels and play a weightless, erotic peek-a-boo dance throughout the day (making me a porn star); or I exhale, letting my body bubble and ooze out of these jeans and fall off of my heels (making an embarrassing blobular "muffin top" of myself). In some cases, current fashion options force women into acquisition of clothing that acts upon them, sexualizing them despite their efforts at modesty. One of our students insightfully commented, "Even a person who dresses modestly, if she purchases clothes that are new, is going to be dressed in a way that draws attention to the bottom and the crotch."

Porn chic literally forces women into certain body shapes and impressions in an attempt to meet an impossible body ideal. Porn chic assumes one size of jeans for all bodies, small and large: a constant frustration of many of our friends is that it is difficult to find cute clothes in any size above a "six," and we acknowledge that, like Dr. Roberts' ideal butts (not too small, but not too large), the female body undoubtedly is idealized as size zero-four.[38]

The body itself—with its ever-so-slight "muffin top"—speaks of the unattainable, always-deferred ideal body toward which she constantly strives, but will inevitably fail, to fully achieve. As Huff elaborates, "the current ideal of thinness . . . is pursued less to achieve thinness itself than to cultivate and continually reinscribe docility on the body. But a perfectly docile body can only be approached, never actually attained, making the struggle for physical self-control an unending battle."[39]

Fashion epithets aid and abet this struggle; one of our students aptly observed: "I think the new 'skinny pant' trend is a good example. . . . The 'skinny' refers to the fit, but the word stresses women out, making them judge and scrutinize their bodies and decide if they are skinny enough to wear the 'skinny pant.'" Again, as a graduate student said,

> I am blessed by genetics and hard work: on the soccer field in high school, the track in college, and now the gym in graduate school and have always been thin. But I am not a stranger to the pressure to be skinny that is fed to us every day through television, magazines, news, and film—I am lucky to be closer to the look that our culture deems as "good," but I am reminded everyday that I had better stay this way, that if one day I change size or shape or wrinkle, I will lose my worth.

One woman of color commented on her perceptions of body expectations:

> I must say though that I do not have as much pressure on me to be skinny by any means. I am part Black and part Hispanic. It's expected of me to "fill out" my clothing. It's like I get kicked out of being Black or Hispanic if I don't. White women unfortunately have the sigma of having to be skinny with big boobs. And [they] must have this body all of their lives and must look this way in [their] clothing.

A "sexy" fit often means "filling out" clothing: excessively popping out of a shirt[40] in all the "correct" places. Fleshy excess is not limited to voluptuous breasts, either—the bum is the current sexy-fit indicator. As the previous student indicated, some women of color feel the additional pressure to shape their bodies according to commonly accepted racially identifying markers. For white women, the well-shaped bum in clothes is not so much a celebration of diverse bodies or a liberation of the fat heinie as it is "something else to desire, to fixate on, to compare and evaluate. After all, it's not just any old big butt—it has to be toned, no cellulite; it's got to have a certain contour. It's a new reigning aesthetic."[41]

While a majority of women who have buttocks augmentation surgery are traditionally just exiting college or might be pursuing graduate work (age 22–35) and the price range for such a procedure equals or exceeds the cost of one or multiple years of a college education ($13,000–$19,000), the seeds of surgery-thoughts likely start in college through magazine ads such as those featured in *Cosmopolitan*.[42] Twice in the *Cosmopolitan* we picked up did the "DoctorsSayYes.net" group advertise in full-page spreads for cosmetic surgery to the masses. "Absolutely no one will be turned down," they promise. "Our company manages a group of Board Certified Surgeons that guarantee financing to any patient who wants *any kind of cosmetic surgery*. . . . Now you can finance your cosmetic procedure for as little as $99 down and $99 per month [emphasis in original]," they say.[43] So on the college campus, young white women are encouraged to dream about bigger booties and live with their own less-than spectacular heinies in the meantime.

If the deflated-booty marks the body as de-feminized, then who/what does this surgery re-mark and transform the body into? For white women receiving this treatment, it could be the appropriation of an exoticized ideal. One white woman receiving buttocks enlargement reported to *Vibe* magazine that "her new figure gets her noticed. 'People think I'm Spanish or mixed,' she says. 'But I don't care. I love it.'"[44] She loves . . . the attention that her newly purchased "Spanish booty" gives her? The desirable behind is notably embodied by the ideal exoticized woman of color—J. Lo's butt-reduction retained just enough toned tushy for a prestigious "baby got back," and Serena Williams's athletic career has been reduced to "you can do back bends or sit-ups, but baby don't lose that butt," to quote SirMixaLot's popular rhyme. Dr. Roberts' website www.betterbuttocks.com reassures us that the ideal buttocks varies from one ethnic group to another. However, the site later contradicts this notion of multiple acceptable bodies by giving us photographs of each ethnicity's ideal; thus, it ultimately prescribes for us what his patients report as the reigning aesthetic. Gazing at this article for an instant all but guarantees that the susceptible reader will label her bum for life.

The current "multicultural" fashion industry feeds on eroticization and exoticization of the black female body. Anne Balsamo writes about the fashion campaigns of supermodel Iman's time up through the late 1990s, when:

"black bodies" serve[d] as mannequins for designer messages intended for affluent white readers. The narrative constructed around *Elle's* black bodies and
white bodies concern[ed] the fashion industry's appropriation of the trope of
primitivism as a seasonal fashion look. In this case, the fashion apparatus de-
ploy[ed] signs of the "primitive" in the service of constructing an anti-fashion
high fashion look.[45]

Affluent white women can appropriate the perception of this exoticized fashion ideal—and, importantly, this is an *enfleshed* ideal. Now, instead of the
fashionable clothing, the fibrous body itself becomes a corporeal chunk to be
purchased—big booties for sale!—inserted, and worn under the skin. This is
not so much a multicultural utopia as evidence that "the politics of representation are [still] very confused."[46] Further, under the guise of "confusion" and
even "multiculturalism," many women of color are reduced to the size of
their butt flesh, which white women are given the power to buy, allowing
them symbolic ownership over this black body (part). Porn chic exoticizes
and commodifies women of color—effectively, the only power they are given
under this fashion rubric is the "power of the bum."

Admittedly and to its credit, porn chic performance troubles the overly-
simplistic Cartesian separation of matter/body and mind/intellect. After all,
these are smart, college-educated women who flaunt their sexualized, fleshy
bodies before peers and professors. Situated within the figurative "bubble" of
the college campus, these performances between fashion and porn "pop" the
invisible membrane separating the (perceptively) sheltered campus environs
and the "real" and sexually explicit world out there beyond KSU's bucolic
borders.

But again, in this campus context, *why* are these women choosing to *emphasize* themselves as bodies to be gazed upon? Are they intending to challenge this body-mind binary? Are they making a statement about women's
sexuality? And/or are they unthinkingly *buying* into an industry and gendered
social system in which others profit from idealized images of women?

Fashion has transformed the icons of pornography into glamorous and
commodifiable reflections. The consumer is seduced into the acquisition of
the *thing* itself (clothing) and learns to disassociate it from the *act* portrayed
in the photo (pornography), thereby disguising the smutty reputation. Those
who embrace "hot" new trends sport them willingly and proudly: this is the
image that attracts! This is what girls are complimented for; this is what
attracts the "gaze" and hence the "mate," to hark back to our earlier discussion of the multiple purposes for seeking a college education (as some have
called it, "She's going for her 'M.R.S.' degree").

Porn chic is not feminism, though it is sometimes taken up as such. Porn
chic reinforces both the power and predominance of the male gaze over wom-
en's bodies by framing individual pieces of women's bodies—the belly, the
booty, the (lack of) muffin top—in much the same way that Laura Mulvey

describes women on film as framed, distilled, and fragmented erotic objects.[47] As one of our conversational partners observed:

> The hipster bottoms we wear are usually paired with lengthening tops, so that our torsos have become longer and longer. This serves to *draw attention to the pelvis*, which these long tops and hipster bottoms define more clearly [emphasis ours]. Where I think many styles from the past may have drawn attention to the shoulders, breasts, or legs, I think that the dominant line in contemporary clothing is designed to draw attention to the central (rather than peripheral, like breasts or arms) area of sex. I think this reflects a shift in sexual attitudes toward increasingly less imaginative ways of thinking about sexuality, even as we are (hopefully) becoming more pragmatic, open, and realistic about the same.

Another student elaborated this important ramification of porn chic culture:

> Most women, I think, dress in a way that calls attention to the most obvious areas of sexual usage and never to the less obvious areas. I think our clothing is rather noisy about genitalia *at the expense of including our whole selves in the sexual, sensual, and very human journeys we are on* [emphasis ours].

Porn chic slices women's bodies into commoditized and individualized bits and pieces, reducing the whole of women students' embodied experience—the "human journey"—to pelvic allure, "the bottom and the crotch."

CONCLUSION

Even as we write these words, the trends are changing: longer tops and rising waistlines on this coming season's new "hot" looks mark the shifts that make fashion what it is: changing, in flux, and dynamic. Perhaps in response to the frustrations some of our conversational partners voiced, fashion is moving away from what we call pornographic looks. But does a change in waistline alter the underlying concerns: that young women are caught up in a system of "fashion" that convincingly induces human beings to commodify their own bodies, and specifically for white women to commodify the bodies of women of color?

For many of the women we interviewed and for ourselves, fashion is intensely personal and powerful. As "the frontier between self and the not-self,"[48] clothing is a simultaneously intimate and public experience, as well as a highly visible marker of personal and social identity.[49] When we participate in the fashion game along with our students, the stakes for all of us are equally high—our very identities are at risk with each choice we make. The matrix of outer gazes wields just as much if not more power than we, transforming the body into an attractive, confident woman, or a smutty porn-star. As one colleague at another university wrote:

Many of my young female colleagues walk the fine line between dressing with confidence and style and dressing in a way that compromises the respect we try to earn in the classroom and in the rehearsal hall. I would have to say that I find myself critiquing this dichotomy a lot. . . .

In our world of increasingly blurry boundaries and slippery dichotomies, the line is not difficult to cross.

In the end, the infuriating point is that, for women, *any* fashion choice may be convincingly narrated as sexual and even pornographic, and increasingly the fashion machine has taken not only a masculinist gaze on woman (labeling her as passive canvas and art object) but now a pornographied gaze (she's porn chic, she's hot) for commercial benefit. The scrutiny with which we monitor and categorize women's bodies as "fashionable" or "pornographic"—judging what's "hot" from what's "trash"—reveals just how deeply embedded the male gaze is in our daily encounters with one another. The fashion machine that now popularly rides the line between fashion/porn purposely sets women up to have their clothing choices (again, supplied by that same fashion industry)—and women themselves—appraised as "hot" or "trash," thus locking them into this dichotomy in which they may only be narrated in terms of sexuality.

Our hope, then, is that our women students would begin to question how they are using fashion, and indeed how fashion is using them. We hope that they question which audiences they are trying to satisfy with their fashions: themselves? Other women? Other men? Or an unattainable ideal that "Others" these women unto their own bodies? We hope that they might take our ruminations here as both homage and call to action—to use their fashions to stare back at the male gaze and embrace their clothed bodies as sexual *beings*, not commodifiable things; as embodied subjects, not objects. Finally, we hope they refashion sartorial expectations on campus in service of women's experience, "including our whole selves in the sexual, sensual, and very human journeys we are on."

———— 5 ————

One Night in Paris (Hilton): Wealth, Celebrity, and the Politics of Humiliation

THOMAS FAHY

F or many Americans, Paris Whitney Hilton washed up on the shores of celebrity in the September 2000 issue of *Vanity Fair*. The article, "Hip Hop Debs," presents Paris and her sister, Nicky, as the new generation of media-hungry Hiltons. Modeling themselves after their great-grandfather, Conrad Hilton, who built the hotel empire and forged a public persona based on his association with celebrities (from L. A. showgirls to his second wife, Zsa Zsa Gabor) and their grandfather, with his short-lived yet highly publicized marriage to Elizabeth Taylor, the Hilton sisters seem to be extending this family tradition with élan. Of course, they have been making appearances at high-society events and parties since the late 1990s, but their debut in *Vanity Fair* marked a new beginning of sorts—an attempt on the part of their family to catapult them into the upper stratosphere of celebrity and to shape the ways in which the media would interpret them.

In many respects, "Hip-Hop Debs" accomplished these goals, albeit ironically. It moved the sisters, particularly Paris, from "Page Six" to cover story material. Yet much to the Hilton family's dismay, Nancy Jo Sales's sardonic text and David LaChapelle's controversial images helped establish the terms that would continue to characterize Paris Hilton as a vapid, narcissistic, spoiled, and highly sexualized figure who desires one thing above all else— fame. Sales reports one anonymous friend as saying that "all [Paris] wants to do is become famous . . . to wipe out the past, to become somebody else."[1] Certainly the accompanying photographs of the nineteen-year-old heiress reinforce this notion. But just like the glaring contradictions between Paris Hilton's ostentatious public image and the ways in which she tries to characterize herself as "a normal kid,"[2] a tension underlies her celebrity status and her privileged place in America's hereditary aristocracy.

Celebrities must continually negotiate the public's desire to both elevate and denigrate the famous. As Leo Braudy explains in *The Frenzy of Renown: Fame and Its History*, "modern fame is always compounded of the audience's aspirations and its despair, its need to admire and to find a scapegoat for that need."[3] Paris Hilton, a celebrity who is both desired and despised, would seem to fulfill these needs. Unlike public figures who achieve recognition from acting, performing, writing, athletics, and/or politics, however, Hilton's fame hasn't come from any discernible talent or skill. It is inherited, like her wealth, and this complicates how we read and understand her image. Not only is there less to admire about Paris Hilton, but she also fails to embody the typical promise of modern-day celebrity—that anyone can achieve the same. If celebrity is a function of birth, it is as exclusive as we've always feared, and supremely undemocratic. Cultural historian P. David Marshall explains the promise in terms of individuality: "Celebrities are icons of democracy and democratic will. Their wealth does not signify their difference from the rest of society so much as it articulates the possibility of everyone's achieving the status of individuality within the culture."[4] Yet in the case of Paris Hilton, wealth *does* signify an important difference. The inherited privilege that she enjoys distinguishes her from the general public and makes her individuality (one largely defined by an elite class status) problematic; it is an identity unattainable, if not impossible, for most to acquire and/or imitate. Despite her claims that any woman can tap into her "inner heiress," Paris Hilton repeatedly acknowledges that "heiresses are born with privileges."[5] She has even claimed to be "American royalty."[6] But who among us will inherit tens of millions? Who has the opportunity to live in the Waldorf-Astoria on Park Avenue and to get unrestricted access to red-carpet events with famous actors and rock stars? If, as Leo Braudy reminds us, fame "requires that uniqueness be exemplary and reproducible,"[7] what exactly is the source of Paris Hilton's appeal? Why does she receive so much public attention?

Two photographs from the *Vanity Fair* article offer a clue about her celebrity. The picture entitled "Sweetie Pie," for example, shows Paris in an act of youthful rebellion as she stands near the entryway of her grandmother's lavish Beverly Hills living room. The elegant, wealthy furniture in the background clearly belongs to another, much older, generation, and a robe lies on the floor as if it has just fallen off her shoulders, revealing Paris's scantily clothed body. Her legs are wide apart. A short, tight skirt barely covers her crotch, and a fishnet tank top reveals her breasts and nipples. The straps of her high-heeled shoes almost blend into a nearby phone cord (the most contemporary and anachronistic object in the room). Reflective sunglasses hide her eyes, and she extends her middle finger to the viewer. On one level, her brazen pose seems directed at members of the media and the general public who both desire her image and criticize her at the same time. On another, perhaps more obvious level (the one probably uppermost in Hilton's mind at the time), the photograph suggests Paris's rejection of her upper-class heritage—leaving behind the values of old money (as embodied in the furniture) and saying "fuck off" to the social propriety expected of someone of her economic class. Even the robe on the floor and her cut-off gloves imply a casting off of sorts. A robe and gloves would hide her body; they suggest an investment in privacy and, arguably, propriety. But Paris Hilton has largely defined herself as the antithesis of these things.[8] Here, she wears an outfit that has more in common with a prostitute than an heiress. It is an outfit that suggests public (as well as sexual) access, not private reservation. And in the context of this Beverly Hills estate, her clothing and exposed body elide class divisions between her and her audience; they promise intimate access to—and even the possible violation of—this world of privilege.

The most striking photograph, "California Girl," also works to mitigate Paris Hilton's elite status through sexual objectification and erotic desire. In this image, Paris's body has washed up onto Zuma Beach. Her eyes are closed, and her mouth is open in an ecstatic smile—perhaps in the hopes of mouth-to-mouth resuscitation from either the nearby men or an anonymous public. The top of her swimsuit has been lowered to reveal her right breast, and her legs, once again, are spread apart. Twenty-dollar bills and a few makeup bottles (trappings of her class or of prostitution) surround her body in the wet sand, while several surfers stand nearby, holding their long, phallic surfboards. These details invite the viewer to watch two things: Paris Hilton's inert, seemingly lifeless body and the surfers who gaze at her. The money reinforces the idea that part of her allure stems from her association with the Hilton family fortune. But her nudity and vulnerability, suggested by the position of her body and the men who surround her with their large surfboards, casts her as an object of desire and potential violation. One might not have riches to inherit, but one can engage in the fantasy of sexual congress with such money through a figure like Paris Hilton.[9] It is both her wealth and sexually exposed/available body, therefore, that titillate the public. Together these things are presented as—and continue to be—defining terms of her celebrity.

Just as these photographs can be read as a critique of the public attention given to such a superficial individual, they also function ironically in relation to the article. Most obviously, they undermine the ways in which Mrs. Hilton insists, for example, that Paris is a "sweet kid" and "the most modest girl."[10] But in many respects, these photographs and the dynamic created by their juxtaposition with the text also set the stage for the ways in which Paris Hilton—and by Paris Hilton I mean all of the people who construct her image (her family, managers, agents, publicists, the media, a complicit public, etc.)—would make immodesty and, more importantly, humiliation significant components of her success. From her autobiography, *Confessions of an Heiress*, and reality television show, *The Simple Life*, to her controversial commercial for Carl's Jr. and her pornographic videos, particularly *One Night in Paris*, Paris Hilton's highly eroticized image promises an erosion of the economic boundaries that typically separate the upper class from the rest of society. As P. David Marshall reminds us, "celebrities reinforce the conception that there are no barriers in contemporary culture that the individual cannot overcome."[11] And Paris Hilton has made this message an essential part of her appeal.

"HOW TO BE AN HEIRESS": DECEPTION, BOREDOM, AND THE NOT SO SIMPLE LIFE

In January 2006, the Economic Policy Institute published a report on the growing disparity between the rich and poor in the United States. Authors Jared Bernstein, Elizabeth McNichol, and Karen Lyons attribute this problem to a number of factors, including wage inequality (which has been exacerbated by globalization, increased immigration and trade, long periods of unemployment, deregulation, and the weakening of unions), investment income that typically benefits the wealthy, corporate profits, and government policies ("both what governments have done and what governments have not done"[12]). The report argues that the economic inequalities of the last twenty-five years have led to a decline in most people's living standards, a decline that has social and political implications:

> The United States was built on the ideal that hard work should pay off, that individuals who contribute to the nation's economic growth should reap the benefits of that growth. Over the past two decades, however, the benefits of economic growth have been skewed in favor of the wealthiest members of society. . . . A widening gulf between the rich on the one hand and the poor and middle class on the other hand can reduce social cohesion, trust in government and other institutions, and participation in the democratic process.[13]

In part, the EPI's report, entitled "Pulling Apart: A State-by-State Analysis of Income Trends," views this widening economic gulf as a corrosive agent for the ideals of American democracy and society—a metaphoric and potentially literal "pulling apart" of the United States. It also implies that this gap can have dangerous consequences, including the weakening of social cohesion and the public trust.

The media quickly characterized this report—along with the conference hosted by the Economic Policy Institute in the same month—as a signal of impending "class warfare."[14] And this interpretation resonates with the analyses of political and economic historian Kevin Phillips. In his book *Wealth and Democracy*, Phillips argues that the United States has long since abandoned

the egalitarianism of the Founding Fathers and has, in fact, become a plutoc-
racy. One dimension of his critique involves the "hereditary aristocracy." He
explains that early-twenty-first-century America is both the "world's richest
major nation" and "the West's citadel of inherited wealth. Aristocracy [is] a
cultural and economic fact, if not a statutory one."[15] And Phillips considers
the ability of the rich to pass on their estates to be a significant factor in this
growing economic inequality: "The United States in turn entered the new
century with the Republican Party having begun the elimination of federal
estate and gift taxes in order to let the great wealth accumulations of the late
twentieth century pass minimally hindered to the next generation."[16] Philips
concludes that this type of disparity often leads to a "politics of resentment"—resentment that is typically manifested in radicalism and sweeping
political reform.

Paris Hilton is a clearly a beneficiary of policies that help safeguard inherited wealth, and as a celebrity who represents this aristocratic culture, a great
deal of public resentment about class inequality has been directed at (and
mitigated by) her image. Oftentimes, upper-class society, just like celebrity
culture, is linked to a democratizing impulse associated with the American
Dream. Both imply that anyone can potentially achieve fame and wealth. At
a time when the gap between rich and poor is greater than at any point in
U.S. history and when political resentment seems to be growing over policies
that favor the rich, however, Hilton's association with hereditary wealth
(which by its very nature is exclusive) could have been a liability for her
public image. Yet it hasn't been. In fact, it has been a crucial part of her
popularity and success. Paris Hilton—at her most glamorous, most erotic,
and most embarrassed—provides her audience, particularly those who feel
disenfranchised by economic inequality, with an outlet for their fantasies and
frustrations. Her eroticized body promises intimate access to the world of
celebrity and upper-class privilege, while images of her that are intended to
humiliate (as evident in the ironic subtext of the *Vanity Fair* article, *The
Simple Life*, and *One Night in Paris*) enact a kind of politics that closes the
socio-economic gap between herself and the majority of those who consume
her image. In this way, Paris Hilton's image is not only an effective tool for
examining contemporary tensions about wealth, but it also offers greater insight into the ways in which popular culture can mitigate—and even defer—
the kind of resentment that would lead to social and political change.

More specifically, both *Confessions of an Heiress* and *The Simple Life* use
eroticism and humiliation to transform "the truth" about Paris Hilton's class
standing into something palatable for consumption. These portraits make Hilton seem more accessible (either to imitation, derision, or desire) and ultimately work to contain some of the broader social problems that her extraordinary inherited wealth creates. P. David Marshall's *Celebrity and Power: Fame
in Contemporary Culture* argues that at some level "celebrities are *attempts* to
contain the mass. The mass is the site par excellence of affective power, a

kind of power that is seen to be very volatile and dangerous but also very desirable if it can be effectively housed."[17] Unlike Marshall's analysis of celebrities who represent the public by attempting to resolve the inherent contradiction in a democratic society between the power of individualism and of collective will, however, Paris Hilton's celebrity contains the mass in a different way; it allows contradictory readings of her (as an object of desire and resentment) that parallels the public's often contradictory responses to wealth (as something that inspires both desire and envy).

Confessions of an Heiress, which has almost as many photographs as words, plays with this tension by offering a range of images that highlight Hilton's glamorous wealth and sexualized body. Her seemingly countless evening gowns, ostentatious diamond jewelry, fur coats, and fashionable accessories appear alongside her bikinis, lingerie, and other revealing clothing. Of course, the wealth and privilege that is evident on every page inverts the more traditional narratives of American autobiographies—the rags to riches, trauma to recovery, rise and fall (only to rise up again) stories. Instead, Paris Hilton's story is one of riches to riches. In this way it offers yet another glimpse into high society life and celebrity culture that continues to intrigue the public. But the book also promises two things that do situate it in the tradition of autobiography: a portrait of the author's "true" self and strategies/secrets that readers can use to achieve the same. This promise of truth (like the illusion of reality in *The Simple Life*) constitutes another aspect of its allure, but neither lives up to these claims. As I will show, the artifice of *Confessions* and *The Simple Life* enables Paris Hilton to remain exclusively in the realm of the interpretable image—the primary vehicle that sustains her celebrity and cultural function regarding class.

Benjamin Franklin's *Autobiography,* which he worked on from 1771 until his death in 1790, begins by setting up his life story as a model for future generations: "Having emerged from the poverty and obscurity in which I was born and bred, to a state of affluence and some degree of reputation in the world. . . . my posterity may like to know [the conducting means I made use of], as they may find some of them suitable to their own situations, and therefore fit to be imitated."[18] The prospect of imitation, in other words, adds a level of import to Franklin's life, for it links the value of his story to its usefulness as a model for other lives. And in eighteenth-century America where the production and consumption of goods was increasingly geared toward a capitalistic market, nothing could have been more important.

Franklin goes on to link this understanding of the American marketplace to the idea of appearance: "In order to secure my credit and character as a tradesman, I took care not only to be in *reality* industrious and frugal, but to avoid all appearances to the contrary. I drest plainly; I was seen at no places of idle diversion. I never went out a fishing or shooting."[19] Franklin understood that one's public identity was often seen as a reflection of the private self, and as a result, he created a public image that would help secure his professional and personal advancement. As historian John Kasson explains in *Rudeness and Civility: Manners in Nineteenth-Century Urban America,* Franklin may not have "directly [advocated] deceit" in the *Autobiography,* but "he was notoriously willing, if he could not 'boast of much Success in acquiring the *Reality*' of a particular virtue, to be more than satisfied by his success 'with regard to the *Appearance* of it.'"[20] For Franklin, projecting an image of success could be just as socially and personally meaningful as the real thing in a society where outward appearances were valued so highly.

On the surface, Paris Hilton's co-written autobiography, *Confessions of an Heiress: A Tongue-in-Chic Peek Behind the Pose* (2004), seems to promote a similar philosophy about appearances and the art of deception, though without Franklin's sophistication, his belief that outward appearances should reflects one's inner merits, and his corresponding emphasis on moral virtues. Hilton begins· by addressing some of the public responses to her image: "Newspapers and magazines write that I'm spoiled and privileged. . . . They think I instantly became famous because I was born into a rich, well-known family. . . . Okay, *I get it.* Everyone can have fun with my image because *I* like to have fun with it too."[21] The main goal of the book is not to defend herself from such attacks but to offer a different, more personal interpretation of her own image: "I've finally decided to give you a sneak peek into my very hyped life—so you can know the real me."[22] Yet based on the book, the real Paris Hilton is no different from the image-constructed one—a young woman preoccupied with clothes, cosmetics, fast food, hair, cell phones, parties, boys, and an insatiable desire to be associated with celebrity. This list does demonstrate one possible facet of her appeal, however. Hilton can claim to be "a normal kid" because she shares the "normal" interests of teenage girls. In fact, Fireside Books initially considered teenage girls the primary market for *Confessions,* which is now in its sixteenth printing. But the range of people who attended various book signings surprised Fireside editor Trish Todd: "We thought it was mostly going to be teenage girls . . . but it was moms with strollers, it was little old ladies, it was gay guys, it was businessmen in suits—it was everyone."[23]

The make-up of this audience is not entirely surprising given the various contexts we have seen for Paris Hilton's celebrity—a celebrity built on the appearance of sexual availability, extraordinary riches, teenage interests (in malls, cell phones, and popular trends), romances with shipping heirs and movie stars, and an unabashed narcissism. Her image encourages a range of responses, in part, because it is not grounded in anything specific. As Leo Braudy reminds us, "those whose fame depends least on anything specific are, in an image-conscious world, the most likely to be emulated. To be famous for yourself, for what you are without talent or premeditation, means you have come into your rightful inheritance."[24] Here, inheritance is personal freedom, the power to stand out in a world where so many people feel anonymous. Not surprisingly, Paris Hilton, who fully embodies this type of meritless fame, wants to establish herself as a model for personal freedom and individuality—qualities that resonate with American audiences of any class.

Hilton's literal inheritance, however, tends to contradict the democratic implications that Braudy finds in her type of fame. Throughout *Confessions of an Heiress*, Hilton tries to glamorize her extravagant, privileged life, while suggesting that class is essentially a state of mind. This absurd message, which isn't offset by her repeated admission that she was born with privileges, is encapsulated in her central theme that everyone has an "inner heiress," the ability to "create [their] own image, and project an extreme sense of confidence."[25] Like Benjamin Franklin, Hilton offers her story as a model, suggesting that anyone, regardless of his or her socio-economic background, can achieve what she has through imitation. As she states at the end of the introduction: "Here are my fail-safe instructions on how to be an heiress and live like you have a privileged life—and I *am* serious about them. Most of them, anyway."[26] Just as this claim is about simulacra, living like you're someone you're not, the playful set of instructions that follow also highlight deception as an integral part of Hilton's public persona: "Always tell everyone what they want to hear. Then do what you want."[27] And later, she advises people to "act ditzy. Lose things. It throws people off and makes them think you're 'adorable,' and less together than you really are."[28] And if all else fails, "you can always reinvent yourself and your lineage if you have to."[29]

It would be a mistake to take these instructions, or any aspect of Hilton's autobiography, at face value. Just when the narrative promises to offer some degree of truth (including her opening claim about getting to know "the real me"), it promotes deceit as a tool for success. Yet the implications of using deception to manipulate people and to achieve recognition remain unacknowledged here. Unlike Franklin's narrative or the autobiography of infamous showman P. T. Barnum in the nineteenth century, Hilton's book does not present a moralistic side to offset her flaws or questionable practices. She simply reminds readers to be kind to animals, which doesn't preclude eating hamburgers or wearing furs.

At the same time, one could see the role of deception in *Confessions of an Heiress* as appealing to—or at least appeasing—those who resent the wealthy corporate culture that she embodies. Certainly, the recent scandals of Enron, Halliburton, Tyco, Qwest Communications, and countless others have kept corporate corruption and unconscionable displays of executive-level greed in the public eye; such scandals serve as disturbing reminder of the pervasive role of deception in corporate America and the lacuna between the haves and have-nots. In this climate, the ways in which Paris Hilton embraces and promotes dishonesty align her with the more insidious aspects of big business—a connection that puts her (with the corporate family name Hilton) in a unique position to operate as an outlet for some of the growing resentment in America over egregious wealth and corporate malfeasance. Specifically, her celebrity status gives people socially acceptable ways to voice their resentment, through television programs, magazines, newspapers, the internet, and even academic collections. Furthermore, the degree of animosity—particularly the tendency to insult, humiliate, and even degrade Hilton—highlights the extent to which her celebrity is about this outlet for contemporary class strife.

In addition to the rather scathing reviews of *Confessions* such as the *New York Post's* "How to Be an Heir-Head. Paris Hilton Dishes Bad Advice in New Book,"[30] many of the over two hundred customer reviews on Amazon.com also make their criticisms personal—and do so by focusing on her wealth and sexualized image. One review, "My Bible," takes the form of a letter:

> Dear Paris,
>   Thank you very much for writing such a wonderful book. It left me with such a strong impression that now I know what I DON'T WANT TO BE, and that is a good for nothing heiress with tons of money and no brains. I don't regret having bought the book in the least; on the contrary, it will be on my bedside table to remind me of my path in life. I want to be creative and do something for others. I don't not want to be remembered just for partying, misplacing videotapes, and acerebral [sic] reality shows.[31]

In part, this response attacks Hilton in terms of class, which is not surprising given the slick images and ostentatious displays of wealth in the book. But it is also an attempt on the author's part to define herself in opposition to privilege: "I want to be creative and do something for others." The reviewer associates this kind of money and lifestyle with selfishness, and she effectively makes Hilton a foil for her own life, which she claims will be dedicated to creativity and communal investment. In another review, "So Bad, I Went Blind,"[32] the writer links his dislike for Paris to her sexual accessibility and humiliation elsewhere: "In my honest opinion, Paris's best work has been in the video industry. Paris's real talent is not writing. If you want to know what her real talent is, rent the best selling video. You will probably find that she is not ever that appealing when doing her video work." Interestingly, this reader doesn't mention the numerous erotic pictures in *Confessions*, as if these images are unsatisfying in a marketplace where one can watch a rentable video of her having sex. Clearly, this association with pornography is meant to degrade Paris (since the video, which I discuss later, was released without her consent and, from her perspective, "was humiliating"[33]), but in fact, pornography is largely responsible for Paris Hilton's unprecedented celebrity.

The animosity expressed in these and dozens of other reviews not only comes from a profound class resentment for the kind of privilege that Paris Hilton has, but it can also be situated in the expectations of autobiography itself—particularly the notion of truth-telling. Autobiographies, and memoirs, promise a kind of truth about the subject/author, and even though audiences recognize these stories as crafted and shaped in various ways, there still is a general expectation of honesty. (Think of the recent controversy surrounding the fictionalized sections of James Frey's memoir, *A Million Little Pieces* [2003], and the public backlash that ensued.) This expectation of truthfulness connects Hilton's autobiography to *The Simple Life* (2003-present) and the problematic illusion of "reality" in reality television more broadly. Both of these "texts" try to lessen the more alienating aspects of Hilton's elite status (with varying degrees of success) by suggesting that a more genuine portrait of Paris will bridge the gap between her and her audience. Even though both of these works fail to provide an understanding of Paris Hilton beyond her photographic image, *The Simple Life* is successful in its explicit use of humiliation to mitigate Hilton's alienating wealth and to make her more palatable for the public as a celebrity.

The opening voice-over for *The Simple Life* establishes the economic and social tensions that will drive the show: upper class vs. working class, urban vs. rural, sophistication vs. simplicity, luxury vs. poverty (relatively speaking), and public vs. private: "Meet Paris Hilton—model, jet-setter, target of the tabloids, and heir to the $360 million dollar Hilton fortune. . . . [She and Nicole Richie] are giving up their plush lifestyle to live on a farm. . . . They've challenged themselves to live the simple life." Throughout the series, "the simple life" is presented as antithetical to a life defined by fortune, extravagance, and jet-setting (which the opening montage equates with men such as Leonardo DiCaprio and Hugh Hefner). In the context of an agricultural community, simplicity also implies a lack of urban sophistication. Hilton and Richie stay with an Arkansas family, the Ledings, in the first season, and this juxtaposition sets up the possibility of poking fun at both worlds (upper-class urban and working-class rural). Yet the Ledings are not constructed as stereotypical Southerners, a portrait that is all too common in Hollywood[34]; instead, they appear to be genuine, caring people who try (unsuccessfully) to help these young women achieve some degree of social and personal responsibility. This starkly contrasts with the characterization of Hilton and Richie as lazy, deceptive, irreverent, rude, ignorant, and childish. In this way, the show highlights the social and intellectual insularity of "the girls," not the Ledings. Money, the series implies, has kept Hilton and Richie from any real or meaningful participation in the world.

The opening sequence in the pilot episode, for example, works to alienate Paris Hilton and Nicole Richie for the audience in terms of wealth: twenty-two-year-old Paris driving a convertible Porsche; Paris asking a salesperson at Dior if her mother's credit card is still on file (before quickly spending thousands of dollars on clothes, shoes, and handbags); Paris sunbathing in a bikini by the pool, Paris and Nicole arriving at a Hilton family party in a helicopter; Paris reluctantly handing over her credit cards and cash to a butler (demonstrating what she is about to sacrifice to live the simple life); and Paris and Nicole taking a private plane to Altus, Arkansas. At quick glance, the world of such money seems glamorous and enticing—her gorgeous car, elegant home, private jet, and freedom from economic worry. But each of these images associates extreme wealth with careless excess and personal irresponsibility. Paris, for example, doesn't have to earn her money; she can spend $1500 on a travel bag for her dog, Tinkerbell, without hesitation.

This kind of excess is also linked with Hilton's and Richie's ignorance and arrogance. While grocery shopping in the pilot episode, Paris asks Nicole what the word "generic" means, and this is followed by their first dinner with the Leding family:

Grandfather: Have you girls ever been to any of this part of the country before?
Paris: I don't know. I only travel like to Europe and L. A. or New York. Yeah. . . . I couldn't imagine living here. I would die.
Nicole: Now do you guys hang out at Walmart? [. . .]
Paris: What is Walmart? Is it like they sell wall stuff?[35]

This exchange pairs Hilton's elitism with her educational and social ignorance. The humor comes, in part, from the contrast between the cosmopolitan image that she tries to establish by referencing her travels to Europe, L.A., and New York and her astonishing ignorance about the world around her. Of course, it is conceivable that someone of Hilton's class has not been to Walmart, but having no knowledge of the largest retail company in the United States says something quite different. It signals a troubling gap between her aristocratic world and the everyday marketplace of middle and working class America—a gap that invites the audience's disdain, judgment, and mockery.[36]

My intention is not to suggest that *The Simple Life* is a realistic portrait of Hilton, Richie, or the Leding family. But for a figure like Hilton, whose celebrity is based predominantly on a superficial, highly readable image, *The Simple Life*—as well as the Fox television network's interest in producing and shaping the show editorially—further pinpoints artifice as a defining aspect of Hilton's appeal. Television scholars have examined the problematic use of "reality" for describing shows like *The Simple Life*. In *Reality Squared: Televisual Discourse on the Real*, James Friedman qualifies the term "reality television" by situating these current shows in the history of reality based programming and emphasizing the important role of dramatic structure. "Rather than 'reality,' these programs are using seemingly 'normal' (real) people rather than professional actors for the production of televisual drama."[37] Of course, Hilton and Richie are far from "normal" people, but as scholars Anita Biressi and Heather Nunn explain, "when celebrities are already a prerequisite of the show . . . the authenticity of the show is marked by the supposed provision of insights into the hidden 'real' aspect of celebrity personality."[38] So like Hilton's autobiography, the reality genre of *The Simple Life* promises to reveal something authentic about Hilton and Richie, but the revelation here is not so much personal as it is socio-economic.

Audiences certainly realize that the participants in these shows are being filmed and, in many cases, are playing to the camera for dramatic effect, but they still watch for signs of something genuine. As critic Annette Hill explains in her analysis of *Big Brother*, "audiences look for the moment of authenticity when real people are 'really' themselves in an unreal environment."[39] In the case of *The Simple Life*, these "truthful" moments rarely occur through Hilton's on-camera behavior. Perhaps this is due to the inversion of real and unreal here; Hilton's "real" world of privilege is completely alien to most, so she seems unreal in a more modest middle and working-class environment. Regardless, an authenticity does emerge in the show's ironic subtext and its explicit engagement with class resentment. While wearing lingerie and sitting on an elegant, canopied bed, Paris Hilton introduces *The Simple Life* with what will become an ironic promise: "Listen. Everyone thinks Nicole and I are these two girls who never worked a day in their life and that we can't do anything. And we're doing this to prove everyone wrong and to show we can do anything."[40] Not surprisingly, *The Simple Life* demonstrates that these young women *cannot*, in fact, do anything—except lie, party, sleep, and complain. If they were capable of hard work, the show would not be entertaining. But more importantly, their incompetence is largely attributed to their privileged backgrounds. The girls admit that they have never had jobs or earned money for themselves; they have no concept of the cost of living; and they demonstrate no work ethic whatsoever. In essence, Paris Hilton and Nicole Richie are merely egregious embodiments of an alienating, disconnected, and irresponsible upper-class culture; they only function as individuals to the extent that they are associated with famous families.

Even the confessional moments—the only vehicle that reality shows provide for a somewhat truthful, and potentially forgiving, glimpse into their characters—is undermined in *The Simple Life*. Unlike the contestants on *Survivor*, *The Apprentice*, or *The Biggest Loser*, for example, Paris and Nicole are never interviewed separately about their experiences or feelings. They not only perform for the cameras that record every interaction with the family, their various employers, and the townspeople, but they also appear to be performing for each other during their joint "confessions." In effect, the lack of privacy or presumed intimacy here makes these moments ring false.

In *The History of Sexuality*, Michel Foucault discusses the personal and social functions of confession in relation to sex, truth, and power:

> The confession is a ritual of discourse in which the speaking subject is also the subject of the statement; it is also a ritual that unfolds within a power relationship, for one does not confess without the presence (or virtual presence) of a partner who is not simply the interlocutor but the authority who requires the confession, prescribes and appreciates it, and intervenes in order to judge, punish, forgive, and reconcile; . . . a ritual in which the expression alone, independently of its external consequences, produces intrinsic modifications in the person who articulates it.[41]

The ritual of confession here involves both judgment and transformation. It "liberates" and "purifies"[42] because the revelation is an unburdening of something hidden. In the context of Foucault's work, sex is "a privileged theme"[43] and hidden burden in Western society.

A rather pedestrian confession about sexual desire does occur on *The Simple Life* when Paris admits to being romantically involved with a local teenager nicknamed "Chops," but the presence of Nicole during these moments foregrounds the performance of the confession. It makes Hilton's sentiments and her other amorous escapades on the show feel as artificial as everything else—from the late night outings to local bars (equipped with stripper poles, mirrors, and strobe lights) to her outrageous behavior at various jobs. As a result, none of these confessional sequences offer an endearing or genuine portrait of Paris and Nicole; in fact, they ultimately heighten the audience's critical judgment because of their inauthenticity.

Another important element that is absent from these confessions, to return to Foucault, is that of transformation. Nothing about Hilton's and Richie's experiences in *The Simple Life* suggest that they have been changed in any way. Their romantic flings are explicitly described as temporary. Their apologies for various transgressions are conscious acts of deception to placate the family and their employers. They are never punished or held accountable for their behavior. And this pattern of deceit also makes their expressions of gratitude seem disingenuous. In the final episode, they ultimately express relief at leaving. "I'm ready to go home," Paris states unequivocally and loudly enough to be heard over Nicole Richie (which is not an easy task).[44]

Judgment and, as Biressi and Nunn point out, derision are essential components of reality television. Not surprisingly, viewers of *The Simple Life* are continually invited to judge Hilton and Richie and to do so in terms of class. When an off-camera voice asks the Ledings' teenage son, Justin, how he will treat the girls when they first arrive, he responds: "It depends on how they're going to treat me. If they're nice to me I'll be nice to them, but it they're like little snotty bitches, I mean . . . payback's hell."[45] In many ways, the entire series can be seen as a kind of "payback" for an audience that is not part of the hereditary aristocracy. We may not consciously align ourselves with Justin per se (he is a minor character), but the show clearly wants us to embrace this sentiment by giving us ample opportunities to mock and criticize these rich, ridiculous girls. In the recurring musical motif associated with Paris Hilton, for example, a rock-and-roll type singer belts: "Miss Hilton, you must be worth a trillion bucks; get the feeling that you don't really give a [fuck]!" The reiteration of this is obviously a conscious attempt on the part of the producers to manipulate the audience, to invite us to see Hilton's money as the reason for her various ineptitudes and deceptions. But the lyrics, particularly the censored word "fuck," implies that Hilton herself feels an aggressive indifference towards others—an indifference that encourages an aggressive response from the viewers/listeners. Interestingly, there is no corresponding tune for Nicole Richie. True, Paris Hilton is the main star/draw for the show, but her name is also the one associated with corporate culture, inheritance, and undeserved fame—characteristics that *The Simple Life* encourages the audience to see derisively.

Perhaps the most telling example of class resentment occurs in the final episode of the first season. In the opening scene, we see Richie getting drunk at a local bar. After misplacing her purse, she starts accusing people of theft and even pours bleach on a pool table. When the owner throws them out, a surprising exchange occurs. The other patrons start jeering at Paris: "Go back to your hotels, Paris!" "Go home, rich bitch, go home." "Go home, little girl, we don't want to see ya." "Get outta here!"[46] Paris Hilton's initial expression might be the only authentic moment in the entire first season—genuine shock and even anger. She immediately leaves, though, calling out to her drunk, absent friend, and the scene fades to black. This collective anger is somewhat misdirected here, since Richie is largely responsible for what happens (though Paris does become indignant when she realizes that her jacket is missing as well). The demeaning phrases "little girl" and "rich bitch" come across as genuine expressions of resentment, and the sudden solidarity of the bar's patrons (who have presumably been witnesses to the antics of these women for thirty days) invites us to agree with them as well. Indeed, there is a certain pleasure in seeing the girls thrown out. They have behaved badly throughout the series, and as Justin warned, "payback is hell." Here, the town gets revenge in the very medium in which these women thrive—television/ photography. Additionally, the reference to the Hilton hotels gives another clue to the source for this working-class community's anger—economic inequality. "Go back to your hotels" is a reminder to Paris that what she has is inherited, not earned. The line also emphasizes the fact that hotels are temporary dwellings, usually associated with luxury, as opposed to the more modest permanent domicile in which Paris and Nicole have been living (as in a hotel) during the show.

As I mentioned earlier, the overriding dichotomy in *The Simple Life* is about class (upper vs. middle and lower), and this contrast is reinforced by the role of labor (what is earned and what isn't) and language. The girls "work" at various jobs, but they aren't fired for gross incompetence. Laziness seems to be the primary problem. In their first job at a diary farm, for example, they simply decide to stop working (because it is so hard) and to sunbathe by a Jacuzzi. (Of course, they just happen to have bikinis with them.) Their laziness is juxtaposed with the real labor being performed in the community of Altus, and this comparison encourages our critical judgment. They aren't capable workers, but they are good at superficiality—putting their bodies on display, spending money, and hanging out with boys. The underlying message of this behavior is that sexuality and status are the only qualities that (self-proclaimed) glamorous women need for success in this world. When Hilton and Richie are confronted by those who do not accept this philosophy and/or validate it, however, these women react petulantly.

Lastly, the language of the show, particularly the repeated use of "boredom" and "bitch," reinforces our personal and socio-economic-based dislike of the protagonists. For Hilton, boredom is constant preoccupation and concern—one that she never bears any responsibility for. She merely complains about it in almost every episode. As she explains in her autobiography, "there is no sin worse in life than being boring."[47] The language of boredom here is presented as the antithesis of fun. But it is also stands in opposition to thought, self-reflection, and the value of community. In the final two episodes of season one, Albert Leding, the father, asks the girls to spend an evening with the family, to stay home so that they can get to know each other better. But Paris rejects the idea on the grounds of boredom and spoiled entitlement: "It's bullshit. . . . It's like we're trapped. . . . Talk about making something out of nothing. . . . I'm going crazy in this house. I can't sit here all the time. . . . I'm so bored!"[48] Hilton seems to equate boredom with familial intimacy because this request puts the family above her own self-interest; boredom, in other words, is something that involves sacrifice (e.g. doing chores around the house) and investing time and effort in others. Hilton's off-putting defiance (with characteristic teenage pouting and dismissiveness) can be seen as youthful rebellion, but her awareness of an audience is also making her act out more. These things give her a freedom that most young kids living at home don't have. Once again, it is her difference from the rest of us that stands out here.

The word "bitch" creates a similar distancing effect. Oftentimes, it operates playfully both as a term of endearment between the girls and more ironically in the subtext of Tinkerbell's role on the show—as Paris's literal bitch. It can also function humorously to characterize most of Hilton's interactions on the show—as complaining or "bitching" about something. At the same time, *bitch* is a hateful word, and there are many instances in the series when it is used hatefully. Like the word "boredom," it also ends up functioning as a statement about appearances and reality. One of the bar owners, Shannon, remarks: "These girls can be the sweetest things. And they can turn on you like they're the biggest bitches in God knows what."[49] Shannon recognizes the role of deceit in the public personas of Hilton and Richie, and she articulates what the audience has seen throughout the series—that these girls behave in nasty, disrespectful, and dishonest ways. Having a lot of money can clearly bring one fame, nice clothes, and the attention of men, but being able to write a check to pay for the damages or to take off one's clothes for photographers and home videos doesn't offset uglier truths about the self. It doesn't prevent one from "being a bitch" or mistreating and abusing others.

HAMBURGERS, WINE, AND HOME VIDEOS:
THE PORNIFICATION OF PARIS

Early in the 1967 film *Cool Hand Luke,* a chain gang is clearing the debris alongside a country road when a young woman with long, blonde hair steps outside her farmhouse and begins washing a dirty car. As the shirtless, sweaty prisoners watch her with increased desire and agitation, a simulated sex scene begins. The camera focuses first on her hands unscrewing the nozzle of the hose as she sprays the car and then lathers it with soap. Though she mostly avoids looking at the men directly, she watches them in the reflection of the hubcap, watching her. At one point, she lies across on the hood at an angle that is preposterous for the cleaning job at hand but ideal for allowing the men to ogle her buttocks and exposed legs. She continues washing with increasing vigor, licking her lips and smiling as the music, which plays from a transistor radio that she has placed nearby, gets louder and faster. She then squeezes the soapy sponge in front of her body, the suds spilling onto her stomach like a "money shot" in pornography films. She wipes it off while her cotton frock clings with increasing tightness to her damp body. Finally, she washes the roof, pushing her sudsy breasts against the driver-side window.

This scene is not just about the erotic pleasure and the power that the woman enjoys by knowing that she is being watched and desired, suggested by her sly smile and performative behavior. This scene is also about perception. The shot/reaction shot sequence enables the audience to observe how these men respond to the woman, how they fantasize and interpret her body in different, self-serving ways. Dragline (George Kennedy) sees her as a Madonna/whore figure, naming her Lucille because "anything so innocent and built like that just got to be named Lucille." Another man defends her purity and innocence, arguing that "she doesn't know what she is doing." But Luke Jackson (Paul Newman), who embodies the nonconformist spirit of the film, recognizes that her behavior is about the power of sexuality: "Oh boy, she knows exactly what she is doing—driving us crazy and loving every minute of it."[50]

It is this scene that commercial director Chris Applebaum used as inspiration for Paris Hilton's controversial Carl's Jr. spot. He told Krista Smith of *Vanity Fair* that "I was one of those people who always felt that glorifying the acquisition of fame and wealth is an ugly thing about our society, and that [Paris] sort of symbolizes that. When I finally got to [the commercial], I found a girl who is so in on the joke and so ready to laugh at herself."[51] What he means by "in on the joke" is a bit unclear here. Is it the recognition that she is playing into the public's desire—not so unlike the chain gang in *Cool Hand Luke*—to see women purely in terms of sexuality? Is it the joke that Paris recognizes her true investment in selling herself as a sexual object for fame and public recognition? Or both? In any case, the Carl's Jr. advertisement recasts this scene in Hilton-esque terms. Instead of walking out of a farmhouse, Hilton walks into a hangar/studio to wash a Bentley (the kind of car that she would presumably be driven around in). Wearing both the trappings of her class (a diamond necklace, jeweled bracelets, rings, and a fur that she drops to the ground in a striptease) and a one-piece leather garment that suggests an association with call girls and strippers, she crawls across the car and the floor in a sudsy fervor. Unlike the woman from *Cool Hand Luke*, Paris looks directly at the audience throughout the scene; in and outside of this advertisement, there is nothing shy about the power and pleasure that Hilton gets from being an object of both sexual and economic desire. The commercial ends after she bites into an enormous, 1000-calorie hamburger and then squirts a nearby hose at the camera with ejaculatory pleasure. The music throughout is fitting for both a strip club and a pornographic film, and much like the videotaped sequences of Paris Hilton in the remake of *House of Wax* (2005), it clearly alludes to her infamous pornographic videos, particularly *One Night in Paris*.[52]

Arguably, it is Paris Hilton's inextricable association with amateur porn that made this commercial controversial. Certainly, one can see half-naked women draped over cars in any number of NASCAR-type calendars, but the Parent's Television Council launched a highly visible and successful campaign to remove this advertisement from primetime television. In September 2005, PTC president Brent Bozell maintained that the Hilton commercial hurt the fast-food chain, citing an Associated Press report that the company recently saw a 30% drop in stock for the year. "Once again," Bozell concludes, "we see the evidence that Carl's Jr. and Hardee's racy Paris Hilton ad failed to increase sales. . . . The soft porn Paris Hilton ad has alienated millions of families and exposed millions of children to raunchy content that has no place on television during primetime hours."[53] Bozell's comments make Hilton's association with pornography and "raunch culture"[54] grounds for censorship here. Paris is bad for families, for children, so she should be banned from primetime. Even in an era when nudity, profanity, and simulated sex scenes are increasingly part of primetime television, Bozell's hysterical response is not entirely surprising, however. As Walter Kendrick argues in *The Secret Museum: Pornography in Modern Culture*, the history of pornography is also a history of censorship. "Once 'pornography' was labeled and its threat identified, the methods employed to control it were borrowed unchanged from the long tradition of political and religious persecution that preceded 'pornography' and outlives it."[55] Yet censoring Hilton's advertisement from television didn't prevent people from reading about it in newspapers and, more significantly, watching it on the internet. The controversy actually seems to have drawn more attention to the commercial as a result. One newspaper report sarcastically points out that a link to the advertisement on the PTC's website ("You can't be outraged if you can't watch it a few times to be sure"[56]) helped contribute to the immense internet traffic promoting it.

Nevertheless, Kendrick reminds us that these acts of censorship expose the ways in which pornography is a highly politicized genre: "The history of 'pornography' is a political one."[57] So what exactly are the social and political implications of Paris Hilton's association with pornography? What explains the extraordinary interest in her video *One Night in Paris*? A four-minute version first became available on the internet in November 2003, one month before the premiere of *The Simple Life*; a thirty-eight-minute version then appeared on Rick Salomon's own website in February 2004 (for $50); and the current tape, which is approximately forty-five minutes long and includes generic footage of the couple from May 2001, is one of the best-selling pornography "films" in the industry. (According to *The New York Times,* for example, Red Light District, which obtained distribution rights and began selling the Hilton tape in June 2004, had sold over 600,000 copies as of March 2006.)[58]

Paris Hilton's amateur home video should be somewhat revelatory in that it is far less edited and constructed than *Confessions* and *The Simple Life*. Home videos often capture spontaneous moments and provide a more nuanced glimpse into the lives of the people on film. Certainly, this was part of the appeal for the notorious video *Pam and Tommy Lee: Hardcore and Uncensored* (1997). The fifty-four-minute Pamela Anderson/Tommy Lee tape, which was stolen from a safe in their garage during their second year of marriage, includes only eight minutes of explicit sex. The rest features rather mundane interactions and conversations, but as Minette Hillyer points out, "the bad camera work and the boring stories the tape tells serve, in this way, to remind us that one or other of the two celebrities is always behind the camera; that—as we might like to imagine with other pornography—this time it really is just them, and us."[59] The illusion of intimacy and reality is a significant part of the fantasy of pornography, and in this case, the amateur quality and the fact that it was never meant for public consumption give the Pamela Anderson/Tommy Lee tape an air of realism. The honest expressions of love and desire on the tape also distinguish *Pam and Tommy Lee: Hardcore and Uncensored* from the porn genre, which has its own conventions and rituals.[60] Critic Chuck Kleinhans argues that "the overall effect of the entire tape is—counter intuitively—not a highlighting of the sensational parts, but a placing of explicit newlywed sex in the context of love and affection, enthusiasm, mutual playfulness, and exploration."[61] Even though the nature of this tape changed when it moved from home video to commercial pornography,[62] it still promises a certain degree of intimate access into the lives of this rock star and former *Playboy* model. So in many respects, shouldn't viewers expect to find similar revelations in the Paris Hilton tape, which was filmed with her boyfriend of several years, Rick Salomon?[63]

As my discussion of Hilton has suggested, pornography seems to be a logical extension of her career; placing her exposed, sexualized body and money on display for public consumption and voyeuristic pleasure. *One Night* in Paris plays into these aspects of her celebrity and has significantly raised her public profile, helping to promote various projects such as *The Simple Life, Confessions of an Heiress,* jewelry lines, perfumes, clubs, video games, and even a music CD whose title song is "Screwed." Specifically, *One Night in Paris* offers both the illusory promise of discovering something beyond Hilton's public image and the desire to see someone of her economic standing humiliated through sexual objectification and exposure.

One of the most striking aspects of *One Night in Paris* is the surprising lack of intimacy on the tape. Rick and Paris do not share deeply personal sentiments (even when they use the word "love," which I will discuss later), nor do they seem invested in mutual pleasure. In fact, they mostly come across as two people with very different desires: Rick for voyeuristic sex and personal pleasure, Paris for posing before the camera and satisfying Rick by complying with his commands. Rick prods—and practically forces—her to perform for the camera and for himself, telling her to strip, to sit on his cock, to lie down, to open her legs, to show her "gorgeous pussy," and to perform fellatio ("suck it"); whereas Paris Hilton looks noticeably bored during inter-course—and heiresses should never be bored, right? This boredom clearly contrasts with the pleasure that she takes in being in front of the camera. Hilton continually seems to pose for and to be fully conscious of how her body is appearing on film. In the opening sequence of Salomon's thirty-eight-minute web version, for example, the camera shows a close-up of breasts and then gradually rises to reveal Paris Hilton's face. She then points the camera back onto her breasts, as if she is taking pleasure in recording herself for later viewing/consumption. This moment of posing, studying, and presenting her own body is when she seems most familiar and, sadly, most comfortable. It is a moment that encapsulates her public and, as suggested here, private life.[14]

After the opening shot of Paris's topless body, the tape cuts to approximately twenty minutes of explicit sex in the greenish hue of night-vision. Their glowing white eyes, which reflect the bright, unnatural light of the camera, and the grainy green-black color make them appear unreal and even ghoulish. These shots (many of which feature close-ups of penetration) could be of anyone; they are so close and/or distorted by the night-vision that they are difficult to "figure out" initially. Once again, this helps to keep Paris Hilton's body in the realm of the ambiguous, interpretable image. She is not individualized here; she is just a set of body parts on display: neck, breasts, back, vagina, legs, buttocks, etc. In fact, without the opening bathroom se-quence, we couldn't be sure who is having intercourse. A few moments later, Rick orchestrates rear-penetration sex, setting up the camera on a nearby surface and ordering Paris into various positions. Her head is off-screen for most of this, except when Rick periodically stops to adjust the camera. During these breaks, Paris crawls into view to smile for the camera—a somewhat eerie image that seems more reminiscent of a photographic negative than a real person, as if her private, sexual life occurs in a kind of darkroom, a place where more poses and images are waiting to be produced for public consumption.

Only when Paris first climbs on top of Rick and faces the camera during intercourse do we get a sustained opportunity to watch Hilton's face. Here she seems utterly bored and far more interested in looking at the camera than in what Rick is doing beneath her. This boredom not only raises issues about the role of women's pleasure in pornography, but it also returns us to the importance of appearances for Hilton's persona. As Ariel Levy sarcastically points out in *Female Chauvinist Pigs: Women and the Rise of Raunch Culture,* "any fourteen-year-old who has downloaded her sex tapes can tell you that Hilton looks excited when she is posing for the camera, bored when she is engaged in actual sex. . . . She is the perfect sexual celebrity for this moment, because our interest is in the appearance of sexiness, not the existence of sexual pleasure."[65] This reading resonates with the portrayal of Hilton's celebrity in her photo-centric autobiography, which is about appearing to be a glamorous, sexually accessible jet-setter and party girl; the pornographic overtones of the Carl's Jr. commercial (where the principal pleasure comes from being watched); her self-involved dancing in *The Simple Life,* and her highly staged romance with "Chops" on the same show. For Levy, Hilton's current cultural function is emblematic of a larger problem among young women today who embrace an overt and public sexualization of the body as a means for empowerment. This critique also resonates with Linda Williams's concerns about pornographic representations of female pleasure in her study *Hard Core: Power, Pleasure, and the "Frenzy of the Visible"*: "[Pornography has] long been a myth of sexual pleasure told from the point of view of men with the power to exploit and objectify the sexuality of women."[66] Both of these analyses point to problematic notions of power in relation to women's sexuality and the consumer marketplace. Exposing one's breasts on the pages of *Playboy,* for *Girls Gone Wild,* or in the context of a pornographic film, for example, does not empower women, yet many women embrace this kind of "raunch culture," as Levy calls it, to assert a certain degree of sexual and personal liberation. Certainly, Hilton has used this type of sexualized exposure to claim her independence from an aristocratic privilege and, by extension, her individuality.

Without a doubt, raunch culture has significantly contributed to Paris Hilton's fame, yet the power and pleasure in *One Night in Paris* center around Rick Salomon. His forceful, often degrading, treatment of Hilton completely plays into the socio-economic politics of the video and her public persona more broadly. The Paris Hilton of this video is submissive, easily embarrassed, and in many ways humiliated—a far cry from her aggressive pose in the 2000 *Vanity Fair* photograph "Sweetie Pie." Given her highly publicized place in America's hereditary aristocracy and her association with corporate culture, this is certainly part of the video's appeal. A quick search of recent pornography titles reveals numerous films that feature settings and/or characters associated with upper-class society and wealth: *Upper Class* (2002), *Rich and Horny* (2004), *Rich Girls Love Anal* (2004), *Filthy Rich* (2005), and not surprisingly, *The Not So Simple Porn Life, Volume 1* (2005). In many ways, *One Night in Paris* can be read as contributing to this genre in that it casts such wealth in the context of pornographic fantasy. As one of the customer reviews of *One Night in Paris* on Adult DVD Empire suggests, the portrayal of the upper class in pornography is often linked to the pleasure of seeing degrading images of the rich: "No matter what, it's nice to know this little trust fund girl can take cock like a champ. It's too bad she takes a shot to the chest in the end, as a facial would have made this home porno even hotter. Buy this video . . . you will not regret it!"[67] Locker-room rhetoric aside, this endorsement suggests that the video's value comes, in part, from the revelation that "this little trust fund girl can take cock like a champ"; to see Hilton performing sexually, erodes some of the distance between her privileged, trust-fund life and her low-brow associations with pornography.

Likewise, Hilton's submissiveness to Rick Salomon contributes to the ways in which the video can be read in terms of humiliation—a pleasure presumably comes from seeing an heiress on her knees, so to speak. I'm not suggesting that pornography is synonymous with humiliation and the misogynistic objectification of women, though much of it does this. But the context surrounding the release of *One Night in Paris* and the ways in which we read Paris Hilton's celebrity and shameless self-promotion contribute to this reading. When Paris Hilton first learned of the tape, for example, she claims to have been heartbroken and humiliated:

> Someone sent it to me and I was, like, crying, I was so embarrassed. . . . It was humiliating. . . . I used to think it was so bad, but it's like, everyone has sex. I'm sure everyone has filmed a tape. It's not like it was some random person. I was in love with that man. I was with him for three and a half years. We were together. I don't even really remember filming it, I was so out of it on that tape. . . . He is making so much money. It makes me so mad. We were suing in the beginning, but everyone has already seen it. . . . I don't want to go to court. He will fight me. I just want to get on with my life.[68]

Hilton highlights two issues here: her emotional and financial violations. On the one hand, she feels that the tape violates the private context in which it was filmed and the love she shared with Rick, who was married to someone else during part of this three-and-a-half year courtship.[69] On the other hand, Hilton expresses resentment about Rick's ability to profit from her image, which she feels more entitled to: "He is making so much money. It makes me so mad." Though she has repeatedly claimed that she doesn't earn anything from the sale of the tape, her lawyer, Peter Lopez, has stated otherwise, explaining in 2005 interview that Paris does, in fact, receive profits from the tape.[70] Regardless, the link between the emotional heartbreak of this exposure for Hilton and the financial exploitation that resulted makes any viewer a participant in this dual violation. We are, in effect, investing money in witnessing and perpetuating this humiliation of Paris Hilton.[71]

The absence of Hilton's own sexual (and arguably emotional) pleasure in *One Night in Paris* can largely be attributed to Rick Salomon's degrading and humiliating treatment of her. Throughout the video, he refers to Hilton as a "bitch," "a fucking scumbag," "a beautiful beast," and "an animal"; even though some of these labels are presented playfully (he doesn't seem capable of speaking without giggling), the terms are degrading nonetheless. At one point, Hilton even protests: "Don't talk to me like I'm an animal." Yet this protest doesn't change Rick's behavior, which is increasingly domineering and objectifying, or hers, which is increasingly compliant. This animalistic and abusive language also undermines the rhetoric of love in the video. At one point, Paris asks Rick to say "I love you," and he only does so because he wants her to show him her "pussy" ("You'd better show me that fucking pussy right now"). He then offers a disingenuous "I love you," mimicking her voice and immediately asking, "Can I please take off your pants?" In fact, Rick Salomon's use of "love" only occurs in tandem with either an objectifying comment about her body, a self-congratulatory remark about his penis, or in the midst of his own pleasure (specifically when she performs fellatio on him at the end of the video). These proclamations of love are ultimately undercut by this behavior, and one never gets the sense that Rick actually loves Paris. Though a certain degree of truthfulness can be heard in Hilton's voice when she proclaims her love for him, these words cannot be understood apart from the sexual gambit that is going on here. Rick is only willing to give her what she wants (a verbal statement of love) for sex. This fairly conventional, almost clichéd division—a woman desiring emotional fulfillment and a man desiring physical gratification—fits into the misogynistic undercurrent that runs throughout *One Night in Paris* and adds another layer to the humiliation that can be read into it.

Prior to the final scenes of missionary sex and fellatio, Paris removes her panties for him (and the camera) while sipping from a bottle of wine and holding it between her legs. At one point, Rick asks, "Are you going to sit on that bottle?" A few moments later his penis will substitute for the bottle that has been between her legs and in her mouth. In the meantime, we watch Paris Hilton on the divans and plush chairs of the elegant hotel room, wearing a black bra and holding that bottle. The white wine and the rest of the furniture function, to some extent, as props for her wealth and class. This isn't Motel 6, and they aren't drinking beer. Normally, this setting would require money to get access to, but through this video, the viewer gets intimate access both to this affluence and Hilton's body. As Rick proceeds to put his penis inside her, first pressing her legs against his chest as she lies on the bed beneath him and then rolling her over, she moans more in pain than pleasure, and says repeatedly that it hurts. Unlike the closing minutes of the video, which provide a close-up of her fellatio, this sex is about not Rick's pleasure but his control. It is a control that comes from Rick's persistent objectification and his forcefulness he slaps her buttocks during this sequence as well, insists that she loves his "big cock," and later presses her head onto his penis even after she protests that he is choking her ("Sorry," he says with a trademark giggle. "I was sort of trying to [choke you]."). It is this kind of dominance that *One Night in Paris* invites and enables us to participate in. It is this kind of dominance that mitigates what is alien, elite, and inaccessible about Hilton's vast fortune and her place of privilege in American society.

CONCLUSIONS: PASSIVITY AND THE PROBLEM
WITH PARIS HILTON

From the photographs in *Vanity Fair* to her exposure in *One Night in Paris*, Paris Hilton's image continues to highlight both her class standing and her sexuality in ways that empower the viewer to desire as well as despise her. Her success, as I have argued, comes in large part from this duality, and is possible because Paris Hilton does not represent or stand for anything outside of herself. Her image, which is both valued in its ubiquitous reproduction and derided, enables her to fill a unique socio-political role today. Particularly, the representation of her privileged, ostentatious lifestyle and the corporate culture of her family name help make her an effective symbol for some of the growing anxiety and resentment surrounding problems with economic inequality in this country. Wealth is not distributed equally, and it is certainly not distributed based on merit.

This privilege, particularly her place in the hereditary aristocracy, also works to exacerbate what is unlikable about Paris Hilton—her ability to have material riches without working for them, to achieve celebrity without talent, to gain access to those with wealth and power simply because of her name, etc. Though her place in celebrity culture may appear be glamorous, fame also invites criticism and resentment. Persistent critiques of her in the media certainly help inform the ways in which people tend to read her image, and Paris Hilton's success can largely be attributed to the fact that she continues (intentionally and unintentionally) to play into and give credence to these criticisms.

Ultimately, this negative publicity, such as demeaning book reviews, the ironic subtext of photographs and *The Simple Life*, and public and private humiliation of her exposure in *One Night in Paris*, enables Hilton's image to serve a social and political function what I have called a politics of humiliation. The prominent role of wealth in her public image continually reminds the public of her association with extraordinary hereditary wealth, corporate culture, and class-based elitism. And at a time of such economic disparity and resentment, our ability to see Paris Hilton in derisive, humiliating terms seems to be part of her appeal.

There is a serious problem with this dimension of Hilton's cultural function, however. In the contemporary climate of growing economic inequality, the disenfranchisement of the poor, corporate malfeasance, an increasing neglect of education, the absence of universal health care, and the astronomical deficit, it seems that we need more than ever to become politically active—whether that means getting more people to vote, rallying communities to protest, writing to our political representatives, supporting social programs and education, or fundraising in tangible and meaningful ways (through education, time investment, and mentorship). The politics of humiliation may allow us to laugh at and to ridicule Paris Hilton as a means of feeling better about ourselves, but it doesn't inspire action or change. In this way, Paris Hilton's image contributes to long-standing and destructive tendencies in America that encourage people to think that they too can get access to such riches—through luck, fame, and/or hard work. It encourages people to be satisfied with the status quo for the time being, instead of inspiring people to act on and demand change in the present.

6

Fear Factor: Pornography, Reality Television, and Red State America

JESSE KAVADLO

America today is living not reality, but reality TV: staged town halls, scripted teleconferences with selected troops, the rescue of Jessica Lynch, the Mission Accomplished press conference 3000-and-counting U.S. deaths ago, the photos of sexual torture at Abu Ghraib. In addition to declaring war on terror, the Taliban, Iraq, civil liberties, dissent, and the budget surplus; George Bush—in the spirit of reality TV—has declared war on the real. At the same time, with *Survivor*, *Big Brother*, *Fear Factor*, continued interest in the *Real World*, and new permutations like *Trading Spouses*, the 2000s will be remembered as popular culture's decade of reality TV.[1] But in the beginning, of course, there was pornography.

Yet the shared ascent of so-called "values voters," reality TV, and pornography is not coincidental; instead, they share a rhetoric that speaks for, and to, a seemingly unlikely constituency: Red State America. Together, the unlikely trinity of reality TV, pornography, and the Bush administration are simultaneously more and less real than reality, as defined by Peter Viereck as "that which, when you don't believe in it, doesn't go away."[2] And that is because Bush, reality TV, and porn, together represent a peculiarly conservative brand of fear-mongering: they reinforce rather than challenge hegemonic codes of gender, power, and the distinctly American Eros of capitalism, while systematically attempting to exclude those who do not agree with their views.

At the same time, the very word "pornographic," perhaps like reality TV, conservatism, and pornography itself, has moved safely into the mainstream.

The late Walter Kendrick prefaces that his book, *The Secret Museum: Pornography in Modern Culture*, "is not a history of pornography; it is a history of 'pornography.' There is a considerable difference."[3] By making this distinction, Kendrick can analyze "an imaginary scenario of danger and rescue" from the "pornographic" rather than try to create connection between all of the things that that "have little in common except that they were once, or are now, called 'pornographic.'"[4] I marvel at what he would think of today's breezy use of the word to which he devoted his study. One cannot read a pop-cultural analysis of the housing market without coming across the mantle of "real estate porn"; the Food Network and spate of subsequent cooking shows, with their lovingly tight close-ups of individual ingredients' pores, has been similarly dubbed, by both detractors and aficionados, "food porn." Kendrick saw the designation of "pornography" as a tool for those in power to keep potentially subversive knowledge away from others; its current casual use suggests the possibility, for some, of reversal, from stigma to radical chic. It is thus unexpected, even ironic, that the Bush presidency has not dampened the appetites to which the porn industry—more than cooking shows—caters, but rather, it has fed it.

Indeed, panting over housing classifieds or salivating in front of Rachael Ray shares elements with pornography; each in its liminal space between real and fantasy seems attainable and seems to take place in real time with real people. Yet the average person viewing a cooking show, or reading the real estate advertisements in the *New York Times*, like the average person watching pornography, possesses the illusion of possible participation more than the actual prospect of making it real. Cooking shows and classifieds engage the viewer in an oxymoronic reality-based fantasy, where the prospect—of the perfect apartment, perfect soufflé, perfect partner—takes the place, even provides the pleasure, of accomplishment. Purveyors of all categories of porn perform so the viewer doesn't have to.

Perhaps this analysis seems too broad. Indeed, talk shows or soap operas, like real estate analyses, cooking shows, or, for that matter, many news programs—and like reality TV and porn—at first appear merely to be two more sigh-inducing indicators for the intelligentsia of a society of the simulacrum in general. However, while there are, I think, links between all of these symptoms, pornography—the old fashioned kind involving visual depictions of bodies engaging in sexual acts—and reality TV share a special affinity. More so than other forms of televisual simulacra, reality TV seems to have taken its cues directly from pornography in three crucial ways: first, in its deliberately duplicitous claims to reality and distinctively ambivalent relationship to the real; second, to its use, for some, exploitation, not just of human desire but also of the human body itself; and, third, crucially, in the way in which both porn and reality TV have moved from the fringe—whether the *avant-* or *derrièr-garde*—into the mainstream not during a time of permissive liberal power but rather in a reaction against such governance.

While Ronald Reagan can be called the first postmodern president, anticipating George W. Bush in many regards, it is the Bush Administration that has more completely co-opted postmodernism's cultural relativism. It has done this, paradoxically, in the name of cultural certainty, codifying completely what Reagan, still waging the last remnant of the cold war, could only aspire to: the substitution of televisual image for reality for the sake of global winner-take-all, dog-eat-dog domination. The S&M-like poses in Iraqi detention center Abu Ghraib are not an aberration from conservatism, as defenders have suggested, as much as the perfect embodiment of the axis of porn, reality TV and conservatism. The poses and humiliations were likely learned from easy-access Internet porn, but the in-retrospect inane documentation and distribution of the images comes directly from soldiers weaned on reality TV's famous-for-anything aesthetic. Finally, the reason for the subjugation in the first place —bad apple theory to the contrary—is nothing short of domination, which, in the end, remains the underlying subtext of porn, reality TV, and the Bush Administration.

Porn and reality TV go back together further. Both distinctly present themselves as "real" to an audience that is extremely, indeed willfully naïve in its consumption of such texts. Indeed, its viewers find themselves engaging in an unspoken moral compromise with the producers: the audience is willing to accept at face value those parts of the show that are coded as real—from emotional conflict to sexual concord—in order to be entertained, but they are distant, indeed, sophisticated enough not to take responsibility for the violence or humiliation that the shows demand. In an essay about a reality TV show called *The Money Shot*, Victoria Mapplebeck begins by quoting Andy Warhol: "Now and then someone would accuse me of being evil—of letting people destroy themselves while I watched, just so I could film of tape record them. But I don't think about myself as evil—just realistic." The author goes on to suggest that Warhol "would have loved Reality TV for its 'access all areas' approach to life."[5]

Yet Warhol is a pivotal figure in the nexus of proto-reality TV with *avant-porn*, especially his film *Blow Job*, in which the central pornographic event— fellatio—is never shown. As Ara Osterweil describes, "the spectator of *Blow Job* must reassemble the details of sexual exchange from clues—facial gestures, murmuring lips, and cigarette smoke—without witnessing the event itself."[6] Likewise, the sexuality of reality TV is, like Warhol's fellator, below the surface but crucial to the viewer's understanding of the event. Both are, in different ways, a kind of ironic pornography—porn without sexual depiction. For Jean Baudrillard, commenting on the first incursion into reality TV, the quasi-documentary *An American Family*, in 1971, reality TV was already like pornography "because it is forced, exaggerated, just like the close-up of sexual acts in a porno film."[7] But Baudrillard may be oversimplifying, and as Linda Williams points out: "in pornography . . . the human body is never superfluous."[8] Indeed, Baudrillard is too quick to dismiss the materiality of the body to the spectacle, a point that, again, reality TV derives directly from porn.

The appeal, then, of reality TV—from misfits thrown together in *Trading Spouses, The Real World,* and *Survivor,* to the gross-out stunts on "*Fear Factor*—and porn are similar, but this appeal is at the same time contradictory. Both are clearly voyeuristic, encompassing the carnival quality that we have a right to look at anything, regardless of the psychic or moral costs, if we can pay for it, because we have no limits on what we find enjoyable if it's happening to other people. Yet because we think it's real, we feel pity and revulsion, but perhaps even heightened excitement. Like porn, reality TV revels in exhibition while also revealing its fundamental banality: no matter how many permutations, reality TV and porn all look about the same after enough viewings, although, as I will soon address, its variations are crucial as well. But rather than feeling satisfied, or disgusted, viewers tune in endlessly, with the frustrated and futile hope that the next time will be the best yet. We are endlessly disappointed by them, but this discontent makes us look again instead of looking elsewhere. On the one hand, viewers are continuously bamboozled, but in part because they want to be. On the other hand, Steven Johnson, in his bestseller *Everything Bad is Good for You,* finds reality TV narratively compelling precisely because, not despite, what he calls its "cringe inducing" moments. As he explains,

> These are people who have spent the last six months dreaming of a life-changing event, only to find at the last minute that they've fallen short. . . . I admit that there's something perverse in these moments, something like the frisson that pornography used to induce before it became a billion-dollar industry: what electrifies is the sense that *this is actually happening.* [author's italics].[9]

Similarly, the viewer's relationship with the reality TV participant and the porn star is contradictory as well. Even as we objectify them, since to see them as full subjects would render us inhumane, we also relate to them: they enact our dearest wishes and darkest fears (or darkest wishes and dearest fears). Porn stars and reality TV contestants lay their stigmas, and everything else, bare for all to see, inviting concomitant pleasures of revelation, envy, scorn, and judgment. Ambivalently, the viewer feels related but revolted—in empathizing with, eroticizing, or stigmatizing the guests, we confirm both our unconscious pathologies and our outward normalcy. We hate the performers, mock them from our armchairs, find them conceited (or modest), identical (or incompatible), contemptible (or occasionally, temporarily, deserving). Yet even "hate" feels too strong, since we also see them as protagonists. In the end, however, despite any feelings of attachment or antipathy, we feel that they deserve whatever they get, because, in true Red State fashion, *they were asking for it.* They are willing to enact taboos ironically to cast off their stigma by the highest validations—the promise of money, Red State

America's incontestable marker of achievement, but even something more, and something equally, and ironically, American: the notion that its contestants can launch a career as a celebrity.

Like porn, *Fear Factor* and other shows put the viewer into the position of power, able to objectify and control the participants on the screen. It's a *Revenge of the Nerds* fantasy on the small screen, a way for the viewer to enjoy the abject humiliation of someone far better looking than he or she. But that, of course, doesn't sound like reality at all. Such criticisms are familiar, meritorious, and endless: that even if the performance is not scripted (a charge currently leveled against MTV hit *Laguna Beach*), it is nonetheless crafted: by meticulous casting, by the thousands of hours filmed that are then cut, edited, and shaped to establish the required narrative arc, and by TV's version of Heisenberg's Uncertainty Principle—the presence of the cameras inevitably alters how the participants behave. The line between the person and persona is irrevocable. Reality TV, like pornography, is not real as much as its very artificiality and artifice are on display as part of the narrative itself. Some viewers choose to ignore the pretenses, of course, but it is a suspension of disbelief, a willfully arrogant unknowing, more than sincere ignorance. Yet the shows—and crucially, like Bush, who also casts his soldiers, screens his questions, and trims any objectionable footage—orchestrate highly artificial conditions in which participants then pretend to act natural, ironically at the same time producers—and Bush—insist that their simulations are authentic. As Frank Rich un-ironically notes of Bush's incessant manufacture of news, from "Karen Ryan and Alberto Garcia, the 'reporters' who appeared in TV 'news' videos distributed by the Department of Health and Human Services to local news shows around the country" to "the fake narrative of 9/11 has been scrupulously maintained by the White House for more than two years," . . . "real journalism may be reeling, but faux journalism rocks. As an entertainment category in the cultural marketplace, it may soon rival reality TV and porn."[10]

Again, the direct antecedent of both reality TV and Rich's "infoganda" is pornography: the plots of porn movies have always been fictional, but they are also frequently beside the point; porn features actors, of course, but they are also always playing themselves, while at the same time what "themselves" even means is called into question though the use of personas, stage names, and fabricated biographies. Like reality TV, then, porn is less than real: the sets, the groans, the stage names, the bleached blond hair, the makeup, the implants, the music that has been lampooned in a thousand jokes, the statistical unlikelihood of so many aroused and attractive housewives, schoolgirls, delivery boys, doctors, et al. But in porn, the artifice is designed to heighten, not diminish, the eroticism, because amidst all of the contrivance, the whole point is that the sex is real and graphic—that is, not concealed (as in Warhol) or simulated (as in erotic mainstream film). The problem with porn for Baudrillard is not that it is simulated, but that it is "disenchanted simulation . . .

When told that she'd that be eating horse rectum, contestant Holli Joy Lamb, whose name sounds simultaneously Christian, like a porn pseudonym, and like an animal pun, replied, "When Joe pulled out the horse rectum and he told us what it was, I didn't think that we were going to be able to perform the stunt. Because, initially, I did not think I would be able to even take one bite, never mind eat over a foot of it." Similarly, the website provides this description of the "Tongue Bob and Transfer":

> During the Tongue Bob and Transfer stunt Amy Haight had to bob for a pig's tongue in a vat of animal fat. She then had to transfer it by mouth to her best friend Christina Martin's mouth, who then dropped it into a bucket . . . As the two friends recount in their Tale of Fear interview, sometimes a little peer pressure is all you need to take care of a dirty situation.

Lamb's nonchalant description of coercion and this glib description of cruelty echo Andrea Dworkin's litany of porn rapes in her book, *Pornography: Men Possessing Women*.[19] But while Dworkin had to argue that sexual abuses and misogynistic attitudes were commonplace and not merely anecdotal (an accusation her critics continue to dispute), *Fear Factor* is unquestionably a mainstream hit, first in prime time and then in syndication. Yet *Fear Factor* and its ilk are, in a sense, more obscene than pornography—at least porn's ostensible reason for being is pleasure, its eroticism from blatant sexuality mixed with elicit sensuality. With reality TV, everything becomes subject to the cold, inescapable light of information: no secrets or ambiguity. Unlike, to use a term that is no longer redundant, "real" reality's elaborate social and personal rituals of concealment, reality TV's operative term is exposure, through the word's multiple meanings: the camera, publicity, spotlight, limelight, revelation, and mere revealing. And not just revelation of the body or intimacy, as in porn, but something more personal, yet strangely depersonalized: our fears, our humiliations, and our wishes. The contestants on *Fear Factor*, like on *Who Wants to be a Millionaire*, frequently risk leaving with nothing—even less than they entered with—without the cash prize, of course, but also without their dignity. They walk away in a slow motion shot of their back, while their own voiceover explains their humiliation and their opponents taunt them, as though all but one of them won't suffer the same fate within the next fifty-two minutes. It becomes, as Baudrillard would put it, a ritual of transparency, in the name of celebrity and dominance.

All this would be amusing, if cynical, if the political machination of the day had not also seized upon the rhetoric of pornography and the redefinition of the real, not in the name of commerce or Nielsen ratings but in the name of morality and poll ratings. While reality TV's predecessors, the talk shows, also offered lurid voyeurism, their hosts, at least, offered enlightened rationales, and they merely exploited their guests' emotions rather than their bodies and souls. For Phil Donahue, the purpose of the show was "to humanize people who have suffered"; for Sally Jesse Raphael, it was "teaching lessons of compassion."[20] Shows like *The Real World* and others may pay lip service to liberalism by featuring gay and minority characters, but in keeping with the mood of the Red States, the politics of reality TV are decidedly conservative, even reactionary, in a change from the inclusive façade of the talk show. On *Survivor*, *Big Brother*, *The Real World*, *Fear Factor*, and *The Apprentice*, the goal again and again is to restore social order by systematically removing the unfit or the dissimilar. Conservatives may not like Darwin, but they still favor Social Darwinism, and the shows enact various scenarios where the least fit are thrown off. Yet only a few contests actually have to do with fitness; most concern how much tripe (or leech-filled sausages) the contestant is willing to swallow. It is a ritual of humiliation on par with what porn's worst detractors accuse it of portraying, and, crucially, it is also precisely the redefinition of patriotism in Red State America: the shows enact and recast "moral values" not as charity, compassion, or social justice, as the left defines them, but rather as marginalizing, scapegoating, and ostracizing the weakest members of a group. Even seemingly less reactionary shows like *Survivor* and *The Apprentice* are in some ways worse than *Fear Factor*'s or game show *Weakest Link*'s or *American Idol*'s straightforward failure to perform on command, the domain of porn and the right wing alike. Here, it is not even the weakest member who is voted off by a judge or host, but a cabal of conspirators inserted into a breeding ground of paranoia where participants must paradoxically work together in order to take each other down one by one. Likewise, Colin Powell and Richard Clarke were voted off the White House's increasingly isolationist island by Dick Cheney and Donald Rumsfeld not for ineptitude, but for dissent.

At the same time, the shows, like porn, and like the mood of the Red States, enact the same raw market forces of capitalism that lead to their own existence: that people will do anything for money, that a TV show will air anything that makes money, and circularly, that viewers will watch anything that reinforces their own ideology that money, coupled with fame, is the ultimate reward. Porn and reality TV represent the power of the free market at its most naked, as it were—capitalism with Adam Smith's invisible hand, and every other body part, rendered palpable. Reality TV's subtext involves increasing competition for decreasing means. On TV, as in contemporary life, the contestants will do anything to win, and, with housing costs and fuel prices up and with the average worker struggling to achieve or maintain a middle-class standard of living, so will the viewers. The problem is that the contestants, like the porn stars, like Red State voters, seem to welcome their own fall. One shirt for sale—there is always more for sale—on the *Fear Factor* website depicts a spider with the words "Bite Me,"[21] in triple entendre: "me" is the spider, who is eaten on the show; "me" is the shirt's wearer, using sarcastic slang for dismissal; but "me" is also the wearer who puts himself in the masochistic object position of not just being eaten, but commanding it.

The viewer is like a participant him- or herself, struggling against oppressive, competitive, and capricious social pressures, but the viewer also identifies with the spider, a living animal and ostensible predator who—in pornographic fashion—finds itself being swallowed whole for grotesque sport.

With the usual array of shirts and mugs, the website also features a banner advertisement for Burger King, with its slogan "Have it Your Way." At first, the ad insinuates our worst post-*Fast Food Nation* fears about what's in the meat. But like the show, Burger King provides a simulacrum of food, served by and for the lowest common denominator, whose workers are increasingly marginalized and expendable. Elsewhere, the website implores viewers to choose their favorite couple of contestants for the upcoming special "Viewer's [sic] Choice" episode.[22] And in current conservative—and, of course, pornographic—fashion, the arbitrary preference represented by viewers' choice— "Have it Your Way"—trumps excellence every time. At least the show's survival of the fittest overtones suggest a meritocracy, if a vicious one. Now instead, the website allows viewers to choose their favorite participants to return, regardless of who won. On these ballots, viewers vote not for competence or ability, even the questionable talent of eating arachnids, as much as dubious and hollow traits of popularity, attractiveness, and self-assurance.

Elected by the same standards, Bush is, Reagan to the contrary, the nation's first reality TV president, continuing to stage and wage our first reality TV war. But as reality TV follows the rhetoric of pornography, so too does this administration: it lays bare the distinction between what is private and public through the Patriot Act and media manipulations, while at the same time imposing a Federalized, top-down, unfettered Social Darwinism in the name of, ironically, privatization. Yet if reality TV makes the private public, the Bush administration has also made the opposite true as well, rendering the public private. At first, the problem with "reality" with which I began seemed like mere reversal: reality TV was supposed to imitate real life; instead, real life is more and more resembling reality TV, itself resembling the worst excesses and exploitations of pornography. In the end, however, through porn, reality TV, and the Bush presidency, we may have moved from such reflections or perversions of reality and inexorably into the last realm of Baudrillard's simulation, in which the image "bears no relation to any reality whatsoever; it is its own pure simulacrum."[23] As Ron Suskind has now infamously reported, an anonymous administration aide explained this new realm of "reality" in a way that Suskind "now believe[s] gets to the very heart of the Bush presidency":

> The aide said that guys like me were "in what we call the reality-based community," which he defined as people who "believe that solutions emerge from your judicious study of discernible reality." I nodded and murmured something about enlightenment principles and empiricism. He cut me off. "That's not the way the world really works anymore," he continued. "We're an empire now, and when we act, we create our own reality."[24]

This neoconservative notion that "we create our own reality" is precisely opposite of conservative Peter Viereck's earlier definition, and it ultimately suggests that, rather than neoconservative, conservative, or even reactionary, Bush is truly our first postmodern president, a simulation for which there is no original. Reagan, at least, it is said, excelled at playing the character "Ronald Reagan."

Henry Giroux introduces his ideas of American and global uncertainty in the post-9/11 era in this way:

> Stripped of its ethical and political importance, the public interest has been largely fashioned as a giant Reality TV show where notions of collectivity register as a conglomeration of private concerns—possessive individualism, the cult of celebrity, and unbridled competition—resulting in communities with nothing in common except for a nagging sense of impending danger.[25]

Giroux could just as easily, however, be analyzing Dworkin's response to pornography. The pornification of America, then, moves beyond the spectacle of the sexual, beyond Baudrillard's height of simulations, and even beyond the individual body, to become, in every sense of the word, incorporated: money making, connected, and multiply embodied. The everydayness of pornography is indisputable. What is more troubling, then, is the way in which the codes and narratives of pornography have embedded themselves into our national collective consciousness.

Yet even putting aside labels and theories, and with all respect to Baudrillard and Giroux, we must realize that Bush's postmodern rhetoric of pornography and reality TV, at its core, subjugates all Americans, to say nothing of Iraqi civilians, in real, bodily, and palpable ways: fantasy has consequences in reality. In keeping, and in conclusion, then, Bush's cultural practices merge with his very real economic policies in the specific term "fear factor." I found the definition below on *Wikipedia*, the online encyclopedia that in some ways is the cultural opposite of Giroux's erudition and Baudrillard's exclusivity, yet it alone inadvertently comes closest to pinpointing the locus between reality TV, pornography, and Red State America:

> The fear factor in occupational terminology refers to the increased per-worker productivity resulting from the threat of impending *layoffs*. The resultant productivity boost is almost always temporary, since *health*-related reasons dictate that workers cannot maintain this level of increased output. Some economists have proposed that the economic growth during the early 2000s *jobless recovery* is a result of this phenomenon.[26]

Before we continue our adventure in reality as reality television, we must remind ourselves of two problems: first, regardless of whether we call the "new reality" a Baudrillardian simulacrum or a Bushian reaction against the "reality-based community," we cannot deny the materiality of thousands dead in Iraq and millions displaced and suffering in America and around the world, just as Dworkin serves as a witness for the women who proclaim that "pornography is not a fantasy, it was my life, my reality."[27] And finally, we must reconsider these programs' generic narratives, and how they inevitably end, once all of the bodily permutations have been exhausted. Porn stars, to Dworkin's outrage, are notoriously disposable or self-destructive; and only one contestant ever remains by the end of any reality TV show. Even then, he or she never makes it to the next season. On TV, and in life, we now have far more to fear than "*Fear Factor*" itself.

Freak Shows in Jesus Land: Howard Stern and George Bush's America

ANN C. HALL

L ove him or hate him, it is difficult to ignore Howard Stern's importance in pop media. Over the past several years, he has been at the forefront of Federal Communication Commission fines, corporate penalties, lawsuits, and finally a departure from the traditional radio format of Infinity Broadcasting to his 500 million dollar SIRIUS Satellite Radio deal. He has been labeled a "shock jock," and his show has been characterized by both supporters and detractors as nothing more than prepubescent-boy-banter, offensive, pornographic, and boring.[1] Ira Glass of National Public Radio's *This American Life* says "There's nobody with the emotional range . . . He's emotionally present and he's emotionally honest more than anybody hosting a program . . . In a typical show, you'll hear him rail like a maniac against the FCC, goad some girl into taking off her top and talk about his girlfriend in an utterly real way." Terry Gross, who admits that she does have trouble with his representation of women, says "he's simply a great talker . . . Funny, colorful. There's a rhythm and style to his speech that makes you want to listen."[2] But Stern is always quick to stand apart from any crowd, political party, or agenda. Even when pitching for 1-800 Mattress, he remains iconoclastic. What most agree on, is Stern's ability to offend, and this ability, to cut through the apathy, to be heard above the commercials, and the political propaganda is noteworthy. Even the most obtuse observer of American politics understands the remarkable ability of the American political and economic system, capitalism, to deactivate threats very effectively, not by oppression or violence, though these are by no means ignored, but frequently through marketing, greed, and glitz. By examining Howard Stern in the context of a conservative, postmodern America, as well as the context of radio and its development, it becomes clear that Stern and his show illustrate the important role pornography plays in political action in a capitalist political system that successfully marginalizes, commodifies, or markets but ultimately deactivates dissent.

At first glance, radio porn seems inherently doomed at worst or absurd at best. As every red-blooded American knows, porn relies on a visual medium. And though we all know about telephone sex, a radio show that interviews porn stars or discusses pornographic content is not the same. Stern's radio show is like many other talk-shows, only his guest are sex stars and playboy models who sometimes wear clothes and who sometimes do not. But without the visual stimulation, who cares if the women or men are dressed or not. We cannot see them. Stern, however, has managed to make this hybrid pornography work. Casting himself as the ultimate director and consummate panderer, the show offers aural descriptions for their listeners. If Stern and his crew label the "babe" hot, then hot she is. All interaction is mediated by Stern and his crew, and this power as our national porno-narrator may account for his tremendous success. We trust him with our porn stars as readily as generations before trusted their news to Edward R. Murrow.

In addition to solidifying Stern's popularity and media ubiquitousness, the role of porno-narrator heightens the already highly intimate relationship established by the radio medium. According to Susan Douglas's work on radio and its effect on the American imagination, radio technology establishes a higher level of intimacy among viewers than television or print media:

> It is clear that with the introduction of the telephone, the phonograph, and then radio, there was a revolution in our aural environment that prompted a major perceptual and cognitive shift in the country, with a new emphasis on hearing. Because sound is dynamic and fleeting, radio conveyed a sense of "liveness."[3]

By compounding the heightened role of the host with the heightened level of intimacy inherent to the medium, the Stern show overcomes the pornographic bias towards spectacle and the visual field. In the case of the Howard Stern Radio Show, sound triumphs over the visual, which is quite a remarkable phenomenon given the proliferation of visual—both pornographic and non-pornographic—images in postmodern America.

In addition to the sense of immediacy afforded by radio, the act of listening to the radio also encourages a sense of community, again making Stern's use of pornography on the radio very different from that of telephone sex hotlines. Douglas argues:

> Some modes of listening have helped constitute generational identities, others a sense of nationhood, still others a sub cultural opposition to and rebellion

against that construction of nationhood. Most modes of listening generate a strong feeling of belonging. Even as background noise, radio provides people with a sense of security that silence does not, which is why they actively turn to it, even if they aren't actively listening.[4]

A sense of belonging and loyalty intrinsic to the radio medium further enhances Stern's popularity. It may, for example, serve to explain the incredible support Stern garners during rallies outside the studio, behavior akin to political activism virtually unheard of and unseen in the last thirty years. As Douglas mentions, talk-radio "tapped into the sense of loss of public life in the 1980s and beyond, the isolation that came from overwork and privatization of American life, and the huge gap people felt between themselves and those who run the country."[5] Stern and other talk-show hosts offered a space to build an electronic community, one denied in regular American life.

Stern's run for political office clearly supports this claim. While joking around on a show one day, Stern said that he could win the New York gubernatorial race on two issues: "fix the roads at night" and "kill the criminals." And with that, Stern was off and running. Ultimately, he pulled out of the race because he did not want to disclose his earnings. He explains in *Miss America*, "If I disclosed my assets, the repercussions would be staggering. . . . If I had less money than people thought, I'd be perceived as an idiot. If I had more money, I could never get a vacuum cleaner fixed again without being robbed."[6] The logic behind his platform and his decision to leave appealed to the disenfranchised.

And given the Telecommunications Act of 1996, it seems more and more are feeling that way. As Bill Moyers reports on "Bigger and Bigger Media":

In 1984, the number of companies owning controlling interests in America's media was 50—today that number is six. Critics of media consolidation say it has led to fewer and fewer voices being heard—and a marked decrease in local news coverage.[7]

Conglomerates like Clear Channel helped build the Stern empire, making his show available nationwide, but they also exerted tremendous creative control. Stern's battles with the FCC highlight the political component of the entertainment industry, as well as capitalism's tendency to render dissent impotent. According to Stern, he was unfairly singled out by the FCC for his show's history of pornographic and distasteful material. His evidence was compelling. He was fined for a discussion explaining certain and cryptically identified sexual practices such as "blumpkin" and "balloon knot," while Oprah Winfrey discussed similar topics with a guest and was never reprimanded or fined.[8] One explanation for the difference is technological. Stern's skill at manipulating the high-level of intimacy afforded by radio technology simultaneously intensifies its offensiveness.

Of course, only the politically naïve would conclude that Stern's novel use of radio technology was the only explanation for the FCC pressure. As Mike Thomas of *The Chicago Sun Times,* notes, prior to and during Stern's difficulties with the FCC, he was most critical of the Bush administration, shifting his allegiance from the Bush administration to its opponents in the 2004 Presidential election.[9] Stern described the situation scathingly in a more recent interview: the FCC "is like racketeering . . . They're like mobsters. You cannot win against the government. . . . When it gets closer to an election, the fines really start flying. It's the only way the government can look like it's doing something.[10] Bob Barr, former Congressman and U.S. Attorney, argued similarly, taking Congress to task on the issue of indecency, murky waters at best, recommending that Congress do something "much easier to resolve. Like Social Security."[11] Ironically, the Bush administration used porn, admittedly their condemnation of it, to their political advantage, but as we shall see later, this strategy generally requires that the conservative party spend most of its time talking about the very issue they are hoping to silence: pornography and pornographic content.

Before continuing, however, it is useful to address the supposed pornographic content of the Stern show. As Mike Thomas writes, "sex is merely a portion of Stern's appeal . . . and a relatively small portion at that."[12] Jokes regarding size aside, it is worth examining what exactly happens on Stern's shows during the "supposed" pornographic sessions. To put it bluntly, Stern's show does not keep it up. Unlike a telephone sex hotline, internet sex rooms, or even porn films, the erotic content is not sustained. A lesbian couple may be making out for the benefit of Stern's listeners; a heterosexual woman may be discussing her most erotic evening; or a stripper might be telling about one of her exploits, but something always interrupts. In what can only be described as *Sternus interruptus,* Stern himself might ask mundane questions about technique or offer an explanation of his own. In *Private Parts,* for example, he not only discusses life with the porn star, but he highlights the correct way to wipe after a bowel movement—far from erotic content.[13] As a matter of fact, the show is notorious for this nuts and bolts approach. At these moments, *The Howard Stern Show* sounds less like an X-rated call-in show and more like a sexy version of *Car Talk.*

Further, unlike the erectile dysfunction ads that appear on American televisions throughout the day, the Stern show does not promise potency and power. Rather, the show chronicles not only his bedroom misadventures but those of the crew. In *Miss America,* for example, Stern recounts his experiences with online sex. The chapter is important because it blurs the boundaries among media—book, radio, and visual—as well as demonstrating the way in which pornographic content is often used on the show. Through his descriptions, online sex looks very much like telephone sex, as well as his radio call-in show. Though the media is clearly visual, the printed emails and chat rooms mimic conversations. The moral of the story is not how hot everyone is or how great the sex online is. No, it is about how Stern himself was having electronic sex with undesirable partners, partners who were some-times men, sometimes ugly, sometimes dangerous. The chapter itself could be presented as a great anti-Internet porn document. Stern vows never to use online sex subscriptions again. Here, porn is clearly limited, and the men who use it are stupid and vulnerable—just like Stern.[14]

Stern is also notorious for his self-deprecating comments about his own virility. Once again, unlike the porn star of the visual field, Stern is not fantastically or freakishly sexually experienced. As a matter of fact, he and his entire radio crew are a bunch of misfits trying to "get laid," with more failures than successes on their scoreboard. Everyone complains about some physical difficulty or ailment. The human body does not cooperate. It is fragile at best and prone to leaks at worst.

Even during the filmed versions of his radio show Stern violates conventional pornographic tradition, as well as the boundaries among media. While we watch a filmed version of his radio show, the women are clearly objectified. They wear very little clothing, while the men are dressed. They are the objects of the male gaze, but the men in the studio are also objectified, and even though they are fully clothed, indicating supposed power, they are not in charge. As a matter of fact, they look pathetic, while the women, thanks to the wonders of silicone, look very formidable.

Further, there is something about this meta-spectacle in which the audience watches men watching women. There is a dismantling of the oppressive nature of spectatorship. The show is clearly contrived. We are watching a film of a radio station. And such contrivance undercuts the privileged position of the camera, as well as the privileged position of the male spectator. Likewise, the radio show also undercuts spectacle, but relies heavily on the porno-narrator, Stern, who always undercuts the erotic for a joke, an interview, a play-by-play analysis, or an interrogation. Clearly, the show has pornographic content, but is the show pornographic? No. In popular culture terms, Stern's shows might be better subtitled, Dr. Ruth meets Woody Allen.

In postmodern terms, the Stern show deconstructs the pornography it invokes. As Sharon Zechowski notes in her extensive dissertation on Stern, "Howard Stern and the Women who Love Him: Working-Class Subjectivity and the Discourse of Male Talk," Stern appeals to more than white men. He appeals to a working-class sensibility in general, which she aligns to theorist Mikhail Bakhtin's carnivalesque:

> Ours is a culture obsessed with physical perfection and the technologies available to transform the grotesque into the beautiful. One need not worry about this if they are a part of the "Whack Pack," the Howard Stern entourage comprised of social outcasts and misfits. . . . Each of these characters became part of the *Howard Stern Show* by pure chance. If the audience liked them, they stayed. Each embodies specific aspects of the carnivalesque. . . . Those who are "different" will always be subject to the gaze; however, within the context of

The Howard Stern Show, members of the Whack Pack share more with Stern's working-class audience than the stockholders or advertisers of the program do. The Wack Pack hyperbolizes what it meant to live as a less-than-perfect-self in a society that reveres and rewards perfection.[15]

Clearly the show emphasizes the body's faults, not its perfection. Even during the competitions for plastic surgery, the human body at its most disgusting is emphasized. The playboy models on the Stern Show do not have brains; the smart women lack playboy breasts; Stern himself has trouble in bed; and nobody is "getting laid." There is always something lacking. Furthermore, there are days when the jokes get weary, even for Stern, who interrupts a dull joke, saying, "we've got to move this along." In this way, rather than emphasizing the culture of the perfect body, the perfect sex partner or experience, or the perfect radio show, Stern's broadcast exposes beauty and perfection for what it is—an illusion, a trick of media mirrors. The body is obsolescent, insubstantial, and like everything else on the show, lacking, incomplete, funny, boring, but sometimes profitable.

Admittedly, and as one of my students pointed out to me, the majority of Stern listeners and viewers would not appreciate these finer arguments regarding the deconstruction of pornographic images.[16] Political conservatives certainly do not. Stern's "shock talk" violates conservatives' obsession with sexuality, an obsession which led some members of congress to drape nude statues in the Capitol and which prompted the passage of the Decency Act following the Janet Jackson "clothing malfunction" during the Super Bowl. Morality in this political context is defined by one criteria only—heterosexual monogamy. Greed, violence, and abuse of the poor are completely ignored. For this political group and for many others unaffiliated with this group, pornography is at the root of all that is wrong with the country.

The problem with this strategy was outlined years ago in Michel Foucault's *The History of Sexuality*. Here is how it backfires. Censorship enhances sexuality through the constant interrogation and discussion in an attempt to discover the "secret of sexuality." Foucault continues saying:

> Sexuality must not be thought of as a kind of natural given which power tries to hold in check, or as an obscure domain which knowledge tries gradually to uncover. It is the name that can be given to a historical construct: not a furtive reality that is difficult to grasp, but a great surface network in which the stimulation of bodies, the intensification of pleasures, the incitement to discourse, the formation of special knowledges, the strengthening of controls and resistances, are linked to one another, in accordance with a few major strategies of knowledge and power.[17]

To clarify, Foucault, for example, notes that "at the beginning of the seventeenth century a certain frankness was still common, it would seem. Sexual practices had little need of secrecy. . . . But twilight soon fell upon this bright day, followed by the monotonous nights of the Victorian bourgeoisie. Sexuality was carefully confined; it moved into the home. The conjugal family took custody of it and absorbed it into the serious function of reproduction."[18] Such continues to be the state of affairs.

What is interesting about Foucault's analysis, however, is that the very power that seeks to silence sex, in fact, talks about it more than any administration in American history. In the face of this censorship, *The Howard Stern Show* continues to talk about sexuality *ad nauseum*, which, in turn, keeps the opposition talking about sexuality. Furthermore, the continued attempts to censor, and thereby continuous discussions of the very pornographic content that is supposed to be suppressed, demonstrates the impotence of the censoring power:

> Underlying both the general theme that power represses sex and the idea that the law constitutes desire, one encounters the same putative mechanics of power. It is defined in a strangely restrictive way, in that, to begin with, this power is poor in resources, sparing in its methods, monotonous in the tactics it utilizes, incapable of invention, and seemingly doomed always to repeat itself.[19]

And though power is everywhere because it is created by everything, says Foucault, one of the effects of the Stern show is to bring power's attempt to repress and control out of the shadows to show itself as basically a "power poor in resources." In the same way that the Stern show demonstrates the limits of the perfectible body, it also highlights the limits of government control, oppression, and communication.

Stern consciously demonstrates the oppressive political and media machine by encouraging his fans to interrupt the seamless broadcasting world in which everything is controlled, rehearsed, framed, and perfumed. An interruption during the 2004 Tsunami coverage by one of his followers clearly illustrated the limits of the media conglomerates as effectively as the Tsunami illustrated humanity's vulnerability to natural disasters. After the usual hype, an eyewitness survivor was promised. After much fanfare and for one brief shining moment, the man screamed, "Howard Stern Rules." Cut. Blackout. Return to Tsunami coverage. No mention of Stern or the interruption again. A tasteless prank worthy of junior high? Certainly. A refreshing departure from the usual packaged, rehearsed, and polished newscasts? Definitely. A cry for freedom of the press in the media wilderness? Perhaps.[20]

Stern himself observes, "we get the most reaction from the phony phone calls that our listeners make to news outlets during natural disasters. . . . I'm of the opinion that disaster calls actually play a worthwhile function. They point out what idiots run our media. The guys call up established news organizations like CNN, claim that they're mayors of local towns affected by the disaster, and without even checking, boom, they put them on the air."[21]

Such behavior may be the only way to reach today's viewers, a generation that finds ignorance charming. *The Nation's* Max Blumenthal, for example, attended the College Republican National Convention in June 2005. He noted:

> By the time I encountered Cory Bray, a towering senior from the University of Pennsylvania's Wharton School of Business, the beer was flowing freely. "The people opposed to the war aren't putting their asses on the line," Bray boomed from beside the bar. Then why isn't he putting his ass on the line? "I'm not putting my ass on the line because I had the opportunity to go to the number-one business school in the country," he declared, his voice rising in defensive anger, "and I wasn't going to pass that up."
>
> When 25-year-old candidate Mike Davidson emerged in the center of the room, the party fell to a hush. "Does everybody know why we're here today?" Davidson asked his supporters, who had huddled around him.
>
> "Beer!" someone shouted. The crowd exploded with laughter.[22]

Compared to this interchange, Stern's commentary and discussions, sexual or otherwise, appear downright intellectual. But this, like it or not, is the political environment of America at this time. High-brow discussions continue, but Howard Stern and Glen Beck are the kings of the radio waves. As a matter of fact, during the 2004 election, Stern was listened to more frequently than Air America in the heavily Democratic North Hamptons. Pollsters boasted that Stern was influential during the last presidential elections.[23] Again, there is something compelling about this data which suggests that while the country may not be persuaded by the issues, Howard Stern's manner of questioning authority speaks.

Of course, there is still the problem of Stern's representation of women, a representation that ostensibly places women in their usual role as objects to be viewed or possessed. True, there are situations in which the women are clearly in power, but for the casual viewer, Stern's porn stars are probably just porn stars, not a means to interrogate speculation or patriarchy. As I ponder this problem, I am reminded of the great line at the end of Billy Wilder's film, *Some Like It Hot*, when Jack Lemmon tells Joey that he is not a woman but a man, and Joey responds, saying, "Well, nobody's perfect." Howard Stern is certainly tacky, indecent, at times sexist, and boring, but he continues to challenge authority, particularly patriarchal authority, in funny, chaotic ways; ways that underscore our limited nature, and our inability to control anything. While the government asks us to trust their findings on weapons of mass destruction, and social security investments, and while corporations ask employees to trust their pensions to the corporate investors, and while the country is continually bombarded with images from plastic surgeons asking us all to trust our faces, bodies, and futures to their skilled hands, Howard Stern asks us to do what he does—ridicule, interrogate, and above all, not remain silent. Find a way to speak, no matter what. If it means using porn, so be it. If it means switching to satellite radio, so be it. During an interview with Stern, which ran days after President Bush had defended his unsuccessful Supreme Court nominee Harriet Miers on the basis of her religious conviction not her abilities as a judge or lawyer, Stern also expressed himself in religious terms, "I thanked God today that I made this deal a year ago [with Sirius]."[24] The conservative political party did not have a market on the divine. Stern had God's ear and ours.

---------- 8 ----------

Toys Are Us: Contemporary Feminisms and the Consumption of Sexuality

DAWN HEINECKEN

In November 2003, Joanna Webb of Burleson, Texas was arrested. Her crime? A sales representative for Passion Parties, Webb was arrested in a sting operation for teaching two undercover officers how to use a vibrator.[1] Such attempts to legislate sexual information demonstrate the ways that certain forms of sexual pleasure continue to be seen as illegitimate for women and that women's access to information about and control over their bodies is still not guaranteed. At the same time, however, women are increasingly being targeted as consumers of a wide range of sexual products. Elexa, Durex, and Lifestyle, to name a few brands, all market to women products ranging from warming lubricants to edible body paints and condoms with vibrating rings. These products have been allotted increasing shelf-space by mass retailers like Walgreens, Walmart, Amazon.com and CVS.[2] A number of women-oriented sex shops have also emerged in recent years, selling everything from vibrators and strap-on harnesses to floggers and anal beads.

In this essay I examine the promotional materials of two such shops, Babeland and The Smitten Kitten. I provide a close reading of the rhetorical and visual strategies at work in their on-line catalogs and print advertisements to consider the ways they encourage women's consumption of erotic products. Founded by young, self-identified feminist women in their twenties and thirties, Babeland and The Smitten Kitten are of particular interest for their explicit association of their products and stores with a contemporary feminist agenda. The stores have a national presence as regular, major advertisers in two of the most prominent feminist magazines for young women, *Bitch* and *Bust*. Their promotional discourses are thus important to examine for the ways they both construct and reflect particular contemporary understandings of feminism, female sexuality, and sexual consumerism for their audience of young consumers.

In her study of the emerging sexual appeals to female consumers in Britain, Feona Attwood notes that the consumption of erotic products is frequently presented as a means by which to signal one's status as a liberated, independent woman.[3] Indeed, the rhetoric of female empowerment has been used to sell everything from running sneakers to make-up cases. As many have observed, a problem with using the language of female liberation to sell products is that it very often trivializes feminism's political goal of social justice.[4] Similarly, the marketing of erotic products often remains informed by "patriarchal understandings of women's bodies and their pleasures."[5] Babeland and Smitten Kitten's promotional strategies are likewise complex and sometimes contradictory. The first section of this essay investigates the ways the stores' promotional materials encourage female sexual agency and enable critiques of traditional notions of female sexual passivity, as well as advance a feminist agenda built around inclusion and social justice. Yet, as I will discuss in the second section, these stores also rely upon rhetoric that can be seen as reinforcing more traditional understandings of female sexuality by selling a sexuality that is carefully contained.

Like many women-oriented stores, Babeland and The Smitten Kitten were founded with the explicit goal to counter the atmosphere of male-dominated adult stores that many women find unsettling. Babeland (originally Toys in Babeland) was founded in Seattle in 1993 by Claire Cavanah and Rachel Venning. Additional stores later opened in New York and L.A. As lesbians, the pair wanted to create "a place that felt comfortable to us" and to give women "a general understanding that women can expect an orgasm and that when it comes to sex it's OK to ask and expect."[6] Similarly, The Smitten Kitten was founded in Minneapolis in 2003 by Jessica Giordani, Jessi Jacobson, and Jennifer Pritchett, in response to the "overwhelming need" for an education-based sex store that would serve as "a safe space for women to access resources, to find out their sexual needs and desire, and to become sexually empowered."[7]

In depicting their stores as safe, liberating alternatives to traditional adult stores, both stores draw from earlier discourses around female sexuality, masturbation and female empowerment that emerged during the 1960s and 1970s. June Juffer, for example, shows how overlapping insights from sociological, scientific, and feminist fields at this time began to redefine the social meaning of female masturbation. The period saw the publication of Masters and Johnson's *The Human Sexual Response*, which debunked the myth of the vaginal orgasm and placed a new focus on the clitoris and female orgasm. This coincided with social changes such as the legalization of abortion, the introduction of birth control, the creation of more liberal divorce laws as well as reduced legal constraints on the publication of porn and a new feminist focus on women's health care.[8] Masturbation began to be viewed as a therapeutic form of self-care, in which "learning about and claiming the body became the vehicle . . . that would allow each woman to revel in her individuality."[9] Within this framework the vibrator came to both symbolize and legitimate "active, female, clitoral sexuality as normal and healthy."[10]

Indeed, the clitoral orgasm, which illustrated the ways the female body could function independently of the male sex, became a fulcrum around which issues of female liberation were debated. As June Juffer writes "masturbation was posited as a political act of individual liberation from confining social structures—the home, marriage, the family. Women need to escape these structures in order to learn about their bodies and boost their self-esteem."[11] Pioneering women-oriented sex shops like Good Vibrations, begun in 1974, started to establish a discourse addressing female consumers that framed the consumption of erotic products as a way to practice resistance against older, male-dominated expressions of sexuality.[12]

Babeland and Smitten Kitten similarly articulate identities built on their opposition to and difference from the rest of the sex industry. Smitten Kitten's website, for example, distinguishes the store from "the all-too-often callous and corrupt adult sex industry" boasting that it is "a working model for operating a successful progressive business . . . responsibly equipped with resources, information and products."[13] Women's consumption of erotic products is constructed by both stores as a means by which to resist oppressive mainstream attitudes towards female sexuality. Babeland's website, for example, places women's orgasms at front and center and as an imperative in good sex. "She comes first and often at Babeland!" the store proclaims, implicitly critiquing sexual activity in which this does not occur.[14]

Babeland and Smitten Kitten very obviously represent the consumption of sexual products as a way for women to enact feminist politics. Babeland's ad for the Hitachi Magic Wand, for instance, presents masturbation as a form of both liberation and self-care. Its model confesses that "I never masturbated when I was younger. . . . Although later I enjoyed sex, I was never sure I was having orgasms. . . . Learning to masturbate has taught me how to love my body and have more intense orgasms with my partner and myself." This ad speaks to the lack of knowledge that many women still have about their bodies, suggests that female sexual pleasure is normal and natural, and that learning about one's own body is a means to start a "personal sexual revolution." Smitten Kitten goes even farther, informing consumers that the store is "owned by three sexy bitches who care as much about our feminist politics as we do about getting off in style." The store's slogan, "Put your pussy where your politics are! Support feminist sex toys stores," makes it clear that sex toys are tools for political transformation.

In his study of Good Vibrations, Dennis Hall points to the ways that erotic commodities are "acquired because the ownership of them defines who we are as individuals."[15] The consumption of erotic products presented here is a means by which to signal one's status as a liberated woman. However, while a number of women's oriented stores may be read as simply co-opting an image of female liberation to sell products, Babeland and Smitten Kitten's address to consumers is considerably more complex. In various ways, they work to confront more traditional understandings of female sexuality, constructing unique images of female sexual agency, utilizing deconstructive techniques to enable feminist critique, and emphasizing a feminist politics of inclusion and social concern.

Babeland's ad for the Rabbit vibrator, for instance, represents a form of female sexual agency that stands in contrast to usual constructions of female sexual assertion. It features a close-up of a woman's leather clad, mini-skirted pelvis against which the model thrusts a bright purple rabbit vibrator. The model's stance is both assertive and active; she appears in the act of spreading her legs and raising the hem of her skirt, while the veins in her hands stand out as she clenches the rabbit, hard. The model here clearly is meant to evoke the defiant, assertive nature of a punk rocker or a dominatrix; the sexual woman is a rebel with a cause.

Obviously, the dominatrix is a widely recognizable figure conveying a sense of female sexual assertiveness, and one that is used to market women's sexual products elsewhere. Yet there are key differences in Babeland's representation of the figure that set it apart from more conventional marketing ploys, like those found in an ad for Xandria.com. The Xandria model, dressed in a black cowboy outfit, also wears clothing connoting strength, masculinity and the rugged individualism of the Marlboro Man, yet she remains curiously passive due to her positioning within the camera frame.

John Berger has shown how throughout the history of Western art and advertising, women are positioned "to-be-looked-at," angled and framed in ways that make clear their value lies in being the object of the observer's gaze.[16] Likewise, the model's sexualized attire, coquettishly tilted head and her gaze, directed outward, implies a relationship with the reader, suggesting that her sexual assertion is at least partly a performance designed for the visual enjoyment of another. Indeed, this representation is in fact quite typical of how the dominatrix appears in male porn—a figure whose sexual aggression is desirable only in so far as it contributes to the pleasure of another. The pleasure promised to female consumers in this ad is based less on the prospect of an orgasm than it is on adopting an aggressive persona for the sexual arousal of another.

In contrast, the Babeland ad is remarkable not simply for its in-your-face use of a "naughty" figure, but for re-presenting it in a way that is truly transgressive—as a symbol of active, assertive female sexuality defined only against itself. The ad commands the reader to "pet your bunny," an imperative that is not justified by any appeal to health or relationships and which

makes clear that use of the Rabbit is strictly about individual physical pleasure. As a fragmented figure, the model lacks a sense of clear individuality,
suggesting that she stands in for some kind of universal "woman." Petting
one's bunny is thus presented as an activity all women do, commonly and
everyday, and at the same time it signals one's independent and rebel status.
Her fragmented body might also be read as reducing her identity to that of
her vagina, but ultimately that identity is closed to us—her vagina covered
by a skirt and the rest of her body and face outside the frame, inaccessible to
the probing eye. The reader has no clear relationship to this woman; we can
not tell if she is performing for us. Indeed, the ad's directive to pet one's
bunny shifts the locus of pleasure offered the consumer from one of looking
or performing, to the pleasure of doing to one's *own* body.

Similarly, both stores employ a deconstructive style borrowed from feminist youth subcultures like those of Riot Grrrl and feminist zine-making that
disrupt traditional understandings of female sexuality. Zines—hand published and distributed magazines—were popularized for young women by the
Riot Grrrl movement of the early 1990s. An outgrowth of early punk subculture, grrl zine makers utilize a number of avant-garde representational practices to critique the signs, symbols and values of mass-consumer, male-dominated culture.[17] Frequently ironic and parodic, they privilege a handmade
and "authentic" look that signifies their distance from consumer-dominated
culture.[18] They invoke taboo subjects, for instance, or celebrate denigrated
parts of girl culture, a form of symbolic inversion that flips the usual distinction between high and low culture.[19] Riot Grrrls' sartorial choice of mixing
and matching frilly dresses with combat boots is one well-known way in
which these activists expressed their contradictory and ambiguous relationship to mass consumer society and traditional forms of femininity. Feminist
zine-makers similarly appropriate texts and images of popular culture, placing
them in new contexts to form new meanings.

All of these techniques are operative in Babeland and Smitten Kitten's advertising, a means by which they hail consumers already familiar with zine
subculture and claim membership in this feminist community. For example,
ads for both stores privilege an amateur aesthetic common to zines, suggesting their distance from mass-consumer culture and stature as "authentic"
feminist shops. Smitten Kitten's ads, for example, always feature a wavery
"handwritten" type while the haphazard placement of copy and pictures, scat-
tered randomly about the page suggests a lack of professional design training.
The ad's cartoon-like bright colors and "Hello-Kitty"-like logo likewise signal
the store's affiliation with popular youth culture.[20]

The zine-inspired aesthetics also are a means by which each store articulates counter-hegemonic attitudes towards female sexuality. For example,
Smitten Kitten's copy, describing the store owners as "sexy bitches," inverts
the meaning of a term that has been negatively used to define women. A
similar inversion occurs with their use of slang and taboo terminology. In

one ad, for example, they reassure readers that Smitten Kitten cares about "getting off in style" and also observe that if a product is "not good enough for us to fuck with, it's not good enough for you," a rhetorical style that humorously disrupts notions of female propriety as well as the more formal language of conventional sales pitches.

Babeland's ad telling readers to "Start Your Own Sexual Revolution" likewise appropriates images from dominant culture and reassembles them in new contexts in ways that subvert their original meanings. The headline evokes the popular "ransom note" zine-style in which words are cut out from newspapers to form new sentences.[21] Its grainy black-and-white photo of the Statue of Liberty also seems cut from a newspaper; however, the meaning of the statue is shifted, altered by the fact that Liberty is holding a vibrator in her hand instead of a torch. This is humorous for the ways it turns this symbol of the male-dominated government on its head, redefining the notion of liberty it represents to include female sexual liberty. The various euphemisms for masturbation running on the vertical and horizontal borders are a tongue-in-cheek way of rendering humorous the "distasteful" meanings of these phrases.

Another Smitten Kitten ad, evocative of the infamous pose of the Charlie's Angels logo, features the silhouette of three people wielding sexual toys. The retro image carries meaning tied to the series' association with 1970s feminism, expressing the liberatory aspects of erotic products at the same time it makes a mockery of the hilariously sexist version of "female independence" that was depicted within the series. Subversive humor is also at work in Babeland's ad for "dual action vibrators." The ad resembles a criminal line up, with a range of pastel colored vibrators lined up under a sign reading "Wanted." The copy parodies the language of such wanted-criminal pictures in the post office, warning readers that "these toys have been known to leave women satisfied and happy" and giving directives for what to do if the criminals are sighted; in this case, however, women are to return "to the safety of your bedroom."

This ad pokes fun at the ways women have been expected to hide from "criminal" threats upon their sexuality, and also inverts the meaning of the home as a place of physical protection and domesticity to a space in which women actively seize control of their own sexuality. Mocking the perspective that sexuality is a deviant, criminal behavior, sex is reframed as a fun and playful activity—a sense only enhanced by the vibrators' doll-like appearance.

While these ads poke fun at traditional understandings of female sexuality, Babeland and Smitten Kitten's ads also emphasize a need for social inclusion and present a clear-cut feminist agenda. While it is obviously in the best interest of sex shops to take a non-judgmental attitude towards consumer preferences, the stores' concern with plurality and inclusiveness is not merely implied by the products they sell. Rather, inclusion is a central aspect of how these businesses define themselves. A recurring slogan on many Smitten Kitten ads, for example, describes the store as "feminist owned, transgender-friendly" and as "a *truly* feminist sex toy store" (emphasis mine). In this brief statement, Smitten Kitten acknowledges the controversy that surrounds transgender people, not just in the straight, male-dominated society, but in gay, lesbian and feminist communities, as well. It works to extend and challenge definitions of what constitutes "correct" gender/sexual orientations, decries the prejudice that occurs even amongst those who themselves are marginalized, and makes clear that any real feminist politics necessitates an open and accepting attitude.

Babeland's print ads similarly embrace alternative sexual identities as well as offer new models of beauty and sexual relationships that speak to a concern for inclusion. For example, the store rarely depicts heterosexual couples in its ads, more often using models who represent a lesbian or ambiguous sexuality or running "neutral" ads that contain no people. When models are used, there is an obvious commitment to "realistic" representations of people that underscore the ways that the products may be consumed and enjoyed by everyone. The models shown by Babeland do not fit mainstream standards of beauty. They are not airbrushed or made-up, nor posed provocatively. The models are also minorities, fat women, or others who have a distinctly alternative, often punk, look. Masculinity is not portrayed in a stereotypical fashion either. In the single Babeland ad I found that featured a heterosexual couple, the man is a skinny "geek," lovingly pressing a kiss to the side of his partner's head as she gazes out triumphantly at the reader. His is a straight masculinity that, unlike other representations of masculinity within popular culture, is not defined by either his muscles or his dominance over a woman.

Babeland's use of "realistic" models shows that the realm of sexual pleasure is one that is, or should be, available to everyone, not just a sexy few straight white people with hot bodies. These ads do not participate, as many ads, TV shows and films do, in representing alternative sexualities in ways that work to excite or reassure straight consumers. Babeland models, for example, are not represented as an exotic "other" whose alternative sexuality is somehow titillating; the ads instead address the reader in a way that takes for granted a readership at least partially composed of lesbians. Babeland's choice of venue is itself notable, placing its ads in third wave feminist magazines like *Bitch* and *Bust* whose feminist agendas likewise target both lesbian and straight audiences. The heterosexual woman who reads a vibrator ad featuring a lesbian model in the pages of *Bust* magazine, for example, must do what lesbians have historically had to do—read through the depiction of a sexuality which is not their own to find their own potential for pleasure in the product or recognize their common bond in wanting self-defined sexual pleasure.

The feminist identity sold by these stores is thus one built around notions of sexual liberation that are not merely about one's own ability to love the self and enjoy pleasure. These stores suggest that the freedom to experience individual pleasure is and ought to be extended to everyone: it is a matter of social concern. Smitten Kitten founder Jennifer Pritchett argues that "Sexual liberation is the basis of all social justice movements," and concern with community well-being is extensively reflected in Smitten Kitten's promotional material which foregrounds health and environmental concerns.[22]

Smitten Kitten's ads in particular are notable for their presentation of an "eco-feminist" perspective. Smitten Kitten's ads and website are examples of "green" marketing—promotional appeals that, according to Anne Marie Todd, emphasize "informed consumer choice" and concern "with the well-being of community," and that focus on details of the production processes and policies, as well as on the effects of manufacturing and consumption practices on people and the environment.[23] To support this commitment, Smitten Kitten's website provides numerous links to environmental magazines as well as its own sister site CATT (Coalition Against Toxic Toys), dedicated to consumer awareness about the dangers of certain sex toys, such as those made of phthalate. According to Pritchett, it is against Smitten Kitten's policies to carry jellies, cyberskins or other potentially toxic toys because "they're dangerous to human health, to the environment . . . it's part of our philosophy to put good things in the world, and it's counter that to sell things that are toxic."[24] These health and environmental concerns are linked to concerns with fair-labor practices, according to Pritchett, since PVC factories employ a workforce of mainly poor, minority people, who are exposed to physical dangers from their exposure to dioxin.[25]

The store's print ads extend the connection Smitten Kitten makes between sexual liberation and social justice, affiliating the store with a range of left-leaning social movements including anti-globalization, labor organizations, and vegetarianism. Each of Smitten Kitten's print ads, for example, features pictures of a globe, a cow, and a handshake, and inform readers Smitten Kitten's products are "environmentally friendly," and "safe for you and the world we live in." Products are "vegan and cruelty free," as well as "ethically manufactured," and "handcrafted by adults in a fair-labor and fair-wage environment." Indeed, one full-page color ad promotes "vegan-friendly strap on harnesses." Consumers who purchase Smitten Kitten's products can be assured that their eco-feminist, pro-labor sensibilities will not be offended. The "green," socially concerned company identity constructed here operates in conjunction with other aspects of the business's self-representation. The punk and zine-inspired aesthetic, and privileging of an amateur look, seen in the company's print campaigns is one that has roots in punk's "DIY" (do-it-yourself) ethos, developed in resistance to mass dominated consumer culture and "the man." It is thus notable that both stores seek to distance themselves from conducting business in traditional ways.

Babeland and Smitten Kitten's depiction of their stores is of casual, happy places, a community made up of valued individuals rather than faceless, nameless automatons. Both websites feature informal photos of the stores'

owners along with short bios. "On any given day," customers may find owners "Jessica and Jennifer at work with canine friends." Photos of these "Smitten Kitten Pooches and their latest hijinx" are sprinkled throughout the web
site.[26] Presumably the dogs are allowed in the office, signaling to consumers
a laid-back and nurturing environment. Obviously, this is not a cutthroat,
uptight company, but a company made up of people who love their dogs, just
like the rest of us. Babeland's staff bio pages present the company as a laid-
back community in which each worker's individuality is respected. The bios,
for example, allow Babeland employees to express their idiosyncratic natures
and are written in an informal, personal style and detail their quirky personal
hobbies and habits rather than their work history.

Certainly, this is a typical strategy by which companies construct a sense
of virtual community for their customers. Yet it is also representative of the
infiltration of certain countercultural ideologies into the business arena that
are consistent with some of punk's leftist, anti-consumerist impulses. "Casual" workplaces are part of a phenomenon that began when the former hip-
pie baby boomers moved into positions of authority and brought their leftist
value systems with them.[27] Nonconformist, anti-institutional, meritocratic
and tolerant people, these boomers formed the members of a new "creative
class" which cultivated an "ethic of creativity at work," valuing "individuality,
self-expression and difference," and found a "magical third way between bohemian values and the Protestant work ethic."[28] The idiosyncratic and casual
virtual communities created by Smitten Kitten and Babeland reflect anti-institutional attitudes and the melding of a Bohemian ethos with the demands of
business.

What is interesting about such workplaces, however, is the way they not
only imply a certain criticism of mass consumer culture (even while participating in it), but they also suggest a non-hierarchical model of business relations in which power is distributed equitably between owners and employees.
In this regard, the business atmosphere they represent coincides, not only
with egalitarian feminist principles, but with each store's continual insistence
that sex must always be mutual and consensual. The fact that Babeland was
voted Seattle's "Best Place to Work" by area employees for being "an inclusive, socially conscious for-profit" with a gay-friendly work environment and
good benefits, suggests that their worker-friendly stance is not a mere advertising ploy.[29] In their self-construction as activist, socially conscious and feminist stores, Babeland and Smitten Kitten attempt a kind of feminist pedagogy,
educating consumers not only about sexual liberation but also what constitutes correct business practices, and by extension, larger social relations.
Babeland, after all isn't just a business, it's "a destination, a lifestyle, a state
of mind."[30]

As the previous discussion shows, Babeland and Smitten Kitten are inter-
vening in popular discussions about sexuality and extending definitions of
feminism in many positive ways. However, I now want to focus on how both

stores also participate in more conventional marketing strategies, reflecting what Dennis Hall has described as part of an "expanding effort to socially sanitize an interest in and the use of a variety of sexual goods, especially apparatus, among middle-class American consumers."[31] In attempting to make their products acceptable to a wide range of consumers, Babeland and The Smitten Kitten also reinforce more traditional understandings of female sexuality as well as participate in contemporary discourses which construct the body and sexuality as sites of knowledge and control.

As Susan Bordo has shown, Western philosophy's historical valuing of the mind over the body continues to permeate contemporary society and is evidenced in the ways that individuals are urged to discipline their bodies—to control, routinize and regiment their bodily processes.[32] The ability to discipline one's body—through diet, exercise, or what have you—is seen as reflecting one's self-control, spiritual state, social worthiness, and even class status. For example, Bordo shows how one reason our contemporary culture valorizes extreme levels of physical fitness is that tight, lean and developed muscles signal an individual's ability to fashion their own bodies, and reflect a mental and moral self-discipline that is required for upward mobility in current economic structures. In contrast, loose, fat or inactive bodies are seen as "out of control," expressive of a kind of moral and mental failure and associated with the poor and working classes who supposedly lack such control.[33] Similarly, Laura Kipnis has observed that while erotica is distinguished as "artistic" and "classy" representation of sexuality, porn has been despised, in part, because its association with excessive, even taboo, bodily practices that threaten middle class notions of propriety and control over the body.[34]

Throughout history women's bodies have been seen as particularly vulnerable to such excesses, their bodies pathologized, and their sexual desires seen as signs of mental illness or moral failing. As a result, they are urged to keep close reign on their bodies by monitoring their physical and social behavior, fitness, as well as their medical and psychological states. As Bordo shows, the feminist movement did little to diminish women's need to discipline their bodies; if anything, contemporary women must demonstrate even more control to make it in the man's world of public work.[35] Indeed, what is apparent about the marketing of erotic products to women, is that although many women-oriented stores overtly promote women's enjoyment of their own bodies and freedom from moral constrictions, their promotional appeals also take great pains to reassure that purchasing the products will not lead to excess—to physical, moral or social failing.

For example, both Dennis Hall and Feona Attwood have observed the ways that female sex shops work to disassociate themselves from the low-brow world of porn by invoking an upscale image.[36] Smitten Kitten's website is no exception, carefully describing the store's location at "the heart of one of the most vibrant of the Twin Cities cultural and commercial centers."[37] It occupies more than 2000 square feet of space "boasting original exposed brick walls and natural slate floors." Smitten Kitten proudly states that it only offers "hard-to find, handcrafted" and "hand-selected" products. Babeland likewise boasts that its toys "all come from small manufacturers with craftslike settings rather than large sex toy plants."[38]

What's interesting about these images is the way they reinforce the store's upscale status by drawing on elitist aesthetic evaluations. Its location in the "cultural center," for example, marks Smitten Kitten as belonging in the world of "high culture." The upscale pitch continues with promises of a "boutique-style shopping experience with complimentary coffee or tea and a personal guide," recalling the habits of the British upper class, complete with personal servant. The description of the store's exposed bricks and slate flooring suggests the site is a reclaimed, restored historical building. Such locations are quite trendy—in part because of the ways in which they express class-based notions of taste in which appreciation for 'original' cultural forms indicates one's difference from the lower class "masses" who mindlessly consume mass produced goods and attitudes.[39] Appeals to good taste reign at Babeland's store, which is brightly lit and airy, "a mix of the serious and spoof"[40] that Venning describes as a "clubhouse of hip sexuality."[41]

This upscale status is bolstered by the way Babeland and The Smitten Kitten stress the educational nature of their products and store mission, in particular their sexual education workshops. These workshops are undeniably one of the chief ways that the stores can be said to be performing a feminist intervention. They are reminiscent of consciousness-raising groups of the 70's, allowing consumers to come together in a group and articulate fears and questions about their bodies in a welcoming context. However, they also demonstrate a middle-class morality in which the processes of the body need to be educated, refined and disciplined through mental study in a socially sanctioned "expert" context.

The Smitten Kitten is particularly forceful about stressing the necessity of education and being "smart." It is "dedicated to educating consumers at making healthy, smart decisions about sex toys."[42] Smitten Kitten claims a certain authority and expertise by attaching itself to professional institutions, informing the reader that its classes have been conducted at "colleges, universities, spiritual organizations, environmental justice, women's health and activist groups." Smitten Kitten's Pussy Parties offer both introductory and advanced "curriculums," and its "Education" page actually provides a syllabus of course offerings. These follow both the lay-out and brief, bulleted, explanatory language of most college syllabi, with "Sex Toys 101: A Smart Introduction" followed by "Sex Toys 102: A Sophisticated State of Arousal," and "Smart is Sexy: Information is Power."

The syllabi indicate that there is a hierarchy of skills and knowledge that must be learned one step at a time. Sex Toys 101, for example, helps participants "understand basic sex toy vocabulary," while 102 helps one "understand advanced sex toy language." Like students learning a language, one must develop sufficient skills and knowledge before moving on to more advanced courses. Notably, the syllabi also construct a hierarchy of specific sexual practices with use of "dildos, vibrator anal toys and cock rings" to proceed before "strap on sex" and the use of crops, clamps and light bondage, or advanced cock rings—a movement from more "vanilla" sexual practices to the more marginalized world of BDSM. The presentation of knowledge of some practices as basic and others as advanced and "sophisticated" portrays these latter forms of sexual activity as desirable. Yet, the construction of a hierarchy of skills and knowledge ultimately represents sex itself as an object of concrete, discernable knowledge. Rather than being a nebulous, bodily, and individual process, the experience of sexuality, like any topic of study, can be apprehended in presumably similar ways by different people sharing a vocabulary and working under the same intellectual frameworks.

Similarly, Smitten Kitten's staff are "the best and brightest in their respective fields." The use of the term "fields" is telling. It's a word frequently used by those in professions with a high level of cultural capital, like medicine or education, indicating a specialized, focused knowledge stemming from years of study. This framing positions the sex trade as a body of knowledge that, like the literature of the Renaissance, can be studied. The "best and the brightest" staff are presented as elite members of a group of professionals with an intellectual rather than prurient interest in sex. Their scholarly activity suggests a kind of disinterested objectivity that works to disassociate the employees—and by extension the store and its products—from the realm of the body into that of the mind. Women may consume sexual products appropriately, it seems, only if their minds are properly educated with the knowledge and skills to operate their bodies properly.

June Juffer notes a similar disciplinary tendency at work in many of the self-help and sexual advice manuals of the 70's that broke down masturbation into a series of instructions. These step-by-step instructions often required women to dedicate substantial portions of their day to practice.[43] The disciplinary attitude was enhanced by the fact that many of these manuals framed masturbation and sexual education as a form of therapy and self-care. Ensuring one's health is a means of monitoring the processes of one's own bodies and avoiding the out-of-control excesses of mental or physical break-down that might disrupt social relations.[44]

While the therapeutic discourses are rare in Smitten Kitten and Babeland's marketing, they do appear in Babeland's aforementioned ad for the Hitachi Wand. The ad's confessional style and before-after structure make it clear that the woman in the ad has moved from a state of illness to health through the proper application of technology—which is important not only for the "personal sexual revolution" it brings to her, but also for the way it facilitates her relationship with her partner. The health and environmental concerns articulated by both companies present the need for women to constantly monitor what goes into one's body. Smitten Kitten, for example, tells its customers that "you should care as much about the ingredients in your sex toys as you do about the food you eat or the air you breathe and the chemicals you use in your home."[45]

What's important to note here, is that such concerns, while certainly legitimate, represent the body as threatened by external perils—in food, air, and the home—that might invade, and over which one "should" be constantly vigilant. Purchasing certain products is a way for consumers to demonstrate a proper level of concern over "health and environmental impacts of the sex toy industry." The consumer should desire the beneficial impact on the environment by the phthalate-free toy at least as much as they desire the sexual pleasure it brings. Concern over protecting the healthy boundaries of one's body becomes a moral imperative that is tied to having appropriate concerns about the environment and larger society.

In this way, Babeland and Smitten Kitten work to undercut the rebellious, revolutionary nature of female sexual desire seen elsewhere in their promotions. Female sexual activity, it seems, needs to occur in an upper-class, intellectual and moral context. Indeed, these aspects of Babeland and Smitten Kitten's marketing are quite consistent with the trend Feona Attwood observed in her study of sexual marketing to women in Britain. Attwood observes that a range of companies from lingerie stores to those for erotic products tend to represent "women's sexual pleasure as fashionable, safe, aesthetically pleasing and feminine."[46] Above all, she concludes, the female sexual consumer is depicted as a "classy self-sufficient subject."[47]

Yet the meaning of "classiness," as we have seen, is tied to one's ability to avoid excess, to discipline one's self, and to control and contain one's body and desires. Themes of containment are at work in several places within Babeland's promotional material. Babeland's parties are particularly strong examples of how certain advertising appeals work to contain women' sexuality in ways that undercut the store's other, more assertive messages. Babeland is, in fact, only one of a number of companies that host such parties, yet its depiction of these events is notable primarily because, despite the feminist agenda of the store, it is so conventional.

Babeland promotes its parties as "Tupperware-style toy parties."[48] The description not only allows instant understanding of how the parties operate, but also places the toys safely in the domestic realm of useful household products. More to the point, however, is that Babeland explicitly delimits the parties' function, describing them as appropriate for "a bachelorette party or girls' night out." Such events are commonly seen as a form of female communal celebrations during which women rebel against normative standards of feminine behavior by engaging in wild, rowdy and sexualized behavior and break free from traditional constraints on their sexual behavior and everyday sexual identifications. Such events initially seem to offer women a space to celebrate the ambiguous and contradictory aspects of sexuality that they may experience.

Yet it is important to note that Bachelorette parties are, in fact, traditions of "carnival"—ritual celebrations in which individuals may overturn the social hierarchy only temporarily. Carnival is a form of play in illegitimate behaviors and sexual and gender identities may be enacted in a way that feels liberating, but does little to change women's social realities. Thus, while sexual play and the adoption of various sexual personae, is experienced by many as pleasurable, and even healing, as for example in the rituals of S&M play,[49] it is questionable whether temporary performances of alternative sexual identities or behaviors may be conceived of as acts of resistance per se. Such parties promise that women may adopt a pleasurable identity of sexual rebel without actually threatening the status quo—one can play at being a "bad girl" while still remaining a lady.

This kind of "naughty" yet unthreatening sexuality is seen yet again in Babeland's most successful ad campaign, judging by the frequency of the placement and its logo-like use throughout its website. Another ad for the rabbit, it features the outline of a handbag set against a pink background. Inside are the pen-and-ink outlines of the various accoutrements of everyday "feminine" life—lipstick, glasses, a pen and even a calculator. Lying amidst these everyday items, rests a solid white-silhouette of the rabbit vibrator. The ad suggests a sexuality associated with the safe world of the everyday and the mundane—the vibrator is meant to be used in the everyday way that one applies lipstick or wears glasses. Set against a pink background and framed by a fashion accessory, it symbolizes a distinctly feminine and stylish world. This is only enhanced by the instant association many women make between the Rabbit and the fashionable and upscale world of *Sex and the City*, in which it appeared and whose protagonists are well-known as the epitome "classy and self-sufficient." By purchasing the Rabbit, consumers are promised a lifestyle similar to that of Carrie Bradshaw.

Thus, in distinct contrast to the earlier Rabbit ad we saw, this ad hints at the ways female sexuality should remain hidden. The ad works by drawing on a sense of titillation stemming from the pleasure in forbidden looking. Women's purses are private, personal objects. We see the contents of the bag as through an x-ray; the vibrator evidence of a female desire we would not see otherwise. Yet again, we do not even really see the vibrator—like a strip tease that ends with panties and bras still in place, the vibrator ultimately remains cloaked. A solid white shape, it is another level of x-ray, set apart and even more secretive. The vibrator here may be for everyday use, but it is for private use. Sexuality done in "good taste" apparently relies on it being fashionable and feminine, in other words politely contained and unseen.

Such ads reveal the ways that contemporary representations of female sexuality remain limited. While Babeland and Smitten Kitten certainly make positive interventions in creating a feminist address, they are affected by the need to render their products acceptable to a wide range of consumers. As a result, they sometimes participate in discourses that seem to work against their self-described feminist politics. In many ways the notions of playful, "naughty" sexual recreation put forth in products like Babeland parties are reflective of what Amber Kinser describes as a kind of "false" feminism. This occurs when "anything that looks like one is casting off any cultural restriction whatsoever . . . counts as feminism."[50]

Similarly, the social justice concerns promoted most strongly by Smitten Kitten, which, while important for framing feminism as necessarily tied to a web of social concerns, are also quite trendy. Their success, as well as the success of other socially conscious stores like Ben and Jerry's and The Body Shop, demonstrates the extent to which marketing appeals based around environmental and ethical concerns have become mainstreamed. In part, the effectiveness of such marketing campaigns lies in their ability to tap into the kinds of "subcultural capital" that is frequently associated with membership in alternative communities like feminism. Heath and Potter, for example, argue that many people identify with environmentalist, anti-globalist, feminist and even punk subcultures as a means of "visibly demonstrating one's rejection of mainstream society" and distinction from the masses.[51] Ironically, this rejection of the consumer-dominated mainstream has become one of the driving forces of contemporary capitalism, as difference becomes a primary signifier of what is cool, with the result that "subculture has become the new high culture."[52] The fact that oil companies like Shell have begun to embrace environmental concerns in their marketing points to the ways such ideologies are frequently implicated in less-than altruistically motivated capitalist processes.

This is not to say that the environmental and ethical concerns expressed by Smitten Kitten and Babeland are insincere, but they do work to invest the company and its products with an aura of coolness that may have less to do with their actual politics than the distinction they promise consumers. Babeland and Smitten Kitten promote women's consumption of sexual goods as a means to access a sense of liberation and to enact new identities based around resisting old limitations on their sexual freedom and concerns with social justice. This is a form of "empowerment through style," a commodification of feminism in which individual consumption substitutes for larger social change.[53] As Dennis Hall has observed, buying erotic products from funky, feminist shops like Good Vibrations or Babeland and Smitten Kitten, may be a way for women to claim a feeling of feminist empowerment in the bedroom, but it does not guarantee their liberation outside.[54] The stores could be said to be contributing to a widely critiqued tendency amongst contemporary third wave feminists to focus on feelings of personal empowerment rather than addressing larger social concerns.[55]

Still, stores like Babeland and Smitten Kitten play an important role in contributing to changing conceptions of female sexuality as well as continuing to expand women's access to sexual materials and information. In her wide-scale study of the spread of pornography in the U.S., June Juffer makes the important point that the growth of the vibrator industry in the 1970s didn't solve the problem of access to sexual products for many women.[56] Despite the growing consumer industry, problems with lack of access continue today, shaped by cultural stigma as well as physical constraints. Most local sex shops outside of centers like New York, Seattle or San Francisco still cater to mainly male clientele. In a trip to a local Midwestern sex shop in researching this paper, for example, I was forced to navigate a store in which I was the only female customer; there were no women-oriented products available for purchase with the exception of a few dildos, and a male client was loudly masturbating in a dark hallway immediately off the main sales floor.

In contrast, Babeland and Smitten Kitten create spaces in both their stores and on-line sites that allow women to easily access sexual products as well as information about the workings of their bodies that remains, shall we say, hard for some to come by in an era of abstinence-only education. They stress the principle that sexuality is and should be part of everyone's life. In addition, during a time in which many young women hesitate to identify with the term "feminist," these stores use punk-inspired aesthetics to present the feminist identity as fun, hip, energetic, and humorous. Commodified or not, the stores' articulation of feminist politics helps to further public discussion of feminist issues, by attempting to shift the focus on sexual liberation from the empowerment of individual women to larger social concerns. Both stores make clear that any feminist politics must be inclusive and address social inequities at a deeper level, and engage with concerns over race, sexual orientation, gender identification and even fair labor practices and the environment.

———— 9 ————

Clean Porn: The Visual Aesthetics of Hygiene, Hot Sex, and Hair Removal

SUSANN COKAL

What was once commonly called a woman's pudendum, a term rooted in the Latin word for "shame," has shed its embarrassment and come out of hiding. In what is sometimes called today's "raunch culture," the ideal of female sexual attractiveness is a firm body with large breasts, flat stomach, and—surprise—a hairless vulva. While big breasts and small waists have been valued for most of Western aesthetic history, the entirely or partially hairless mound is a relatively new innovation. Only over the past ten years or so has it become fashionable to spend hours and dollars removing hair from the pubic bone to the anus. Perhaps the most popular of these styles, the Brazilian, leaves a narrow stripe leading to the vulva's slit; other options include the "landing strip," a somewhat wider swatch; a stencil that will shape the patch into a tulip, arrow, heart, or other coy design; or complete baldness, a choice that *Cosmopolitan* magazine recently reported is growing in popularity.[1] We live in a culture of exposed vulvas, naked to the world, hairless as the day they were born, and paraded endlessly in front of our faces. Or so it might seem to viewers of pornography and readers of popular advice-giving magazines.

For several years now, the pubic coiffure has been a hot topic for discussion in venues such as *Cosmopolitan*, the *Village Voice*, and the online magazine Salon.com. In fact, there is a wealth of Internet discussion; typing in "shaving pubic hair" to Google on September 2, 2006, resulted in 4,694 hits. These discussions usually lead to talk of porn. In August of 2006, a woman

wrote in to Cary Tennis's advice column on Salon.com: "I know that nowa-
days, the style for women is to shave their pubic hair, maybe leaving a tiny
strip, à la Brazilian wax. . . . So now I am curious. Do most women do this
today? Are there guys who don't mind pubic hair au naturel?"[2] Tennis admitted he was nonplussed, saying only that the "shaved look" could mean "the
infantilizing of the female genitalia, etc." and that pornography "has transformed the pussy into a legitimate object of style, like legs or lips; it's so
widely represented that it has become public—though it is still viewed largely
in private. He asked readers for their insights and, in less than a month,
received 342 letters in response, 27 of which appeared online as the "editors'
choice."

Tennis makes the two obvious connections: shaving pubic hair returns the
vulva to a more adolescent appearance (though the swelling of the labia in
puberty guarantees that a grown woman will never look like a little girl Down
There again), and the fashion is the direct result of pornography's influence
on popular culture. Most people, in fact, will offer the same observations. In
Cosmopolitan, journalist Sara Bodnar speculates that "The proliferation of
porn could be one reason for the bushwhacking bonanza"; she quotes a Ph.D.
psychologist who says, "Women sometimes assume men want them to look
like porn stars, who are often completely bare."[3] We might disagree only with
the psychologist's tempered phrasing, and it is perhaps unnecessary to bela-
bor the connection.

As a visual medium and a culturally produced text, pornography can be
considered a form of art, though the relationship between high art and porn
is a tricky one. As long as there have been people working with visual media,
they have represented female genitalia, but very few have offered a full bush
to public view. As John Berger wrote in 1972, this hair has traditionally been
"associated with sexual power, with passion," and "woman's sexual passion
needs to be minimized so that the spectator may feel that he has the monop-
oly of such passion."[4] The elision of sexuality created a popular aesthetic.
Even some of the most sophisticated male spectators have been horrified at
the sight of what's normally there. Meanwhile, counter to the current of high
art, some pornographers and their clients were comfortable with the sight of
that hair, particularly as the camera, not the paintbrush, began capturing
images. But, as current DVDs and *Cosmopolitan* magazine show, we've swung
back around to the bare aesthetic for pornography as for popular culture.
This time the key is a notion of cleanliness: Our culture particularizes and
aggressively markets hygiene, and these days, one of the ways for a woman—
traditionally considered the "impure" sex—to show she's clean is to remove
her private hair.

Thus, in the current culture, pornography, female shaving, and the American ideal of cleanliness being next to godliness all converge between a woman's legs. The shaved pubis fuses current conservative prudery and American
squeamishness about the body with a pornographic culture that considers

this particular type of hygiene to be sexy. What we might call "clean porn" is our current ideology, and the shaved or waxed vulva is sexy, hip, and modern. In this one regard, then, the two culturally opposing views of women, the completely clean Victorian angel in the house and the porn star who is considered practically a prostitute, now become one.

"THE SPECTACLE WAS ALL THE MORE STRIKING": GAZING OVER THE ABYSS

Often criticized for being at best uncomfortable and at worst objectifying, pubic coiffures are driven by the interests of visual culture. We like to look, and removing the pubic hair gives us both more and less to see. By page 161 of Pauline Réage's *Story of O*, for example, the eponymous and willing sex slave has seen and experienced more than most adventuresses can imagine: a chateau where the libertines torture and ravish each other's mistresses; a lover who consigns her first to those libertines and then to his half-brother; a cruel Englishman who loves against his will and whips what he loves; and various adventures both sapphic and sublime. But she is actually surprised by what she sees when observing "the torture of little Yvonne":

> Her thighs, like her breasts crisscrossed with a green network of veins, spread to reveal a pink flesh which was pierced by the thick iron ring, which had finally been inserted, and the spectacle was all the more striking because Yvonne was completely shaved.
> "But why?" O wanted to know . . .
> "He says I'm more naked when I'm shaved. The ring, I think the ring is to fasten me with."[5]

This literary-pornographic classic, first published in France in 1954, offers the one supreme reason for shaving a *mons veneris*: Shaving yields up the vulva's secrets to the male gaze, makes the woman more naked, the spectacle—for the female body is always a spectacle—more striking.

Thus the shaved mound has entered pop culture, and it does so as a new means of expressiveness. Whether they shave or wax, use a stencil, leave a "landing strip," or go all-bare, women who remove their pubic hair are catering to a particular version of sexiness that is focused on the viewer (one might even say "the consumer") and his expectations. These are the women poring over advice in more popular sources such as *Cosmo* and *Salon.com*; relishing story lines about nether do's on *Sex and the City* and, like the characters on that show, chatting about pubic hair with their friends. At the very least, they go online and post their own theories and feelings about the fashion.

Many—if not most—women and men connect this ideal to the porn models and actresses who make their living displaying every bump and crease of their bodies for the devouring gaze of a mostly male audience. That "mostly male" is important: While the generalization would be difficult to prove, shaved pubic areas seem to be a largely heterosexual phenomenon.[6] Men, in fact, tend to assume that the pubic coiffure or shave has been performed for their sake—which is one reason why it's sexy ("the fact that it's partly on my behalf is very exciting"[7]). As Berger argued in *Ways of Seeing*, the real subject of the nude painting—one of the staples of Western art and the precursor to porn—is not the female on the canvas but the "spectator in front of the picture," who "is presumed to be a man. . . . It is for him that the figures have assumed their nudity."[8] Striking as O might find little Yvonne's shaved pubis, it is not O's gaze that matters.[9] The visual exists for the male.

What was unusual in the 1950s is becoming common practice now, thanks in part to the ideology that spawned *Story of O* and its less literary cousins. In 1997, Slavoj Zizek was perhaps the first to theorize that ideology and the nuances of various pubic hairstyles:

> Wildly grown, unkempt pubic hair indexes the hippie attitude of natural spon-
> taneity; yuppies prefer the disciplinary procedure of a French garden (one
> shaves the hair on both sides close to the legs, so that all that remains is a
> narrow band in the middle with a clear-cut shave line); in the punk attitude,
> the vagina is wholly shaven and furnished with rings (usually attached to a
> perforated clitoris). Is this not yet another version of the Lévi-Straussian semi-
> otic triangle of "raw" wild hair, well-kept "baked" hair and shaved "boiled"
> hair?[10]

Convincing as his triangle may be, the ideology has changed somewhat in the last decade. Pubic coiffing has become so popular that by now most of the styles are "baked," including the naked *mons*. Even the bald treatments that have become fashionable in recent years belong not to punks but to professional women, college girls, and housewives. In the new visual culture, the shaved mound is an everyday aesthetic standard.

In our current popular culture, with its interest in self-empowerment and self-help, there's also an apparently narcissistic aspect to the pubic coiffure; magazines push it not only as a way of appealing to men but also as a way of pampering the self. A nether-do requires a lot of attention and upkeep, and it gives a woman an excuse, perhaps even a command, to pay attention to herself. The authors of the e-book *Hot Pink: The Girls' Guide to Primping, Passion, and Pubic Fashion* declare their intent is "to give women a resource for feeling great about themselves, whatever their personal style."[11] Even the men surveyed by *Cosmo* said that they like that the woman who shaves or waxes has decided to "lavish so much attention on herself" and is "looking after herself"[12]: that kind of attention to the self is sexy. It would appear that it is all right, and even arousing, to be self-involved if the part of the self that attracts one's attention is one's vulva—and the activity in question is readying the body for the gaze of the other.

L'ORIGINE DU COIFFURE: AESTHETIC HISTORY AND STATISTICS

The visual arts, in which we might include pornography, thrive on a certain deceptiveness. Previous visual culture tended to obscure what was actually going on around the genitals. Michael Castleman noted those murky origins and art's ability to mislead on Salon.com: "It's not easy to track the history of pubic presentation. Ancient Chinese, Greek and Roman erotic art generally depict genitals—both male and female—without pubic hair. Did the ancients remove it? Or did the artists simply not include it? Art historians are silent on the subject." In fact, Castleman's rule doesn't quite hold; flipping through a book on Chinese or Indian erotic art, for example, will yield as many pictures with pubic hair as without.[13] The hair is mostly sparse, a mere shadow around the *mons* or penis, but it is there. Most of this art came miniaturized, on vases and scrolls for private viewing; perhaps the scale of the work itself may have had something to do with how much hair was represented.

Other writers claim to possess more hard facts. Sketching a history is, of course, a way of normalizing and establishing a practice, very much in-line with the goals of authors who gain readership by urging women to reinvent their looks and their selves. On their Web site, Deborah Driggs and Karen Risch, authors of *Hot Pink*, assure potential buyers that nether coiffures have a long and varied history. They, too, cite the ancient Greeks and Asians, saying they "actually plucked their pubic hair to shape it into an aesthetic ideal"; they also declare that "aristocratic women in the sixteenth century grew their curlies as long as possible so they could pomade and decorate them with bows."

Cosmopolitan reporters seem to have performed most of the historical research (or speculation) done on the nether coiffure. In 1999, *Cosmo*'s "Irma Kurtz's Agony" column again mentioned the example of ancient Greece.[14] In 2004, Paula Szuchman described ancient Egyptian and contemporary Middle Eastern methods of removing hair with honey or sugar and strips of fabric.[15] She also noted that the Sears catalogue advertised razors and depilatory creams in 1922, and that reduced availability of cloth for swimsuits during World War II meant scantier styles and increased potential for stray hairs; women used razors or even sandpaper, and sometimes burned the hairs away.[16] This determination to remove hair at any cost shows again that the hair was considered scandalous and intolerable; to let a stray curl peek through would have been to demonstrate an execrable lack of self-control and a louche, dirty sexuality. Worst, it would have been ugly.

In any event, the removal of body hair, particularly through salon procedures such as waxing, has clearly become more popular in recent years, fed by media that recognize and perpetuate it. To explain the popularity of waxing, *Cosmopolitan* claimed in 2004 that "the number of people employed by salons has jumped 24 percent since 1999, while, according to the market research firm ACNielsen, razor sales for men and women have dropped 18 percent in the last two years."[17] In an area in which statistics are hard to come by—even *Cosmo* can't say how many women are shaving, or how much they take off—the magazine has made a valiant effort to put the new fad into a context of scientific and historical data. By doing so, the writers make readers more comfortable with the practice and even create a certain amount of pressure to participate in it.

"QUITE DIFFERENT TO WHAT HE SAW": HIGH ART AND CLOUDY EXPECTATION

No matter what actual women were doing Down There, visual culture and artistic aesthetics have long been creating discomfort with the hairy female pubis. Before the twentieth century, representing any pubic hair at all (or, for that matter, the slit over which it grows) was out of the question for high art, and consequently some naïve persons were led to false expectations.

The case of John Ruskin, for example, is legendary. The Victorian art critic and essayist married Euphemia Gray on April 10, 1848, but never managed to consummate the marriage. As Euphemia would write to her father when seeking an annulment some years later, Ruskin offered a variety of excuses before he "told me his true reason (and this to me is as villainous as all the rest), that he had imagined women were quite different to what he saw I was, and that the reason he did not make me his wife was because he was disgusted with my person the first evening 10th April."[18] In fact, Ruskin had never had sex before, and his experience of the unclothed female body was limited to artistic representations. He had not, in short, expected pubic hair, and he found it revolting. He fled the room and thereafter treated Effie with a distant kindness.[19]

The arts had led Ruskin to expect a sort of blank area between a woman's legs, based on versions of the female nude that had been a popular subject since the Renaissance. Often in the service of some abstract allegory about virtue and purity, these pictures satisfied both prurient and moral interests. Representations of Susannah and the Elders, for example, were particularly well loved in Germany. Viewers got to see young Susannah's white flesh exposed to the gaze of the two lecherous old men—and, lest the painting's viewers become overstimulated, a number of pictures also showed the elders being punished not just for looking at Susannah or for attempting to seduce her, but for telling others that *she* had tried to seduce them. Nowhere, even in a full-frontal depiction, did Susannah's pubic hair come into play. While women had to have legs and bellies, and the sight of those things could certainly arouse, the woman's private hair was *too* private, too animal, for anyone to view.

As we will see below, this high art is not exactly comparable to today's pornography.[20] First, the artistic bare pudendum is completely featureless; there is no slit, no clitoris, no vagina—none of the elements so aggressively on display in pornography. High art manifests an aesthetic of elision rather than of revelation. In their day, these female nudes were usually considered instructive and uplifting, because of their beauty alone if not some added moral message. Even ladies could examine paintings and sculptures of naked women, even though most of the models were assumed to be prostitutes, but they would never look at a picture that featured a hairy mound. Such pictures were available as engravings and, in the nineteenth century, photographs, sold clandestinely to men who used them for the same purposes men use *Penthouse* and *Hustler* today.[21] Writing of the Gilded Age, M. H. Dunlop mentions "bulky peepshow books with the words *Gems* and *Masterpieces* in their titles"[22]—essentially, pornography masquerading, however feebly, as art. Even then, there seem to have been relatively few representations involving pubic hair; it just wasn't something that people wanted to see.

There is one notable exception in nineteenth-century art. Perhaps the earliest modern artistic representation of female pubic hair, Gustave Courbet's *L'Origine du monde* (*The Origin of the World*), was painted in 1866 for the Turkish diplomat Khalil Bey. Starting mid-thigh, the painting offers a view between a woman's legs, showing sparse black hairs near the vaginal opening, increasing in thickness and curliness as they move up the mound of Venus. The view ends at the breasts, with a sheet draped just above nipple height. In the era of the gently clouded *mons veneris*, this painting was never displayed publicly and became the stuff of legend. After Bey's bankruptcy, the painting was sold—but still considered so incendiary that it had to be hidden beneath an outer panel. In the twentieth century, *L'Origine* was lost for a while, then resurfaced; it belonged briefly to Jacques Lacan and ended up at Paris's Musée d'Orsay in 1995.[23] It still draws giggling crowds today. The fact that only the erogenous zones are displayed, coupled with the inclusion of both hair and a subtle clitoris, make *L'Origine* shocking even now, particularly when it's surrounded by the more sedate works of Courbet and his contemporaries.

Still, the bush displayed in *L'Origine* does not appear entirely *au naturel*. No hairs stray down into what we now call the bikini line, the creases by the thighs, and the growth thins dramatically below the clitoris—as if it's just too appalling to think of hairs growing abundantly down and around the vagina itself. We seem to have an early version of the landing strip, or in any case a somewhat manicured mound: The world may have originated between this woman's legs, but she cleaned herself up a bit first.

"I LIKE WHAT YOU HAVE GOING ON DOWN THERE":
INTIMACIES OF THE SMALL SCREEN AND PERVERSION

With its single, uncomplicated sexual message, porn is one of our most visually driven cultural products, even more so than the high art that tends to deliver a more philosophical message. Porn's popularity is well established and widely acknowledged; Pamela Paul writes that it is "so seamlessly integrated into popular culture that embarrassment or surreptitiousness is no longer part of the equation"[24] and cites a 2004 poll that found 75 percent of men and 41 percent of women[25] had "used" (in common parlance, people use porn rather than merely see it) pornographic films from the Internet alone. In her theoretical classic *Hard Core: Power, Pleasure, and the "Frenzy of the Visible,"* Linda Williams takes a phrase from Jean-Louis Comolli to dub "the visual, hard-core knowledge-pleasure produced by the *scientia sexualis* [Freud's sexual science] a 'frenzy of the visible.'"[26] Despite the "extreme" phrasing, she writes, "this frenzy is neither an aberration nor an excess; rather, it is a logical outcome of a variety of discourses of sexuality that converge in, and help further to produce, technologies of the visible."[27] We might consider pubic coiffure fashions to be one such "technology of the visible"— part of a culture increasingly oriented toward the use of mass-produced images destined exclusively to arouse.

From the days of silent stag films, visual stimulation has always been paramount; no one rents or downloads porn to listen to the dialogue, the moaning, or the "bow-ch-ch-bow-bow" music in the background. Williams writes that the "principle of *maximum visibility*" has evolved over the history of hard core, with the intent, among other activities, "to privilege close-ups of body parts over other shots; to overlight easily obscured genitals; to select sexual positions that show the most of bodies and organs."[28] Pornography's interest in strong visuals of the genitals is indisputable. But the visual stimuli have not always included hairless *mons*; in fact, the stars of 1920s stag movies and soft- or hard-core 1970s hits such as *Emmanuelle in America, Deep Throat,* and *Behind the Green Door* had full bushes that spoke to a different kind of femininity. Retired porn model and actress Kelly Nichols says that when she started out in the early 1980s, "I posed with a full bush. No one in adult entertainment shaved back then. Now everyone does."[29] So how, then, did the fashion change in porn—and thus in our popular culture?

The answer may lie in the shift from big movie screens to the much smaller screens of television and computer. Peep shows and porn shops always featured loops, short films run in private booths, but the fanciest porn—long-running and (often sketchily) plotted—played in theaters. *Deep Throat* and *Behind the Green Door,* for example, made their mark on big screens in packed houses. But in the early 1980s, the industry made the change to VHS. A smaller screen makes for decreased visibility, and camerawork had to change in order to display those hard-to-find "naughty bits." The naughty bits had to be compelling, too, as with video came the fast-forward button: Former actor Tim Connelly says that while there was "craft . . . a certain element of art" in pornographic films for the big screen, "Now you can't even think about porno without thinking about fast-forward, which is really a testimonial for why people didn't want to do videos."[30] It seems inevitable that, in order to keep the viewer's hand from wandering to the fast-forward button, the action's pace had to pick up and the objects of interest be more prominently displayed than ever before. The narrative art was lost and the visual component made more prominent.

This is around the time the actresses began to shave and wax consistently. Though no one seems to have made the connection between shaving and the small screen specifically, it is true that, as Nichols said, hair removal is now expected of the women in porn.[31] They may also be expected to conform to more consistent images than previously: Almost all are now blonde, pneumatic, and waxed, with collagen lips and plenty of eye makeup. While Linda Lovelace, star of *Deep Throat*, was generally considered rather plain and had a long disfiguring scar on her chest, Connelly says the 1980s brought "the concept of the 'Video Vixen' a girl who appears in videos and has got sort of a style [that] comes across as incredibly telegenic."[32] Playing on the relatively small screen of a television, then, video required a special look of its actresses.

Part of that look would be a kind of intimacy; this is, after all, pornography showing in someone's home, his private space. As Horace Newcomb has written about the difference between cinema screens and television more generally, the TV screen is a personal and intimate thing;[33] intimacy is impossible in a movie theater but absolutely required in the living room or bedroom. And with its close look at what's usually concealed, a shaved or otherwise groomed vulva creates deeper intimacy as well as improved small-screen visibility.[34]

Pubic hair has always, and perhaps ironically now, been one of the determining factors when defining pornography. *L'Origine du monde* is shocking in large part because of the hair depicted. Theater owner Dave Friedman says that in the 1960s, "you didn't dare show pubic hair. An L.A. vice squad cop told me, 'If we see pubic hair, then it's pornographic—and that gives us an excuse to pick up the print.'"[35] What was forbidden, and thus especially erotic then, has been banished again—this time, in order to increase a visually driven eroticism. The porn industry has erased one mark of perversion and, in the eyes of some commentators at least, substituted another: To some people, the hairless mound is more fetishized than the hairy one, and fetishes are not just perverted—they're dirty.

An informal survey of women who don't shave comes back with comments such as "I don't have the time," "It would itch too much," and "I think there's something wrong with men who want women to look like little girls." Writing for Salon.com in 1998, Joan Walsh expressed the psychological discomfort many women feel: "creating the illusion of a hairless pubis seemed like one more example of how we glorify the sexless child's body over what's womanly, a step in the direction of kiddie porn." Even men often declare themselves uncomfortable with the idea of confronting a vulva that looks like Lolita's—and yet another informal survey indicates that they are invariably fascinated with a shaved vulva when they encounter one; they call for more light and will delay intercourse in order to explore with their eyes the secrets laid bare. Jschinn1, who answered Cary Tennis, dismissed the child-*mons* accusation as "idiotic": "A full-grown woman . . . does not suddenly become like a 12-year-old simply by shaving her crotch." She remains full-grown, her hairlessness adding a new layer of sexual mystique.

People who frown on pornography don't do so merely because they see it as exploitative; some suggest it is ruining sex. A 28-year-old man told Pamela Paul, author of *Pornified*, that he stopped watching Internet porn because "I began to find it more difficult to stay aroused when having sex with a real woman."[36] One "Anonymous" respondent to Tennis claimed that pornography has led the "younger generation" to an unsatisfying sense of performance rather than participation: "The men are less present . . . then [sic] they used to be. The preference for shaved pussy goes along with this." A lack of hair and a lack of individualized inspiration go hand in hand, and it's easy to blame porn.

There is another potential model for the top heavy, bare-mounded feminine ideal, one with a historical tie to the sex industry. Another of Tennis's respondents, Anne, says that a shaved *mons* reminds her not so much of a little girl as of a Barbie doll—the toy with which a little girl might play in order to fantasize and learn about being a woman—and there is some relevance to the observation. Barbie herself was copied in 1959 from a naughty German doll called Lilli, which was marketed primarily to men and based on a comic-strip character who devoted her life to teasing men and to "mildly sordid double entendres."[37] She is thus an early pop product of the modern sex industry, one who infiltrated the culture in a more subtle and pervasive way than production companies like Vivid Entertainment could ever hope to do. People who compare the airbrushed women in *Playboy* and *Maxim* to dolls and "dollies" are tapping into the ideology that created Barbie.[38]

So here are connections to porn and to adolescence. Are men who like their women shaved then to be considered perverts and pedophiles—that is, dirty old men? It depends on whom you ask. At the very least, this preference plays into the visual culture that makes most women feel insecure about their bodies. A poll conducted for *Pornified* found that 51 percent of Americans felt that porn "raises men's expectations of how women should look."[39] One of the author's informants, for example, says, "porn's prevalence is a serious hindrance to my comfort level in relationships. . . . my body image suffers tremendously. . . . I wonder if I am insecure or if the images I see guys ogle every day has [sic] done this to me."[40] *Cosmopolitan*'s advice columnist Irma

Kurtz assured a letter writer that a man who wants his lady to sport some kind of style isn't necessarily a pervert and that she should "Play along for fun."[41] Interestingly, in the very same column, Kurtz tells a flat-chested woman whose boyfriend likes big breasts that she should not consider getting hers augmented "Because what really turns the poor jerk on is the idea of seeing women as objects." Some fetishes—or preferences—are acceptable; but a line is being drawn. A woman might shave to please her man, but she should not have surgery. Perhaps shaving means a proclivity and surgery means perversion.

The somewhat contradictory message in Kurtz's column speaks to a trend that Ariel Levy discusses in *Female Chauvinist Pigs: Women and the Rise of Raunch Culture*, a book aimed at a popular audience. In our present state of mind, pornography and its easily acquired accoutrements are often seen as empowering to women; some people even say the trend is a natural outgrowth of feminism, as it shows we don't need to rebel against male ideals anymore. Levy reports hearing women say that "We'd *earned* the right to look at *Playboy*; we were *empowered* enough to get Brazilian bikini waxes. Women had come so far, I learned, we no longer needed to worry about objectification or misogyny. Instead, it was time for us to join the frat party of pop culture."[42] Objectification is perhaps the greatest problem that Levy perceives: "The women who are really being emulated and obsessed over in our culture right now—strippers, porn stars, pinups—*aren't even people*. They are merely sexual personae, erotic dollies from the land of make-believe."[43] Under this view, pubic hair styling plays into an ideology by which women give up their personhood in order to conform to an abstracted, Barbie-like idea of sexiness.

There is another wrinkle to the debate, as some people say that shaving offers pleasures beyond the visual stimuli that one gives to one's partner. The big advantage for the woman is increased sensation and convenience; without hair, the skin receives direct stimulation that increases many women's pleasure. And as jschinn1 wrote to Tennis, "Cunnilingus is far more pleasant for both giver and receiver when it's performed on a trimmed or bare vagina." "Magpie Malone" also wrote in to say that porn stars shave "for practical reasons": The longer a sex scene lasts, the easier it will be if "you are fully shaved and lubed." Shaving can be not only arousing but also practical, a way of achieving pleasure for the self as well as for the other.

Still, even when the woman acknowledges increased sensation, it is impossible to escape the insistence on male visual pleasure. In an episode of HBO's television show *Sex and the City*, Carrie and her friends go to Los Angeles for a week of fun—part of which entails Carrie getting a Brazilian wax that leaves her, as she says several times, "bald" and hyperconscious of her own sexuality: "I'm so aware of 'down there' now. Now I feel like I'm nothing but walking sex."[44] Samantha, who seems to have some experience going bare, says that a Brazilian "makes you do crazy things." In this condition, Carrie spends the night with a man named Keith, who refers to her pudendum when he tells her in the morning, "I like what you have going on down there." Carrie giggles and passes it off with, "That would be a whole lot of nothing," but perhaps the greatest pleasure we see her take in this episode is in receiving Keith's compliment. Her satisfying sexual adventure is enabled by her daring new do, something the script takes pains to associate with LA's film-and-beach culture, as opposed to New York's more conservative milieu. However, Keith is never presented as wrong or perverted for liking a naked vulva.

Shortly after Keith's remark, Carrie Fisher (playing herself) walks in and exposes him as a personal assistant, not the Hollywood agent he claimed to be. Carrie Bradshaw's adventure becomes a misadventure, proof (like her new coiffure) of LA's shallowness. When she returns to her own apartment at the episode's end, she's glad to be "inside," where "it was all real" and "I was starting to feel like myself again. And the rest of me would grow back. Eventually." The half hour's trajectory takes first Keith and then Carrie to an authentic interior. Keith is too shallow to appreciate the genuineness of Carrie and the true "inside" of her vagina, but despite the external changes, Carrie is smart enough to know she remains the same person and has enough self-esteem enough to appreciate herself and her vulva, which she expects to return to its natural state. Thus, the episode ultimately devalues the pubic coiffure, and it celebrates the real woman who might choose to alter her appearance "down there." The wax is a novelty (except perhaps to Samantha), serving mostly to attract viewers whose interests may be as false as Keith's.

The bookend to this episode comes three seasons later, when Samantha, the most sexually promiscuous and experimental of the four main characters, decides to honor her boyfriend's request to grow a "full bush."[45] As the hair comes in, she is surprised to find a gray one. As a result, she tries to dye everything she has, accidentally ending up with a fluffy carnival red tuft that makes her call herself "Bozo the Bush." Samantha shaves everything off and tells her boyfriend that, as a working woman, "I don't have time for you to be down there searching for it [her clitoris]. So I wanted to make everything nice and simple." (The efficiency factor was mentioned in the earlier episode, too, when Miranda explained the Brazilian's West Coast popularity: "L.A. men are too lazy to have to go searching for anything.") Within three years on the show, then, a full pubic wax or shave went from a sign of LA's counter-culture (or hyperculture) to a matter of convenience and efficiency for a high-powered woman on-the-go. It has been normalized to such an extent that no one now feels the need to comment on the fact that Samantha normally shaves herself, probably bare.

Samantha's bush-loving boyfriend is not alone. Even as the bare vulva has grown in popularity in both porn and the culture at large, the unshaved woman has come in for her share of fetishization as well—and in fact, if the men's magazines are any indication, it is the natural bush that's now the locus of perversion. Some Web sites, such as Fuzzywomen.com, offer contempla-tive, sometimes philosophical or quasi-scientific essays about the abundance or removal of pubic and other body hair. The effect is, however, altered in that they also feature photographs of hirsute vulvas and ads for "hot movies" and sites such as HornyHairyGirls.com. Other ads for pornographic videos in magazines such as *Penthouse* make lavish promises: "This 21-year-old is so hairy that you can't see her pussy until she pulls herself open!"[46]; "Their hair has been growing wild their whole lives and they don't want to shave any of it now!"; "definitely the hairiest vaginas ever seen!!!"[47] Granted, the hirsute vulva gets fewer pictorials and less attention in porn than the naked one—but even in pornography, it is not an entirely bald world. The relegation of the full bush to "dirty" fetish-type pictures and videos only highlights the acceptance of the coiffed vulva, the new industry standard.

NAKED, CLEAN, AND HAPPY: OR THE NEW HYGIENE

Certain concepts of cleanliness may be related to the jokes about efficiency and giving men quicker access. Perversion is dirty, and hygienic ideologies have come to motivate the waxing or shaving to such an extent that we are removing perversion and instating a kind of morality when we remove the hair. Americans' obsession with cleanliness and sterility is notorious worldwide.[48] It seems to come from a combination of our reformist heritage and our position as leader of the industrialized world; we have the belief that cleanliness is next to godliness, and we have the technology and medical understanding to enforce it. At our cultural roots, we also have a Puritanical discomfort—and fascination—with sexuality, and that sexuality can be made "cleaner," more moral, by adjusting the body's appearance. As Mary Douglas has argued, getting rid of what seems dirty is a way of "imposing system on an inherently untidy experience" and "making an environment conform to an idea"[49]; if we label the hair as dirty, we can gain control of our bodies and our sexuality by removing it. Given our ardently reformist background, too, it is perhaps natural that we translate our fetishization of pornographic *mons* style into a concern with hygiene: We're just more comfortable doing something, especially something sexual, if we can cite cleanliness as a motivator.

Even the dirty-picture industry has expressed an interest in the virtue next to godliness. In 1967, before the era of extensive genital topiary, Hugh Hefner described his ideal model in terms of a happy, clean, nakedness: "The *Playboy* girl has no lace, no underwear, she is naked, well-washed with soap and water, and she is happy."[50] In the same interview, Hefner described another feminine type, the femme fatale: she "wears elegant underwear, with lace, and she is sad, and somehow mentally filthy."[51] Even in the erotica business, to be clean is to be happy; a mind that acknowledges its sexuality straightforwardly is unsoiled. And the eponymous sexpot of *Emmanuelle in America* says that when sex is natural it's "clean"; she then unzips the fly of her would-be killer and fellates him until he flees.[52] Lust, then, and nakedness are clean—

now it's just a matter of defining how, in our contemporary culture, that clean body should look.

The eighteenth-century Reverend John Wesley, founder of Methodism, is responsible for dubbing cleanliness the virtue "next to Godliness." Whether the god in question is Venus or the Christian version is currently open to interpretation. Suellen Hoy, author of *Chasing Dirt: The American Pursuit of Cleanliness,* writes that this handy saying is somewhat misleading: "Clergy of that time favored cleanliness to promote not piety but Christian respectability, and eventually, health."[53] Hygiene was thus conceptualized perhaps rather like the cup and saucer that represented some souls in nineteenth-century sermons, clean on the outside but dirty within; and in this case the outside— the appearance or impression of cleanliness—was what mattered. Some years after Wesley, Benjamin Franklin's *Autobiography* called cleanliness one of the thirteen virtues.

A proper shave was part of that purity. Franklin wrote, "if you teach a poor young Man to shave himself and keep his Razor in order, you may contribute more to the happiness of his Life than in giving him a 1000 Guineas."[54] Shaving the face, like shaving the genitals, is motivated by visibility— and by reducing the number of vermin who might hide among the hairs. If it is hygienic to have a clean-shaven face, it may be even more important to have a clean-shaven mound (though, of course, Franklin dispensed no advice about this area, and in fact none seems to exist for the era).

From the beginning, women have been responsible for America's domestic cleanliness. It has been their job to make sure that their homes and their families' bodies are kept as clean as possible according to the standards of the day. For all that, conditions in the early days were not what we could consider truly clean; the technology just wasn't ready, and only the wealthy were able to maintain even minimal standards of hygiene. In the mid-nineteenth century, reformers began working to bring cleanliness to the masses. Writing books and proselytizing about the healthful effects of a dirt-free home, women such as Catharine Beecher were key players. Male health reformers again, as always, entrusted women with the health and cleanliness of their families.[55]

The perfection and dissemination of the microscope in the second half of the nineteenth century revolutionized the medical profession and the way we think of hygiene. Visibility achieved new levels. Suddenly doctors and scholars everywhere could see what lives in a drop of pond water—or on a half-inch of human skin. In the 1880s, for example, it turned out that consumption was caused by bacilli that created tubercles in the lungs and other flesh (hence the disease's new name, tuberculosis); the discovery spawned new cleansing technologies such as pasteurization and increased vigilance with personal hygiene. The hitherto hidden world of germs and parasites created a new unease with dirt, and a new interest in washing. If the skin itself could hide so much, just think what might lie behind a tuft of hair.

Women, the Victorian Angels in Houses, are the traditional gatekeepers of American good hygiene (and the goddess Hygeia herself is a woman), so it is natural that current ideas of cleanliness should be writ largely on the female mons. We might speculate that today, with a heightened fear of potentially fatal sexually transmitted diseases, perhaps some of the appeal of clean and clean-shaven genitals is that they give the impression of nothing to hide, no diseases to catch. Thus shaving confers another kind of respectability and virtue. And the arousing narcissism of this kind of personal attention is part of the ideology of hygiene. Notions of cleanliness are often focused outward, on making the body fit for social interactions, whether those interactions take place in the office or the bedroom.[56] Under this kind of thinking, a woman who wants to express herself with a clean body is not such a narcissist after all; she is a thoughtful partner.

In fact, a lack of pubic hair can be read as either dirty or clean, depending on who's looking. In 1999, a *Cosmopolitan* reader wrote in to ask if shaving pubic hair increases the risk of STD's; the answer was no.[57] It's a common concern, and not every doctor would agree with the article's answer; a general practitioner once told me that the hair is necessary for keeping out germs— it's the body's way of keeping clean. In 2003, *Cosmo* addressed the same issue in slightly different terms: "Back in caveman days, we needed pubic hair to keep germs out of the body, but now that we bathe and wear underwear, we no longer have much use for it."[58] In 2001, the magazine made virtually the same point: "In prehistoric times, this patch of hair probably helped keep germs and dirt away from genitals . . . now women usually wear underwear, which protects their privates."[59] The hair can be a useful tool in the fight against disease, but these days other innovations can take over that role. We're free to shed the part of our bodies that filtered out those germs.

By far the most common opinion is that a hairless body is a clean one. *Cosmopolitan*'s "History of Bikini Waxing" argued that Middle Eastern women remove their pubic hair to "appear clean and pure for their husbands."[60] Medical science, too, would support this idea; traditionally, nurses have shaved a woman's pubis when she is about to give birth—a way of keeping the area clean and the visibility good (the patients, however, sometimes complain that razor burn and itching from the hair growing in are the most long lived problems of childbirth). Removing the pubic hair, then, can give that impression of cleanliness, even if the cleanliness comes with a certain degree of inconvenience.

The happy hygiene of contemporary pornography, unlike that of Hefner's conception, also turns on hairlessness. One of Tennis's respondents speculated about "slick pornography, where actors' pubic hair shaving is pretty much a practical necessity for hygiene on the set." That claim may have been conjecture, but the prostitutes on HBO's *Cathouse*, a documentary series examining the Moonlite Bunny Ranch in Reno, Nevada, explain that they shave—sometimes twice a day—in order to be "clean" for their customers.[61]

A happy star or hooker is a hairless one; as throughout American culture, hygiene leads to good sex and to general contentment.[62]

This happy, hygienic nakedness is not, however, uncomplicated. Discussions of the potential benefits and drawbacks for both the woman and her partner, featured *ad infinitum* in the media, seem to be rationalizing one particular stance on the shaving question—that is, that shaving is desirable, its pitfalls avoidable, and a few basic techniques and products available to combat the discomfort. The side-effects of shaving or waxing can be uncomfortable as well as infectious. If the goal of a close shave is hot intercourse, the end result might disappoint expectations built up by watching porn: A bare *mons* is vulnerable to chafing, the downside of increased sensation. One gynecologist quoted in a 1999 *Cosmopolitan* calls pubic hair "a 'dry' lubricant, a barrier that prevents uncomfortable bare-skin friction during intercourse."[63] The article recommends "trimming unruly down-there hair rather than taking it all off." Waxing is painful and can irritate the skin just as badly as shaving; see, for example, Joan Walsh's article "From Happy Trails to Landing Strips."[64] Skin usually grows over the shaved hair as well, and some unsightly red bumps can pop up. Another drawback is oft-mentioned itching; as hair grows back, it can turn against the skin and cause irritation. In short, a woman who wants porn-quality sex has to be willing to put up with a bit of discomfort on her way to pleasuring herself and her man. No pain, no gain; everything worth having is worth suffering for.

In response to these irritations, a new culture has grown up around this type of self-care, and that new culture, again, refers us to hygiene. If the discomfort sets in, plenty of advice—and plenty of merchandise—is available in the popular arena. The University of Iowa Student Health Service, for example, has a web page explaining how to avoid ingrown hairs and other discomfort.[65] American enterprise has also sprung to the breach, and there are plenty of products available to circumvent these problems. Buying products is part of the self-care ideology; shaving, inspired by the porn industry, is made cleaner and more legitimate by purchasing accoutrements such as triple-blade razors and specially formulated lotions at the local drugstore. The woman who shaves or waxes again gazes at her vulva, evaluates it, as she takes measures to avoid infection and applies the recommended products: more of that healthy, sexy narcissism, and this time a narcissism truly directed toward hygiene and the public good.

Some of the advice given is quite basic, and yet it speaks to an endless process, chasing an elusive perfect pubic complexion. Exfoliation with a loofah or other rough scrubber is important; it is also advisable to moisturize, particularly with a product made for sensitive facial skin. And as specialized shaving has become part of our culture, so have specialized after-shave lotions such as Bikini Zone and TendSkin, which keep the follicles open and prevent ingrown hairs and unsightly red bumps. Thus, this new kind of hygiene associated with a new kind of beauty, itself explained in part by a desire for good

hygiene—a goal forever receding on the horizon, and becoming more and more impossible as art and fashion make new demands on it.[66]

CONCLUSION: STRANGE BEDFELLOWS

So our Victorian forebears and our pornographer contemporaries are, in fact, not so far apart. The Angel in the House of one and the whore of the other are joined at the *mons*. While they may have advocated different kinds of cleanliness, their ideologies have permeated popular culture and fused in the image of the hairless vulva. While the trend may have begun with the increased demands for visibility as porn moved from the silver screen to the small one, the shift was quickly justified with a rhetoric already in place, equating perceived cleanliness with morality and positive participation in the life of the culture. If we can see the vulva clearly, we can believe it to be clean and healthy in a way that will ease potential discomfort with sexuality itself.

There is a common denominator enabling the changes in all of these areas: new technologies. Some of these innovations let consumers watch pornography in the home, and some let them wax and shave with greater efficiency and comfort. These technologies converge to make the naked *mons* more possible, more normalized, and more visible; they also make it a form of technological innovation itself. Rendered hairless through science and consumerism, the bare (or topiaried) vulva of the contemporary "dollie" becomes itself a kind of machine that helps drive the pleasures inspired by mass-produced pornographic materials. Current standards may say that we're sexy, and that we're clean, but this is a manufactured kind of sexy-cleanliness that has rendered the vulva an artifact, an aesthetic product that perhaps might lead to even less realistic expectations than the elided genitals of pre-twentieth-century Western artwork.

While aimed primarily at a male gaze, the pubic coiffure is still called a matter of personal choice and self-expression in women's magazines. The notion of expression, particularly of the ever-elusive, always constructed self, calls into question the constructed nature of sexuality, of hygiene, and even of the distinction between natural and artificial. In this age of strong visual media and of grooming products for every area, is it possible to be truly *au naturel*? Even if a woman allows her hair to grow to a full bush, as Samantha does on *Sex and the City*, she seems to be conscious of it as a "look" or a style. That very attentiveness means that even the natural becomes, to some degree, artificial. We are both more and less naked down there now than before—more exposed to the gaze and more visibly manipulated. All of us now dollies, we wander through our own English gardens, admiring the topiaries and dreaming of the real.

Your Privacy's Showing: Pornography at Your Local Library

SUE BANKS

I f the internet is for access to porn, and public libraries are for internet access, then do public libraries equal access to porn? The internet is for porn, that's common knowledge. Cultural icons trumpet it on late night comedy shows, Broadway musicals celebrate it in song, and the federal legislature confirms it—the internet and pornography are inextricably linked. After more than 20 years of internet history, pornography on the internet characterizes the average citizen's concept of the online experience. Way back in 1998, candidate George W. Bush referred to the "dark dungeons" of the internet as an irresistible magnet for wayward children. The federal government has made efforts to control public access to adult material, including the establishment of the Child Internet Protection Act (CIPA), which restricts federal funding to public libraries that do not filter internet material to block pornography. Even with filters in place, it is not difficult to access sexually-oriented material, particularly in written form, chats and message boards.

Public libraries all over the world provide internet access to millions of citizens. Communities have made it clear that internet access is an important part of their library's role. But if the internet and porn are inextricably linked, how reasonable is it to hold public libraries responsible for controlling a medium which by its very nature is uncontrollable? When the litmus paper that is the public library is dropped into the volatile chemical broth that is community standards, it is the acid (or base) of internet pornography that separates the red from the blue. In the twenty-first century, public libraries stand at the center of the cultural battlefield between the secular humanists and the religious right fighting over the exercise of personal responsibility versus the defense against the dark side of human nature.

According to the Statistical Abstract of the United States, a majority of Americans, 61 percent in 2003, have computers of their own and access to affordable internet service for most households, compared to 54 percent in 2003.[1] However, the Bill and Melinda Gates Foundation produced a report in 2004 that sheds great light on an alternate reality: how individuals use the internet in their public libraries.[2] In 2002, 95 percent of public libraries in the U.S. provided internet access to the public. So, despite the numbers of those with access to computers and the internet at home, more than 14 million people spend hours every day accessing internet resources at their local library. Among those 14 million are individuals who spend upwards of 10 hours a day in the library, often so deeply immersed in the experience of online erotica and a community of adult content consumers that what most of us consider the "private" nature of the experience is immaterial to them.

Every library has policies that state the limits of acceptable use of the internet resources of the library. The New York Public Library's policies are a good example of the structure built to support and restrict access to material.[3] Most acceptable use policies delineate the responsibility of the patron to stay within the law of the land and the policies of the library. They amount to "don't do illegal things, hurt anyone else or the computers." In response to CIPA, any library that needs or wants federal funding of any kind, including those discount programs that allow us to purchase discounted telecommunications services to provide that high-speed internet access, has implemented some filtering solution. In a 2004 study by Florida State University, nearly 50 percent of all public libraries employed some filtering solution. Interestingly, in the 2006 update of the Florida State study of internet access in the public library, internet filtering wasn't even measured.[4] That subtle fact raises the question of whether the library research field has somehow resolved to its satisfaction an issue that continues to vex practitioners; or is content control and internet security simply so prevalent that there is no need to measure it?

Regardless of those controls, no library is a utopian haven for adults of the highest moral fiber where children can roam free in a perfect cloud of learning and literature. It is not a place where you can drop off your 10-year-old, drive off to the gym and be sure they're not going to be confronted with what some consider adult-only material. Whether it's language in a conversation, a book from the adult non-fiction collection or a picture on the internet computer, there are just as many materials that some would find offensive as there are to celebrate and embrace. There aren't enough tax dollars in the world to support the kind of professional library staff it would take to make every person's experience in the public library appropriate. Of course, the question of appropriateness is open to debate. But more importantly, the public library is free and open to all—not just those who are "like us" or who agree with our particular standards of decency.

DEFINITIONS

This examination of public access to adult material on the internet will be limited to the "legal" aspects of the activity. This will not be a discussion of the effect of consumption or suitability of access to obscene material including child pornography or the consumption of adult materials by people under 18 years of age. Those specific instances tend to be illegal in most state and federal statutes. Rather, the discussion will focus on the actions of adults and their access to material and interfaces that *may* be restricted by a library's acceptable use policy or violate community standards, but are not restricted by the law. Filtering will also not be an issue since CIPA has made filtering internet access a reality in most public libraries and libraries deal with it as they must.

How does the conversation begin about what is acceptable information-seeking behavior in adults and what is not? Joseph Slade articulates the nature of pornography as constantly shifting "along a vast continuum moving between two equally slippery concepts, the *erotic* and the *obscene*."[5] The studies and statistics related to the production and consumption of "pornography" on the internet are subject to the same slipperiness. For the purposes of this essay, we will use the term "adult material" for information and "online sexual activity" (OSA) for the broader sense of communications between and among users. These terms more accurately reflect the reality of internet pornography: what is pornography for one is erotic for another and obscene for a third.

A REVIEW OF THE LITERATURE

Before discussing OSA in the library, it is useful to examine the psychology at work among users. Cooper, Putnam et al. established three types of online users of sexual matter: recreational users, sexual compulsives, and at-risk users. The authors make the point that anyone pursuing online sexual activities is engaged in paraphilia—experience that reduces the individual's ability to make real and intimate connection with another person. Internet sexuality may, in their words, "lead a person who is prone to intrapsychic and interpersonal difficulties down a slippery slope."[6] The first type of user, recreational, is unlikely to experience any adverse effects from his or her online activities. They may have accidentally seen adult material and become intrigued enough to return to view it or communicate in a chat room, etc. The second type, sexual compulsives, are those who pursue online activities at the risk of their jobs, relationships and social lives. Compulsives deny, attempt to control, repeat, and ultimately continue to pursue those behaviors to an extent that can have extremely negative consequences. Compulsives can lose their jobs, their families and their self-respect, like any other addict. Compulsive behavior can be seen at times in the library—the patrons, primarily men, who spend many hours each day on the internet, often tucked away in a corner with their monitor adjusted so that others cannot see it. Those users exhibiting compulsive behavior are the most disturbing and problematic for the library employee to manage. The third type of users are those at risk of problematic behaviors because of their use of online sexual activity to treat either depression or stress. These users find OSA to be an outlet to reduce stress produced by other factors in their lives—a sort of "self-medication" to take their minds off of other problems. That analgesic property of OSA is exactly what puts them at risk to move to the compulsive category.

But is every user who accesses adult material or pursues sexual relationships through interactive interfaces a possible compulsive? Michael Ross took a much more equitable approach toward the engagement in online sexual activity. He speculates that the internet is a powerful tool for all sorts of individuals and groups—"internet sexuality as reflecting a change in the locus of power, where the internet has become a dense transfer medium for those relations of power." Ross speaks of the emergence of "plastic" sexuality, "where personae can experiment with sexual behaviors that may be considered perversions . . . without being considered perverse."[7] He also examines the acceleration of intimacy on the internet, noting that the site through which users interact make clear that the goal of their interaction is a romantic or sexual encounter. It is common for those who interact through specifically adult sites to skip to highly intimate discussions, leading those who connect to feel as though they know each other well.

In their study of the psychosocial aspects of consumers of sexually explicit material on the internet, Fisher and Barak found that many of the claims commonly accepted that internet pornography is a "gateway drug" for rapists and sociopaths are not sustained by research.[8] Consumers of internet pornography tended to reflect their innate sexual and sociological orientation when exposed to sexually explicit materials through the internet. According to the researchers, it is reasonable for library employees to assume that if their patrons accessing adult material were not pedophiles or exhibitionists to begin with, their activity in the library will not make them so. On the other hand, it is equally easy to assume that the bad people who trolled the library stacks before the days of the internet are just as likely to be sitting at a computer today. The positive aspect of that concept is that it is easier to monitor their behavior in a sedentary state.

There are countless studies of how the use of adult material, particularly through the internet, affects the users. The dangers of addiction, the damage to personal relationships, the difference between the consumption patterns of men and women are all well-mined, although the conclusions those researchers draw vary wildly. There is also a wealth of claims available freely by

"Googling" of how internet pornography is destroying the moral fiber of our society. There are plenty of anecdotes about "perverts" in the library conveniently collected by organizations like the Illinois Family Institute, one of the many organizations throughout the nation formed to battle the irresistible dark power of internet pornography (and adult material in any format) in libraries.[9] Sadly, there are no scholarly studies—quantitative or qualitative—that examine the psychology of those consumers of adult material who choose to do their consuming at the public library. A deeper understanding of the motivations of the problem patrons may go further in protecting users of all ages than filters could ever hope to.

ONLINE SEXUAL ACTIVITY AT THE PUBLIC LIBRARY

Al Cooper of the San Jose Marital and Sexuality Center has been the seminal researcher of the study of behaviors of participants in online sexual activity (OSA). OSA encompasses everything from viewing pornographic images, reading erotic writing and communicating via chat and email with other users. He identified a construct that frames the rise of the use of the internet for OSA—"the Triple A Engine" of accessibility, affordability and anonymity—that describes the appeal of the internet as a medium for the consumption of adult material. Cooper et al. refer to that "Triple A Engine" as the features that serve to "turbo charge" consumers' experience of OSA and can "facilitate compulsive and other problematic behaviors in users."[10] This "Triple A Engine" also serves as a fitting structure for an investigation of the confluence of OSA and the public library.

Access

The American Library Association sets standards for the mission of public libraries in the Library Bill of Rights. Primary to these tenets is that of unrestricted access to information for all users, regardless of age:

> The American Library Association affirms that all libraries are forums for information and ideas, and that the following basic policies should guide their services. . . . Books and other library resources should be provided for the interest, information, and enlightenment of all people of the community the library serves. Materials should not be excluded because of the origin, background, or views of those contributing to their creation. . . . A person's right to use a library should not be denied or abridged because of origin, age, background, or views.[11]

So why do libraries let those perverts do what they do? The answer is a simple one: in the case of those library users who are consuming legal material, it is the library's mission to do so.

There are aspects to OSA which are freeing and redeeming for adult citizens, regardless of where that activity takes place. OSA provides the opportunity for affiliation and community-building for those who otherwise might not have the ability to find like-minded people. Adult material and interactive interfaces that allow people to communicate with others provide an accessible outlet for those for whom "face-to-face" (FTF) or "in real life" (IRL) experiences are not an option. It also allows for a consumer to stay outside of the "industry" that produces adult material. "Porn consumers . . . are engaged in multiple lines of communication. Sexual adventures and amateur porn exchanges create complex social and ethical communication codes alongside the profit-oriented goals of the porn industry."[12]

Another aspect of access to adult materials that fits neatly into the central mission of libraries is support for the information and educational needs of users of all ages including teens and older adults. "The internet is a powerful tool for older adults . . . (it) does not discriminate based on physical appearance . . . allowing older adults to avoid some of the initial prejudices they might otherwise encounter. . . ."[13] As more and more seniors become proficient in the use of computers and the internet, their use of the internet to connect and communicate with others increases as well. The internet can aid those with limited mobility. It is also a boon for those who may want to break free from the restrictive social traditions associated with sexual activity in which they were raised.

Similarly, the internet can be a likely tool for young adults who seek information and affiliation while exploring their sexuality. As stated earlier, this essay will not address the access to adult materials available to children under 18. Allowing minors access to sexually explicit materials is not acceptable use in most libraries and thus tends to be controlled to one extent or another. In their study of the OSA of young adults, Boies et al. found correlations between college-aged adults' difficulties in developing and maintaining relationships and their attraction to the social distance the internet provides.[14] They warn against the tendencies of OSA as a primary method of relating to sexual partners to increase their isolation and further harm their relationships in real life. On the other hand, there is no doubt about the ease of access to a wide range of information that can help young adults formulate their emerging sexuality.

Affordability

Free and open to all, the public library in America is the golden door for the huddled masses who yearn to read free. The Library Bill of Rights again gives direction:

The American Library Association opposes the charging of user fees for the provision of information by all libraries and information services that receive their major support from public funds. All information resources that are provided directly or indirectly by the library, regardless of technology, format, or methods of delivery, should be readily, equally, and equitably accessible to all library users.[15]

Why do people use the library for internet access? As public librarians, we ask ourselves why people who want to access erotic materials or images want to do it in public—if it's such an important part of their lives, why don't they invest in a computer and internet connection of their own? The answer to that question is not quite as simple as one might think. The study commissioned by the Bill and Melinda Gates Foundation explains the role of public libraries in bridging the "digital divide" between internet users and non-users.[16] According to that study, 48 percent of Americans who do not use the internet cite cost as the reason. Other obstacles to internet use were lack of skills and barriers to access. Nearly every public library provides free access to the internet, generally to a high-speed connection. Additionally, many libraries offer classes in using computers and the internet, or at least one-on-one instruction and aid to new users. The library then is again a perfect storm of affordability for anyone who needs a facilitated and free connection to their source for adult material.

Anonymity

What happens in the public library, stays in the public library. Once again the Library Bill of Rights states outright whos business it is what anyone consumes:

> The ethical responsibilities of librarians, as well as statutes in most states and the District of Columbia, protect the privacy of library users. Confidentiality extends to "information sought or received, and materials consulted, borrowed, acquired," and includes database search records, reference interviews, circulation records, interlibrary loan records, and other personally identifiable uses of library materials, facilities, or services.[17]

It is part of every librarian's training and ethical orientation that the confidentiality of patrons' information consumption is of primary importance. In our world, it is no one's business but the patron's what information an adult consumes or why. This tenet informs our work every day as we are confronted with those accessing adult materials on the internet. In most cases, a librarian intervenes only when a patron's behavior in some way imposes on another's ability to use the library. At the center of each occurrence is a judgment call by the librarian, making for enormous variation in practice.

It is reasonable to assume that anonymity is perhaps the most salient factor to explain why adults, particularly those who could afford to have computers and internet access at their homes, use the public library. In the minds of those who engage in OSA in the public library, there is no one there to check up on their activities. No one knows or even cares what they consume. And there is no record and no interest in with whom they communicate or what they send to and receive from other people. For anyone who would be embarrassed or get in trouble if a loved one found out about their online sexual activity, the library is perhaps not a perfect solution, but serviceable.

Anonymity is particularly important when an adult is seeking information about sensitive issues or non-traditional practices. If a person lives in a situation in which alternate lifestyles, information about sexually transmitted diseases, or questions about anything outside a conservative, "normal" sexuality are unacceptable, there could be dangerous repercussions to gathering information about those things. Also, someone accessing information about those things in the library might very well be considered as accessing "pornography" if overseen by another person with delicate sensibilities. Librarians tend to take a "live and let live" approach—it is not our job to dictate to an adult what is and is not appropriate to do with their life.

PROBLEMS WITH FUELING THE "TRIPLE A ENGINE"

As Cooper and Delmonico pointed out, the "Triple A Engine" can be the very reason those consumers who are prone to problematic or compulsive behavior begin to go overboard with online sexual activity. It is not the role of the library or its employees to "save people from themselves" by controlling their access to the internet or the material they access over the internet. On the other hand, Cooper et al. found that the small percentage of users in their studies that used the internet more than 11 hours per week for OSA experienced difficulties in other areas of their lives.[18] Under those circumstances, one would think it was easy to identify the people who are exhibiting problematic behaviors. Patrons spending many hours at a computer however are not necessarily suffering from online sexual problems (OSP) or online sexual compulsivity (OSC) as defined by Cooper et al. Interfering with those patrons could just as easily be construed as treading on their civil and personal rights.

Misuse of Library Resources and Library Patrons

In April of 2006, two Montgomery County, Maryland security officers saw a man viewing what they judged to be pornography and approached him directly, citing his actions as a violation of the county's sexual harassment policy. Library staff intervened, informing the security officers that the library supports the rights of patrons to consume information of their choice, but the veteran officer continued to prosecute his case with the patron. Ultimately, both officers were reassigned but not before the library was embroiled in a messy and contentious public debate.[19]

In another case, police and a library in Salem, Oregon banned a man from the city library, public parks and parking decks when he was observed viewing pornography on two consecutive days in violation of library policy. He had been ordered from the library on the first occasion and returned the next day to the same effect. When the police were called after the second offense, it was discovered that the man in question had been recently released from jail after serving 18 years for abduction and sexual assault of a minor. In that case, the policies of the library and the judgment of the library staff worked in concert to address a problematic user.[20]

Parental Involvement with the Information-seeking Behaviors of Minors

An argument commonly used by patrons who report the activities of their fellow users in the library is that "he's looking at porn—any kid can come by and see that." As discussed in the beginning of this chapter, it is difficult to draw clear lines between erotica, pornography, and obscenity and there is very little will to create an atmosphere in every public library in which all material available is appropriate for every possible audience. With the exception of violent or degrading pornographic images, it is often a matter of personal taste and orientation as to whether what someone is viewing on their computer screen is even against a library's acceptable use policies, much less labeled as "porn." In a carefully executed and well-balanced study of the issue of access and exposure of children to sexually explicit material via the internet, the Markkula Center for Applied Ethics came to several conclusions that extend beyond the library they studied in their applicability to concerned adults who think children are at risk of accidentally viewing porn in the library. The report strongly advocates for both freedom of access to those users who have a legal right to any information they choose to consume and the responsibility of parents to teach and monitor their children whenever and wherever they use the internet.[21]

"Hostile Workplace" Issues for Library Staff

There have been cases in which library staff have lodged complaints against the board and administration for allowing patrons to access materials on the internet that disturb and disgust them—and since they have no choice but to stay in the area in which the disgusting behavior is taking place, the lack of controlled access to adult material on library computers constitutes a hostile workplace for those staff members whose sensibilities are damaged by exposure to images and behavior. In May of 2000, 12 staff members of the Minneapolis Public Library filed an EEOC complaint against the library on the grounds that they were regularly and egregiously being exposed to images that created a hostile workplace. Those librarians experienced a great deal of criticism within the library community for their stance.[22]

The debate about free and open access versus community standards and the rights of patrons and staff to not be exposed to images, materials and behaviors they find abhorrent is not just an American debate. The board and administration of the city library of Ottawa, Ontario, Canada found themselves on the losing side of the argument when their staff and community made it clear that the prevalence of patrons accessing pornography was not tolerable in the name of freedom of access.[23]

CONCLUSION

It is undeniable that the internet is a powerful tool for information retrieval and dissemination. As a communication device, it has transformed our world. It makes the world a smaller place and gives every individual the power to "be" almost anyone and learn almost everything. Libraries embraced the internet with great zeal in the 1990s and did not necessarily see that the very foundation of library ethics would make a cozy haven for the consumers of adult material via the internet. For those who engage in OSA, for good or evil, the internet connection at their public library is an unlimited charge account at the world's largest adult bookstore and sexual emporium where, unlike *Cheers*, *nobody* knows their name. Are libraries empowering a sexual revolution where anyone can find their community of like-minded sexual partners or are we underwriting a demi-monde of perverts and sexual obsessives who lurk in the computer carrels, searching endlessly for the next image, word or chat session that will satisfy them? Perhaps both, but probably neither.

At the heart of the argument is the heart of democracy—what are citizens willing to sacrifice or compromise to live the life they choose? If Americans want internet access in the public library, they're going to have to put up with a little porn. Even the best filters don't filter everything. The library can initiate a number of practices to control the negative impact of adult materials on young children, and every library understands its responsibility to attach each user with the information that most suits their needs. Ultimately, it is the responsibility of the individual to exercise judgment in consuming information and it is the responsibility of the parents of young children to teach their children how to be safe and how to evaluate what they see, whether on a computer screen, a page, a television screen, or on the street.

For some organizations and individuals, the public library is now the drain down which our morally bankrupt society is swirling, because of the porn people access. For others, the public library is the last bastion of freedom of thought in an aggressively conservative society bent on moral homogeneity. But cultural orientation is a pendulum, and it is much more likely that the next decade will show a decline in society's interest in internet pornography, rendering these heated arguments quaint, if not moot. We may yet see a future in which the "family friendly libraries" organizations are placed next to the hatchet-wielding bar-wreckers of the Temperance Movement in the annals of history. In the meantime, libraries and librarians will bravely straddle the line between saving the world from itself and letting it go to hell in a hand basket, just as we've always done.

Notes

INTRODUCTION

1. David Holmes, *Faiths of the Founding Fathers* (New York: Oxford University Press, 2006).

2. Ariel Levy, *Female Chauvinist Pigs: Women and the Rise of Raunch Culture* (New York: Free Press, 2005).

3. Pamela Paul, *Pornified: How Pornography Is Transforming Our Lives, Our Relationships, and Our Families* (New York: Times Books, 2005).

4. Brian McNair, *Striptease Culture: Sex, Media and the Democratization of Desire* (New York: Routledge, 2002).

5. Linda Williams, ed., *Porn Studies* (Durham: Duke University Press, 2004).

6. Joseph Slade, *Pornography and Sexual Representation: A Reference Guide*, vol. 1 (Westport, CT: Greenwood Press, 2001).

CHAPTER 1: PUSHING THE ENVELOPE: THE ROLE OF THE MASS MEDIA IN THE MAINSTREAMING OF PORNOGRAPHY

1. Fenton Bailey, as quoted in Steven Daly, "Blue Streak," *TV Guide*, August 2–8, 2003, 32.

2. Jeannine Amber, "Dirty Dancing," *Essence*, March 2005, 162–66, 203.

3. Ariel Levy, *Female Chauvinist Pigs: Women and the Rise of Raunch Culture* (New York: Free Press, 2005).

4. Jane Caputi, "Everyday Pornography," in *Gender, Race, and Class in Media.*, 2nd ed., ed. Gail Dines and Jean Jumez, 434–50 (Thousand Oaks, CA: Sage Publications, 2003).

5. Several television markets refused to air the ad. As of this printing it was still accessible online at www.SpicyParis.com.

6. Morality in Media, "The Rogues' Gallery of Television 2003" http://www.moralityinmedia.org/mediaissues/rogues2003.htm (accessed June 28, 2006).

7. Amber, "Dirty Dancing," 162–66, 203.

8. Leonard Pitts, "Oprah Gets Hip-Hoppers' Goat," *The Atlanta Journal-Constitution* (June 28, 2006): A17.

9. Kenneth Jones, "Are Rap Videos More Violent? Style Differences and the Prevalence of Sex and Violence in the Age of MTV" *Howard Journal of Communication* 8 (1997): 343–56.

10. Amber, "Dirty Dancing," 162–66, 203.

11. Federal Trade Commission, "Marketing Violent Entertainment to Children: A Fourth Follow-up Review of Self-regulation and Industry Practices in the Motion Picture, Music Recording & Electronic Game Industries," http://www.ftc.gov/os/2004/07/040708kidsviolencerpt.pdf (accessed July 18, 2006).

12. Barry S. Sapolsky, "The Attraction and Repulsion of Media Sex," *Journal of Broadcasting and Electronic Media* 47 (2003): 296.

13. S. Liliana Escobar-Chaves, Susan R. Tortolero, Christine M. Markham, Barbara J. Low, Patricia Eitel, and Patricia Thickstun, "Impact of the Media on Adolescent Sexual Attitudes and Behaviors" *Pediatrics* 116 (2005): 303–26.

14. Michael Bradley, as quoted in Janet Kornblum, "Porn 'Tidal Wave' Puts Parents to Test; Solutions Are High-tech and Old-fashioned," *USA Today*, January 30, 2006, 10D.

15. The U.S. Justice Department has subpoenaed data from Google, Yahoo, and Microsoft MSN in an effort to show that filters currently in use are ineffective in protecting consumers from porn. The 1998 Child Online Protection Act, which would make it a federal crime to make porn accessible to non-adults and require age verification systems, has never been enforced, due to lawsuits from search engine providers and blocks from the Supreme Court, which sent the issue back to a lower court to resolve, now scheduled for trial in October 2006.

16. Dale Kunkel, Keren Eyal, Keli Finnerty, Erica Biely, and Edward Donnerstein, *Sex on TV 4: A Kaiser Family Foundation Report* (Menlo Park, CA: Henry Kaiser Family Foundation, 2005).

17. David Walsh, Douglas Gentile, Erin Walsh, Nat Bennett, Brad Robideau, Monica Walsh, Sarah Strickland, and David McFadden, *Tenth Annual MediaWise Video game Report Card*, National Institute on Media and the Family, 2005, http://www.mediafamily.org/research/report_vgrc_2005.shtml (accessed July18, 2006).

18. Cheryl Miller and Katherine Kinnick, "Toxic Speech: A Content Analysis of Top 50 Song Lyrics," conference presentation, Association for Education in Journalism and Mass Communication Midwinter Conference, Kennesaw, Georgia, February 12, 2005, and Carol J. Pardun and Kathy B. McKee, "Strange Bedfellows: Symbols of Religion and Sexuality on MTV," *Youth & Society* 26 (1995): 438–49.

19. Tom Reichert and Courtney Carpenter, "An Update on Sex in Magazine Advertising: 1983–2003," *Journalism and Mass Communication Quarterly* 81 (2004): 823–37.

20. Kunkel et al., *Sex on TV 4*.

21. Reichert and Carpenter, "An Update on Sex in Magazine Advertising," 823–37.

22. Pardun and McKee, "Strange Bedfellows," 438–49.

23. Miller and Kinnick, "Toxic Speech."

24. For a review of media effects, see Escobar-Chaves et al., "Impact of the Media on Adolescent Sexual Attitudes and Behaviors," 303–26.

25. Juliann Sivulka, *Soap Sex and Cigarettes: A Cultural History of American Advertising* (Belmont, CA: Wadsworth, 1998).

26. David A. Cook, *A History of Narrative Film* (New York: Norton, 1991).

27. Joyce N. Sprafkin and L. Theresa Silverman, "Update: Physically Intimate and Sexual Behavior on Prime-time Television, 1978–1979," *Journal of Communication* 31 (1981): 34–40.

28. Barry S. Sapolsky and Joseph O. Tabarlet, "Sex in Primetime Television: 1979 versus 1989," *Journal of Broadcasting and Electronic Media* 35 (1991): 505–16.

29. Brian McNair, *Striptease Culture: Sex, Media and the Democratization of Desire* (London: Routledge, 2002), 61.

30. Peter Bogdanovich, as quoted in Cynthia Lont, *Women and Media: Content, Careers, Criticism* (Belmont, CA: Wadsworth), 264.

31. Ron Leone, "Contemplating Ratings: An Examination of What the MPAA Considers 'too far for R' and Why," *Journal of Communication* 52, no. 4 (2002): 938–54.

32. Betsy Streisand, "Lawyers, Guns, Money," *U.S. News and World Report*, June 14, 1999, 56.

33. Rodger Streitmatter, *Sex Sells: The Media's Journey from Repression to Obsession* (Boulder, CO: Westview Press, 2004).

34. Barbara Lippert, "From Sexy to Sleazy," *Adweek*, January 3, 2005, 8.

35. Frederick, S. Lane, *Obscene Profits: The Entrepreneurs of Pornography in the Cyber Age* (New York: Routledge, 2000).

36. Motion Picture Association of America, Research and Statistics, http://www.mpaa.org/researchstatistics.asp (accessed July 14, 2006).

37. Richard C. Morais, "Porn Goes Public," *Forbes*, June 14, 1999, 214. One such company on the NASDAQ stock exchange is New Frontier, a Boulder, CO-based corporation that distributes pornographic movies on cable, satellite and hotel networks nationwide.

38. Vicki Mayer, "Soft-core in TV Time: The Political Economy of a Cultural Trend," *Critical Studies in Mass Communication* 22, no. 4 (2005): 302–20.

39. Lippert, "From Sexy to Sleazy," 8–10.

40. Sut Jhally, *Dreamworlds: Desire, Sex and Power in Music Videos*, documentary video (Northampton, MA: Media Education Foundation, 1991).

41. Julie Andsager and Kimberly Roe, "'What's Your Definition of Dirty, Baby?': Sex in Music Videos," *Sexuality and Culture*, 79.

42. Jean Kilbourne, "The More You Subtract, the More You Add: Cutting Girls Down to Size," in *Gender, Race and Class in Media*, ed. G. Dines and J.M. Humez, 2nd ed. (Thousand Oaks, CA: Sage, 2003), 262.

43. Stuart Potter from *Jacobellis v. Ohio, 1964*, as quoted in Neil M. Malamuth, Tamara Addison, and Mary Koss, "Pornography and Sexual Aggression: Are There Reliable Effects and Can We Understand Them?" *Annual Review of Sex Research* 11 (2002): 27.

44. See D.L. Hudson, *Pornography and Obscenity*, http://www.firstamendmentcenter.org/speech/adultent/topic.aspx?topic=pornography (accessed July 24, 2006)

45. Anne L. Clark, "As Nasty as They Want to Be," *New York University Law Review* 64, no. 6 (2001): 1481–531.

46. Walsh et al., *Tenth Annual MediaWise Video Game Report Card*.

47. Ibid., 9.

48. Ibid.

49. Robert Peters, as quoted in *Morality in Media*, November 15, 2005, www.moral ityinmedia.org/obscenityenforcement/suppcrackdown.htm (accessed June 28, 2006). More than three out of four adults support the U.S. Justice Department's crackdown on illegal obscenity.

50. The pro-porn faction believes women have a right to do whatever they want with their bodies; restrictions on earning a living as a porn star or prostitute represent men's control over women's bodies. The anti-porn camp focuses on the harm to individual women who work in the sex trade as well as generalized harm to all women caused by the objectifying and demeaning depictions of women.

51. Streitmatter, *Sex Sells*.

52. George Gerbner, Larry Gross, Michael Morgan, and Nancy Signiorelli, "Growing up with Television: The Cultivation Perspective," in *Media Effects: Advances in Theory and Research*, ed. Jennings Bryant and Dolf Zillman (Hillsdale, NJ: Erlbaum, 1994), 17–42.

53. Nancy Signorielli, "Sex Roles and Stereotyping on Television," *Adolescent Medicine: Adolescents and the Media* 4 (1993): xx.

54. Media Education Foundation, *The Electronic Storyteller*, videotape (Northampton, MA: Media Education Foundation, 1997).

55. Laura L. Jansma, Daniel G. Linz, Anthony Mulac, and Dorothy J. Imrich, "Men's Interactions with Women after Viewing Sexually Explicit Films: Does Degradation Make a Difference?" *Communication Monographs* 64 (1997): 1–24 and D. McKenzie-Mohr and M.P. Zanna, "Treating Women as Sexual Objects: Look to the Gender Schematic Male Who Has Viewed Pornography," *Personality and Social Psychology Bulletin* 16 (1990): 296–308.

56. Anthony Mulac, Laura Jansma, and Danuiel G. Linz, "Men's Behavior toward Women after Viewing Sexually Explicit Films: Degradation Makes a Difference," *Communication Monographs* 69 (2002): 311–28.

57. See Neil M. Malamuth, Tamara Addison and Mary Koss, "Pornography and Sexual Aggression," *Annual Review of Sex Research* 11 (2000): 26–94, for a meta-analysis of these studies. In one example, male college students who viewed sexually explicit interactions that were demeaning to women were more likely to express attitudes supportive of rape than those who viewed neutral videos (Jeffrey A. Golde et al., "Attitudinal Effects of Degrading Themes and Sexual Explicitness in Video Materials," *Sexual Abuse: A Journal of Research and Treatment* 12 (2000): 223–32. The effects of viewing softcore vs. hardcore porn remains a point of controversy among researchers, with some researchers maintaining that negative effects on men's attitudes and behaviors toward women result only from viewing porn containing a combination of sex and violence against women.

58. Christy Barongan and Gordan N. Hall, "The Influence of Misogynous Rap Music on Sexual Aggression against Women," *Psychology of Women Quarterly* 19 (1995) 195–07.

59. Victoria Rideout, Donald F. Roberts, and Ulla G. Foehr, *Generation M: Media in the Lives of 8–18 Year Olds* (Menlo Park, CA: Kaiser Family Foundation, 2005).

60. Ibid.

61. Ibid.

62. Donald F. Roberts, "Media and Youth: Access, Exposure and Privatization," *Journal of Adolescent Health* 27 (2000): 8–14.

63. Rideout et al., *Generation M*, 39.

64. Ibid.

65. Roberts, "Media and Youth," 8–14.

66. Victoria J. Rideout, Elizabeth A. Vandewater, and Ellen A. Wartella, *Zero to Six: Electronic Media in the Lives of Infants, Toddlers and Preschoolers* (Menlo Park, CA: Kaiser Family Foundation, 2003).

67. Rideout et al., *Generation M*.

68. Roberts, "Media and Youth," 8–14.

69. Rideout et al., *Generation M*.

70. Ibid.

71. Dale Kunkel, Keli Biely, Keren Eyal, Kirstie Cope-Farrar, Edward Donnerstein, and Rena Frandrich, *Sex on TV 3: A Biennial Report of the Kaiser Family Foundation* (Menlo Park, CA: Kaiser Family Foundation, 2003).

72. Jane D. Brown, "Mass Media Influences on Sexuality," *Journal of Sex Research* 39 (2002): 42–45.

73. Jeffrey Arnett, "The Sounds of Sex: Sex in Teens' Music and Music Video," in *Sexual Teens, Sexual Media: Investigating Media's Influence on Adolescent Sexuality*, ed. Jane D. Brown, Jeanne R. Steele, and Kim Walsh-Childers (Mahwah, NJ: Lawrence Erlbaum, 2002), 253–64.

74. Bradley S. Greenberg and Rick W. Busselle, "Soap Operas and Sexual Activity: A Decade Later," *Journal of Communication* 46 (1996): 153–60.

75. Kunkel et al., *Sex on TV 3*.

76. Leone, "Contemplating Ratings," 938–54.

77. Rideout et al., *Generation M*.

78. Walsh et al., *Tenth Annual Media Wise Video Game Report Card*.

79. Rideout et al., *Generation M*.

80. David Finkelhor, Kimberly Mitchell, and Janis Wolak, *Online Victimization: A Report on the Nation's Youth* (Durham, NH: National Center for Missing and Exploited Children, 2000).

81. While the National Association of Theatre Owners agreed in 1998 to restrict placement of movie trailers to within one MPAA rating of the feature film being shown, the FTC says this policy allows involuntary exposure of children younger than 17 (for instance, those seeing a PG-13-rated movie) to be exposed to R-rated content (Federal Trade Commission, "Marketing Violent Entertainment to Children: A Fourth Follow-up Review of Self-regulation and Industry Practices in the Motion Picture, Music Recording and Electronic Game Industries," 2004, www.ftc.gov/os/2004/07/040708kidsviolencept.pdf (accessed July 18, 2006).

82. Victor Strasburger, "Clueless: Why Do Pediatricians Underestimate the Media's Influence on Children and Adolescents," *Pediatrics* 117, no. 4 (2006): 1427–31.

83. L. Monique Ward, "Does Television Exposure Affect Emerging Adults' Attitudes and Assumptions about Sexual Relationships?: Correlational and Experimental Confirmation," *Journal of Youth and Adolescence* 31 (2002): 1–15.

84. Jennifer S. Aubrey, Kristin Harrison, Leila Kramer, and Jennifer Yellin, "Variety Versus Timing: Gender Differences in College Students' Sexual Expectations as Predicted by Exposure to Sexually Oriented Television," *Communication Research* 30 (2003): 432–60.

85. Laramie D. Taylor, "Effects of Visual and Verbal Sexual Television Content and Perceived Realism on Attitudes and Beliefs," *Journal of Sex Research* 42 (2005): 130–37.

86. L. Monique Ward and Rocio Rivadeneyra, "Contributions of Entertainment Television to Adolescents' Sexual Attitudes and Expectations: The Role of Viewing Amount Versus Viewer Involvement," *Journal of Sex Research* 36 (1999): 237–49.

87. Stacy Davis and Marie-Louise Mares, "Effects of Talk Show Viewing on Adolescents," *Journal of Communication* 48 (1998): 69–86.

88. Taylor, "Effects of Visual and Verbal Sexual Television Content," 130–37.

89. David Mosher, "A Script Theory of Human Sexual Response: A Glossary of Postulates, Corollaries, and Definitions," in *Knowing Feeling: Affect, Scripts and Psychotherapy*, ed. Donald L. Nathanson and Andrew M. Stone (New York: Norton, 1994), 105–31.

90. Aubrey et al., "Variety Versus Timing," 432–60.

91. Ariel Levy, "Dispatches from *Girls Gone Wild*," *Slate Magazine*, March 22, 2004, www.slate.com/id/2097485/entry/2097496 (accessed September 11, 2006).

92. Ariel Levy, *Female Chauvinist Pigs: Women and the Rise of Raunch Culture* (New York: Free Press, 2005), 33.

93. Jane D. Brown, Kelly Ladin L'Engle, Carol Pardun, Guo Guang, Kristin Kenneavy, and Christine Jackson, "Sexy Media Matter: Exposure to Sexual Content in Music, Movies, Television and Magazines Predicts Black and White Adolescents' Sexual Behavior," *Pediatrics* 117, no. 4 (2006): 1018–27.

94. Rebecca L. Collins, Marc N. Elliott, Sandra H. Berry, David E. Kanouse, Dale Kunkil, Sarah B. Hunter and Angela Miu, "Watching Sex on Television Predicts Adolescent Initiation of Sexual Behavior," *Pediatrics* 114, no. 3 (2004): 280–89.

95. Rideout et al., *Generation M.*

96. Cheryl L. Somers and Joshua J. Tynan, "Consumption of Sexual Dialogue and Content on Television and Adolescent Sexual Outcomes: Multiethnic Findings," *Adolescence* 41, no. 161 (2006): 15–38.

97. Megan Rauscher, "Oral and Anal Sex Increasing among Teens," *ABC News*, May 9, 2006, http://abcnews.go.com/health/wirestory?id=1941903 (accessed July 31, 2006).

98. Levy, *Female Chauvinist Pigs.*

99. Jamie Malernee, "S. Florida Teen Girls Discovering 'Bisexual Chic' Trend," *Fort Lauderdale Sun-Sentinel*, December 30, 2003, B-3.

100. Sapolsky, "The Attraction and Repulsion of Media Sex," 296–302.

101. Ibid.; Dolf Zillman and Jennings Bryant, "Effects of Massive Exposure to Pornography," in *Pornography and Sexual Aggression*, ed. Neil M. Malamuth and Edward Donnerstein (Orlando, FL: Academic Press, 1984), 115–38.

102. Zillman and Bryant, "Effects of Massive Exposure to Pornography," 115–38.

103. Cited in Morality in Media, "More Than Three out of Four Adults Support the U.S. Justice Department's Crackdown on Illegal Obscenity," November 15, 2005, www.moralityinmedia.org/obscenityenforcement/suppcrackdown.htm (accessed June 28, 2006).

104. Federal Trade Commission, "Marketing Violent Entertainment to Children."

105. Walsh et al., *Tenth Annual MediaWise Video Game Report Card.*

106. Federal Trade Commission, "Marketing Violent Entertainment to Children."

107. Robert Abelman, "Preaching to the Choir: Profiling TV Advisory Ratings Users," *Journal of Broadcasting and Electronic Media* 43 (1999): 529–50.

108. Rideout et al., *Generation M.*

109. Walsh et al., *Tenth Annual MediaWise Video Game Report Card.*

110. Federal Trade Commission, "Marketing Violent Entertainment to Children."

111. Cited in Morality in Media, "The Rogue's Gallery of Television 2003."

112. Robert Peters, "The Importance of Making Complaints," 2006, http://www.moralityinmedia.org/fightbadtv.htm (accessed July 29, 2006).

113. As quoted in David Everitt, "TV's Getting Dirtier, and Bozell Angrier," *Media Life*, July 23, 2001, http://www.medialifemagazine.com/news2001/july01/july23/2_tues/news5tuesday.html (accessed July 29, 2006).

114. Rebecca L. Collins, Marc N. Elliott, Sandra H. Berry, David E. Kanouse, and Sarah B. Hunter, "Entertainment Television as a Health Sex educator: The Impact of Condom-Efficacy Information in an Episode of *Friends*," *Pediatrics* 112, no. 5 (2003): 1115–21.

115. Keren Eyal and Dale Kunkel, "The Effects of Television Drama Shows on Emerging Adults' Sexual Atittudes and Moral Judgments" (paper presented at the annual conference of the International Communication Association, New York, NY, May 2005.

116. Kunkel et al., *Sex on TV 4*.

117. American Decency Association, "Howard Stern Information Action Page," December 16, 2005, http://americandecency.org/stern/ (accessed July 29, 2006).

118. Carol King, "More Retailers Blocking 'Offensive' Covers in Response to Moral Watchdog Group," *Circulation Management*, February 1, 2000, http://www.keepmedia.com/pubs/circulationmanagment/2000/02/01/158466?extID=10026 (accessed July 29, 2006).

119. D. Aileen Dodd, "Tees with a 'Tude Kindle Competition from Mom," *The Atlanta Journal-Constitution*, June 5, 2006, B1, B5.

CHAPTER 2: PANDA PORN, CHILDREN, GOOGLE, AND OTHER FANTASIES

1. "Panda Porn to Cure Bedtime Blues." *CNN.com*. (http://archives.cnn.com/2002/TECH/science/06/27/giant.panda/index.html). Posted June 27, 2002. Accessed December 22, 2006.

2. In *Child-Loving: The Erotic Child and Victorian Culture* (New York: Routledge, 1992), James Kincaid shows the multiple, contradictory cultural functions of the figure of the child and the divisions between childhood and adulthood in nineteenth century culture. As he shows, "the child is not simply the Other we desire but the Other we must have in order to know longing, love, lust at all." He continues this argument in *Erotic Innocence: The Culture of Child Molesting* (Durham: Duke University Press, 1998), showing the ways the figure of the Child works as a necessary part of the elaborate construction of the category of the erotic in western culture, including the category of the pedophile or sexual predator. This argument extends Kincaid's by suggesting that the status of representation itself is also at stake in preserving the category of the Child as innocent.

3. In *Three Essays on the Theory of Sexuality* (trans. James Strachey, New York: Basic Books, 1962), Sigmund Freud asserts that very young children indeed have a sexuality, which he terms "infantile," but which is nonetheless sexual. The second essay of the collection, "Infantile Sexuality," begins with a caveat that still holds today: "One feature of the popular view of the sexual instinct is that it is absent in childhood

and only awakens in the period of life described as puberty. This, however, is not merely a simple error but one that has had grave consequences, for it is mainly to this idea that we owe our present ignorance of the fundamental conditions of sexual life." The idea that young children have a sexuality does not necessarily justify showing them pornography, but Freud's formulation points out one of the biggest problems with the cultural formulation of the child. The developmental differences between young children and adolescents, which are often treated by public policy as if they are exactly the same, are not the same at all and represent entirely different sets of feelings and capabilities.

4. The "general" acceptance of children's imitation is more a cultural opinion than perhaps a scientific fact. How children learn is a complex matter, but public discussions of materials deemed harmful to children assumes children's response to media images as a somewhat undefined combination of imitation, sullying knowledge, attraction, and confusion. General public opinions about the capabilities of children have very little relation to what children actually do and how they do it. On the one hand news reports feature the disastrous ends of children who have imitated superheroes, professional wrestlers, executions, or pornography. One case in Ontario, reported by The *Hamilton Spectator* ("Hamilton School Children Imitating TV and Internet Porn in Sexual 'Experiments'" April 5, 2004, http://www.hamiltonspectator.com/NASApp/cs/ContentServer? Accessed December 30, 2006), involved children who were imitating the sexual acts they had seen in pornography. The expert prognosis in this case, delivered by a forensic psychiatrist and expert in sexual psychopathology, was "that children who are exposed to pornography can become desensitized to it and begin to think that is normal behavior." The mechanism of desensitization would seem to be somewhat different from the issue of imitation, suggesting that repeated viewing of pornography somehow eliminates the moral judgments that typically accompany learning. It is apparently an accepted fact that children imitate superheroes. "Children naturally imitate fearless superheroes who overcome any obstacle in their path," the KidSource Parenting Website ("Imitating Superheroes." *Kidsource* http://www.kidsource.com/parenting/imitate.hero.html December 30, 2006), announces. An opinion column, written by the Rev. E. F. Bennett in the *Corpus Christi Caller Times* is certain that children learn by imitating. "Monkey see, monkey do," it begins ("Children Learn by Imitating Adults Around Them." *Corpus Christi Caller Times*, November 6, 1999, http://www.coastalbendhealth.com/1999/november/06/today/contribu/581.html. Accessed December 30, 2006). Those who study media violence make their own assumptions about how watching violence may affect behavior. The "Facts About Media and Violence" web page offers this factoid: "Longitudinal studies tracking viewing habits and behavior patterns of a single individual found that 8-year-old boys, who viewed the most violent programs growing up, were the most likely to engage in aggressive and delinquent behavior by age 18 and serious criminal behavior by age 30" ("Facts About Media Violence and Effects on the American Family." http://www.babybag.com/articles/amaviol.htm. Accessed December 30, 2006.)

On the other hand, psychologists such as Jean Piaget and B. F. Skinner do not include simple imitation as a central part of their theories about children's learning. Piaget understands childhood learning as a series of stages during which children acquire various skills and build on them. Skinner sees learning occurring with reinforcement, but also occurring only when a child is ready. Psychoanalysts such as Jacques Lacan and Melanie Klein tend to see child development as a series of identifications and/or relationships.

Experiential testimony, the hardest of all to dispute even if tainted with preconceptions, shows different parents with different children observing different capabilities. See Jean Piaget, *The Child's Conception of the World* (New York: Routledge, 1998) and B. F. Skinner, *The Technology of Teaching* (New York: Appleton-Century-Crofts, 1968).

5. In *The Secret Museum: Pornography in Modern Culture* (New York: Viking, 1987), Walter Kendrick maps the emergence of the "young person" as the imaginary object in relation to which pornography is produced, both as a concept and as a set of circulating representations.

6. See for example, Jack Samad's comments about Google at the end of this essay.

7. "Vets Give Panda Crash Course in Sex Ed." *CNN.Com* http://cnn.com/2004/TECH/science/03/16/china.pandas.ap. Posted March 16, 2004. Accessed December 22, 2006.

8. "Panda Porn Helps Spark Birthing Boom in Captive Breed." *FoxNews.com* http://www.foxnews.com/story/0,2933,231578,00.html. Posted November 23, 2006. Accessed December 22, 2006.

9. In *The Secret Museum*, Kendrick locates the rise of the category of pornography in the late-eighteenth century, spurred in part by the discovery of salacious Pompeiian artifacts.

10. The evolution of the "community standard" by which obscenity that is not protected by the First Amendment of the Constitution is defined eventually arrived at the following formulation: "whether to the average person, applying contemporary community standards, the dominant theme of the material taken as a whole appeals to prurient interest." Cited in Roth v. United States, 354 U.S. 476 (1957).

11. In *Harmful to Minors: The Perils of Protecting Children from Sex* (New York: Thunder's Mouth Press, 2002), Judith Levine argues that negative education tactics such as ignorance and abstinence-only espoused by recent governmental entities cause the problems they are imagined to resolve, while damaging children's understanding and attitudes towards their own sexuality. Milton Diamond and Hazel Beh make a similar argument in a legal context, suggesting that public censorship laws protecting children are harming them. See *"Children and Education: The Failure of Abstinence-Only Education: Minors Have a Right to Honest Talk About Sex,"* 15 Colum. J. Gender & L. 12, 2006.

12. The Ginsberg case (390 U.S. 629, 1968) held that "The area of freedom of expression constitutionally secured to minors is not invaded by a state statute making it a misdemeanor knowingly to sell a minor material "harmful to minors," and defining this phrase as meaning that quality of any description or representation of nudity, sexual conduct, sexual excitement, or sadomasochistic abuse, when it (1) predominantly appeals to the prurient interest of minors, (2) is patently offensive to prevailing standards in the adult community as a whole with respect to what is suitable material for minors, and (3) is utterly without redeeming social importance for minors."

13. In August, 2005, the Attorney General of the United States issued a subpoena to several internet search engines, including Google, Inc, the largest. The subpoena was issued in relation to *ACLU v. Gonzales* (23 F.R.D 120, 2006), a case that had been bouncing around the Federal Court system in the Eastern District of Pennsylvania since *ACLU v. Reno* (521 U.S. 844, 1998). The case involves ACLU's challenge to the constitutionality of the Child On-Line Protection Act. Google has never been a party to the case. The subpoena asks for "the production of documents identifying all queries conducted on . . . the company's search engine, and all URL's identified through such queries, within a specified time period" which was the month of July, 2005. As might be expected (but not really since all of the other subpoenaed search engines complied), Google ob-

jected to the government's subpoena, and even though the government had, in the period between August and October, narrowed the request to a mere "random sampling of one million URLs" Google persisted in its objection on every available ground from the subpoena's being "overbroad," burdensome, vague, and harassing, to the claim that the material is irrelevant to the underlying lawsuit, that the material is privileged and confidential, and that the subpoena would force Google to divulge trade secrets. Google further claimed the following: "In Google's understanding, Defendant would use the one million URLs requested from Google to create a sample world-wide web against which to test various filtering programs for their effectiveness. Google objects to Defendant's view of Google's highly proprietary search database—the primary reason for the company's success—as a free resource that Defendant can access and use, some levels removed, to formulate its own defense." Google argued further that if it acceded to the request such cooperation "would suggest that it is willing to reveal information about those who use its services. This is not a perception that Google can accept." These latter objections raise the spectre of the uneasy and potentially dangerous relation between the property rights of the owners of the Internet and governmental functions, here perhaps the invasiveness of a self-serving subpoena, but in another context imaginably the problem of a limitation of expression permissible precisely because the Internet is privately owned. These issues all arise because the Internet looks like a vector of public discourse.

14. Samad is quoted in Declan McCullagh and Elinor Mills, "Feds Take Porn Fight to Google," http://news.zdnet.com/2100–9588_22–6028701.html. Posted January 19, 2006. Accessed December 22, 2006.

CHAPTER 3: THE MAKING OF A PRE-PUBESCENT PORN STAR: CONTEMPORARY FASHION FOR ELEMENTARY SCHOOL GIRLS

1. One such article is J. Leo's "Haute Porn, Hard-core Couture," in which Madonna is credited with popularizing "many porn styles—pointy bras, tight bustiers." See J. Leo, "Haute Porn, Hard-core Couture,' U.S. News and World Report, June 3, 1991, 20.

2. A typical article is "Britney Brigade," which begins with "The race pop icon is now a style setter. Is it bad that millions of young girls, from post-toddlers to teens, want to look like her?" and continues by discussing the "skimpy" fashions that Spears is credited with popularizing. See Nady Labi et al., "Britney Brigade," Time, February 5, 1991, 66.

3. Susan Driver, "Pornographic Pedagogies?: The Risks of Teaching 'Dirty' Popular Cultures," M/C Journal 7.4 (2004), http://www.media-culture.org.au/0410/03_teaching.php (accessed September 1, 2005).

4. Most notable is Ariel Levy's research on fashion, pornography, and sex for high school girls in which she describes contemporary fashion choices for high school girls and interviews them regarding their feelings towards pornography, sex, their boyfriends, and their body image. See Ariel Levy, Female Chauvinist Pigs: Women and the Rise of Raunch Culture (New York: Free Press, 2005), 139–69.

5. Victoria Steele, Fetish: Fashion, Sex and Power (Oxford: Oxford University Press, 1996), 4.

6. One store display I observed had mannequins dressed in camisole tops and shrugs. The mannequins were positioned right underneath a sign that said "Girls 7–11," which would be for girls aged 7–11. The mannequins had large breasts.

7. Levy, Female Chauvinist Pigs, 142.

8. Ibid., 143.

9. Ibid., 142.

10. Quoted in Lindsay Beyerstein, "Padded Bras for Six-year-olds?" (September 14, 2006), http://www.alternet.org/bloggers/lindsay (accessed October 5, 2006).

11. I have also seen this style called "stripper wear" and "porn star" fashion.

12. Brynn Chamblee, personal interview, September 1, 2005.

13. In my investigation of girls' clothing, I spent one day perusing stores at the mall. Two days later I went back to take photographs (clandestinely) of what I observed. In that time, Children's Place had sold their entire supply of faux-leopard skin mini-skirts for babies.

14. The actual title of Rivenbark's book is *Stop Dressing Your Six-Year-Old Like a Skank: And Other Words of Delicate Southern Wisdom* (Boston: St. Martin's Press, 2006).

15. I did not identify nor define "porn" fashion until after the survey concluded. At the beginning of the survey, I had the teachers identify and describe what they considered inappropriate clothing for school. While the majority of their comments focused on "porn" fashion, other types of clothing that were mentioned were, in the teachers' words, "gang-related" dress and "rap" dress, which they described as pants that were too big and shoes that were not tied.

16. Henry A. Giroux, "Teenage Sexuality, Body Politics, and the Pedagogy of Display," in *Youth Culture: Identity in a Postmodern World*, ed. Jonathan Epstein (Oxford: Blackwell, 1998), 41.

17. Levy, *Female Chauvinist Pigs*, 33.

18. Naomi Wolf, *The Beauty Myth: How Images of Beauty Are Used Against Women* (New York: Morrow, 1991), 12.

19. Ibid., 12.

20. Thomas F. Cash, "Cognitive-Behavioral Perspectives on Body Image," in *Body Image: A Handbook of Theory, Research, and Clinical Practice*, eds. Thomas F. Cash and Thomas Pruzinsky (New York: Guilford Press, 2004), 41–42.

21. Nita Mary McKinley, "Feminist Perspectives and Objectified Body Consciousness," in *Body Image: A Handbook of Theory, Research, and Clinical Practice*, eds. Thomas F. Cash and Thomas Pruzinsky (New York: Guilford Press, 2004), 57.

22. The magazines include *Cosmogirl!* and *TeenVogue*, which are targeted at "tweens," girls aged 8–12.

23. Linda Smolak, "Body Image Development in Children," in *Body Image: A Handbook of Theory, Research, and Clinical Practice*, eds. Thomas F. Cash and Thomas Pruzinsky (New York: Guilford Press, 2004), 71.

24. Marika Tiggemann, "Media Influences on Body Image Development," in *Body Image: A Handbook of Theory, Research, and Clinical Practice*, eds. Thomas F. Cash and Thomas Pruzinsky (New York: Guilford Press, 2004), 91.

25. Ibid., 94.

26. "Marketing a Way of Life to our Youth," ObscenityCrimes.org, http://www.obscenitycrimes.org/espforparents/espforparents2003–01.cfm (accessed October 6, 2005).

27. Terry Bravender quoted in "Help Little Girls Develop Healthy Body Image, Experts Say," *Schneider Children's Hospital Newsletter*, August 2005, http://www.schneiderchildrenshospital.org/sch_news_aug_2005.html (accessed October 10, 2006).

28. Pamela Paul, *Pornified: How Pornography Is Transforming Our Lives, Our Relationships, and Our Families* (New York: Times Books, 2005), 184.

29. Chamblee, personal interview, September 1, 2005.

30. Smolak, "Body Image Development in Children," 66.

31. Ruth H. Striegel-Moore and Debra L. Franko, "Body Image Issues among Girls and Women," in *Body Image: A Handbook of Theory, Research, and Clinical Practice,* eds. Thomas F. Cash and Thomas Pruzinsky (New York: Guilford Press, 2004), 185.

32. McKinley, "Feminist Perspectives and Objectified Body Consciousness," 56.

33. Ibid., 57.

34. Smolak, "Body Image Development in Children," 70.

35. Ibid., 70.

36. Judity Coche quoted in Paul, *Pornified,* 180.

37. Paul, *Pornified,* 180.

38. Ibid., 186.

39. Gary Brooks as quoted in Paul, *Pornified,* 187.

40. Patricia Adler as quoted in Kay Hymowitz, "Kids Today Are Growing Up Way Too Fast," *Wall Street Journal,* October 28, 1998, http://www.manhatten-institute.org/html/_wsj_kids_today_are_growing.htm (accessed October 7, 2006).

41. Steve Kroft, "Porn in the USA," September 2004, http://www.CBSnews.com/stories/11/21/60minutes/main85049.shtml (accessed January 21, 2007).

42. Sut Jhally, "Image-Based Culture: Advertising and Popular Culture," in *Gender, Race and Class in Media,* eds. Gail Dines and Jean Humez, 2nd ed. (Newbury Park: Sage, 2003), 252.

43. Giroux, "Teenage Sexuality, Body Politics, and the Pedagogy of Display," 32.

44. Ibid., 34.

45. Adler quoted in Hymowitz, "Kids Today Are Growing Up Way Too Fast."

46. Giroux, "Teenage Sexuality, Body Politics, and the Pedagogy of Display," 32.

CHAPTER 4: HOT BODIES ON CAMPUS: THE PERFORMANCE OF PORN CHIC

1. It only takes momentary glimpses of other popularly dressed bodies across this campus to confirm the fact that many sartorial elements associated with pornography, striptease, and fetishism have interpenetrated everyday dress in numerous ways. And yet, they are consistently framed in the media as "fashion." How conscious are college women that their choices have pornographic resonances that transcend mere mirroring of contemporary "hot" trends—are they conscious that they may, indeed, be performing porn?

2. William Shakespeare, *As You Like It,* ed. Louis B. Wright and Virginia A. LaMar (New York: Simon and Schuster, 1959), 42.

3. These questions are drawn from Kenneth Burke's method of studying human behavior through dramatistic analysis, delineated in his *Grammar of Motives.* See Kenneth Burke, "A Grammar of Motives" in *The Rhetorical Tradition: Readings from Classical Times to the Present,* ed. Patricia Bizzell and Bruce Herzberg (Boston: Bedford Books, of St. Martin's Press, 1990), 992.

4. Our questions included:
    1. Pick two of your favorite outfits—ones that you'd wear to school. These could be outfits that reflect different aspects of yourself. Describe them and how they feel on your body; and how you behave in them. What does this clothing make you do/feel? Are you someone different/more in this outfit?

2. Write a love letter to one of these outfits—or even an individual piece of clothing (my favorite pair of jeans, etc.) Tell that outfit why you love it!

3. From what sources do you draw your inspiration for the clothing you purchase and wear to school? (And what do you give yourself 'permission' to wear to school that you might not wear elsewhere?)

4. What do you find yourself critiquing in the clothing choices made by other female students you see on campus and why? What do you think about popular fashion today? What are the dominant images related to fashion in the media that have an impact—of any sort—upon you?

5. What are some contemporary expressions and/or bits of slang you've heard and/or used that are used to describe:

a. contemporary women's clothing (outfits and/or separate pieces),

b. the *interrelationship* of contemporary clothing and women's bodies. (Or, put another way: pieces of women's clothing and how they look on women's bodies—what does clothing 'do' to our flesh?)

For example, we recently learned about the expressions "muffin-tops" and "whale-tails."

6. Anything about hair/make-up preferences and fashion you'd like to add?

7. Do you notice or feel any differences in racial or ethnic expectations in fashion?

Note: These can be "pieces" of thoughts, not necessarily fully-formed theses—and they can be about the joys, frustrations, or anything at all related to college clothing/fashion today. Hope to hear from you!

5. Herbert J. Rubin and Irene S. Rubin, *Qualitative Interviewing: The Art of Hearing Data* (London: Sage Publications, 1995), 10–12.

6. Norman K. Denzin, *Interpretive Interactionism, 2nd ed.* (London: Sage Publications, 2001), 39.

7. Here, Rubin and Rubin quote performance studies scholar Clifford Geertz. See Herbert J. Rubin and Irene S. Rubin, *Qualitative Interviewing: The Art of Hearing Data* (London: Sage Publications, 1995), 8.

8. This follows Madison's concern about not "privileging the written work at the expense of shunning the poetics, oral rhythms, and improvisational expressions of subaltern communities" See D. Soyini Madison, "Performance, Personal Narratives, and the Politics of Possibility," in *The Future of Performance Studies: Visions and Revisions*, ed. Sheron Dailey (Annandale, VA: National Communication Association, 1998), 276–86. Similarly, Conquergood argues for "another way of knowing that is grounded in active, intimate, hands-on participation and personal connection: 'knowing how,' and 'knowing who.' This is a view from the ground level, in the thick of things." See Dwight Conquergood, "Performance Studies: Interventions and Radical Research," *The Drama Review* 46 (2002): 145–56. Thus, the focus of this project is on the local knowledge of participants.

9. The designation "non-traditional" at KSU refers to students who fall outside the "traditional" age range of 18–23.

10. Kennesaw State University, "About KSU," http://www.kennesaw.edu/prospective/u/about.shtml (accessed January 15, 2007).

11. See *The Devil Wears Prada*, Feature Film, directed by David Frankel (20th Century Fox, 2006).

12. Loredana Buonopane, "Back-to-School Preview!" *Seventeen,* August 2006, 39.

13. In a marginalized region, rural women may transcend the criticisms of their homesite as provincial or behind the curve by pursuing supermodels ("super"--in its full meaning as above and beyond—here, beyond regional boundaries or identifying markers) as "hot" images.

14. Ariel Levy, *Female Chauvinist Pigs: Women and the Rise of Raunch Culture* (New York: Free Press, 2005), 31.

15. Joseph W. Slade, preface to *Pornography in America: A Reference Handbook* (Santa Barbara: ABC-CLIO, 2000), 2.

16. Valerie Steele, *Fetish: Fashion, Sex, and Power* (New York, Oxford: Oxford University Press, 1996), 9.

17. Naomi Wolf, *The Beauty Myth* (New York: Anchor Books, Doubleday, 1992), 132.

18. Calvin Klein Jeans (advertisement), *Vanity Fair*, March 2006: 50–51.

19. We originally found the photograph we describe when we "Googled" soft porn and located: Mravac Kid, "Soft Porn of the day!" http://forums.keenspot.com/viewtopic.php?start=1640&t=41823 (accessed on July 31, 2006). However, when we tried to return to the site, it no longer "existed." Subsequently, we searched for the subject of the photograph and learned that she is a Japanese porn star. (See Sola Aoi Official Website, "Solar Power," http://www.aoisola.net/.) On February 14, 2007, we again located the photograph through an image search for Sola Aoi. See gals and idols, "Les Asiatiques les Plus Belles et les Plus Sexy du Moment," http://galsandidols.blogspot.com/search/label/Sora%20Aoi.

20. Dennis Hall, "Delight in Disorder: A Reading of Diaphany and Liquefaction in Contemporary Women's Clothing," *Journal of Popular Culture* 34, no.1 (2000), 65–69.

21. Though a thorough investigation is beyond the scope of this article, it is interesting to note the correspondence here to the principles of striptease and pole-dancing.

22. Michelle Stacey, "Are Butts the New Boobs?" *Cosmopolitan*, August 2006: 154.

23. Fred Davis notes that the "theory of the shifting erogenous zone" is the best known of several "explanations of fashion that locate its source in a desire to heighten sexual allure." He adds, "The most fully developed statement of it . . . is to be found in . . . *The Psychology of Clothes* . . . by J.C. Flugel." Davis quotes Flugel:

> But perhaps the most obvious and important of all the variations of fashion is that which concerns the part of the body that is most accentuated. Fashion, in its more exuberant moments is seldom content with the silhouette that Nature has provided, but usually seeks to lay particular stress upon some single part or feature, which is then created as a special centre of erotic charm.

See Fred Davis, *Fashion, Culture, and Identity* (Chicago: Chicago University Press, 1992), 25.

24. Not too long ago (2005), the *Atlanta Journal and Constitution* featured a front-page article about breast augmentations bestowed as high school graduation gifts.

25. Michelle Stacey, "Are Butts the New Boobs?" *Cosmopolitan*, August 2006, 156–57.

26. Levy writes, "The thong is a literal byproduct of the sex industry. In 1939, New York City mayor Fiorello La Guardia insisted that the city's exotic dancers cover their genitals for the World's Fair, and the thong was born to placate his decree while exposing the maximum amount of skin. Now they are the underpants of choice for pubescent girls." See Ariel Levy, *Female Chauvinist Pigs: Women and the Rise of Raunch Culture* (New York: Free Press, 2005), 142.

27. As we shared stories about scantily clad women in the classroom, a colleague who teaches costume design at another university stated, "We've actually had to tell some women who report for work in the costume or scene shops that they must go home and change; not only is their near-nakedness distracting; it is downright dangerous." On another campus, a male professor commented that his female students' attire "distracted" him to the extent that he found it difficult to concentrate on the delivery of course content. And when we mentioned the words "soft pornography" in connection with certain student fashion selections, colleagues' and students' eyes widened in recognition of something they had intuited perhaps, but not yet articulated using those terms.

28. Jozworld.com, "Sisley Photos, 2005–6 Campaigns," http://jozworld.club.fr/sisley_2006.html (accessed 31 July 2006).

29. Ibid.

30. Dolce and Gabbana (advertisement), *Vanity Fair*, March 2006: 104.

31. Nicola Bockelmann, "Porn Chic," www.nicolabockelmann.de/ (accessed July 31, 2007.

32. We owe our understanding of "dirt" as "matter out of place" to Mary Douglas. See Mary Douglas, *Purity and Danger: An Analysis of Concept of Pollution and Taboo* (New York: Routledge, 2002), 44.

33. More and more often this is directly stated in fashion marketing: even Oxford-inspired white shirts are currently marketed as the "sexy shirt" at local Limited stores; jeans are sold as "the sexy jeans" as well.

34. By referencing *Psalms*, we acknowledge that Jewish women, too, may include themselves in this call to fashion. *Psalms 45: 10–13*, in *The Bible: New Revised Standard Version*, ed. Bruce M. Metzger and Roland E. Murphy (New York: Oxford University Press, 1991), 712.

35. Richard Schechner, *Performance Studies: An Introduction* (New York: Routledge, 2002), 45.

36. NPR's *This American Life* offered an interesting parallel in 2002 with their spot on conservative Pentecostal teenagers who vigorously competed for who got to play the roles of the "sinner" (abortionist, druggie) and "Satan" in their annual Halloween haunted house, Hell House. See NPR's "This American Life" with Ira Glass, Aug. 17, 2002.

37. Nicola Bockelmann, "Porn Chic," www.nicolabockelmann.de/ (accessed July 31, 2007).

38. This message runs rampant in *The Devil Wears Prada*: the bane of Andrea's existence—in hers and her colleagues' eyes—is her size six body. Later in the film when she coyly confides to her fashion friend that she has attained a size four, Andrea clearly is celebrating a major accomplishment: her life, at that moment appears to be at its apex.

39. Joyce L. Huff, "A 'Horror of Corpulence': Interrogating Bantingism and Mid-Nineteenth-Century Fat-Phobia," in *Bodies out of Bounds*, ed. Jana Evans Braziel and Kathleen LeBesco (Berkeley and Los Angeles: University of California Press, 2001), 49.

40. As one of our white, smaller-cupped girlfriends complained, "I have very *submissive* breasts—they don't fight against my bras and shirts like they should!" This same friend keeps a menagerie of breast-enhancing devices—a veritable museum of her college-age attempts at building "better" boobs.

41. Quoted in Michelle Stacey, "Are Butts the New Boobs?" *Cosmopolitan*, August 2006, 157. To have a nicely-formed *feminine* butt, Cecilia Hartley reminds us that

the construction of the body is undoubtedly a social act insofar as gender (that is, the construction of a body that is recognizably masculine or feminine) is performed for the satisfaction of both performer and audience. In characterizing femininity as "spectacle," something performed for a watcher, Bartky admits that 'under the current "tyranny of slenderness' women are forbidden to become large or massive."

Hartley follows this by noting that women *do* get fat, do "let themselves go," and hence (somehow this logically follows) are treated with derision in society. What does fat—particularly bum and waist fat—mean in a contemporary college campus environment? What can we say about this culture's rejection of the fat waist—and embrasure of the well-toned and, indeed, sometimes *enlarged* bum—as "fashionable?" See Cecilia Hartley, "Letting Ourselves Go: Making Room for the Fat Body in Feminist Scholarship," in *Bodies Out of Bounds*, ed. Jana Evans Braziel and Kathleen LeBesco (Berkeley and Los Angeles: University of California Press, 2001), 63.

42. Stacie Stukin, "'Paying for Booty' in *Vibe Magazine*," Better Buttocks.com. See http://www.betterbuttocks.com/article_vibe.htm (accessed July 31, 2006).

43. "Cosmetic Surgery" (advertisement), *Cosmopolitan* (August 2006): 174, 225.

44. Stacie Stukin, "Paying for Booty" in *Vibe Magazine*.

45. Anne Balsamo, "Forms of Technological Embodiment: Reading the Body in Contemporary Culture," in *Feminist Theory and the Body* (New York: Routledge, 1999), 281.

46. Ibid.

47. Laura Mulvey, "Visual Pleasure and Narrative Cinema," in *Film Theory: An Anthology*, ed. Robert Stam and Toby Miller (Malden, MA: Blackwell Publishers, 2000), 488.

48. Elizabeth Wilson, "Selections from *Adorned in Dreams*," in *Performance Analysis: An Introductory Coursebook*, ed. Colin Counsell and Laurie Wolf (New York: Routledge, 2001), 147.

49. We are grateful to Jeanne Entwistle and Fred Davis for our understanding of fashion as a deeply embodied "situated" practice that can, among other functions, communicate "a kind of visual metaphor for identity." See Fred Davis, *Fashion, Culture, and Identity* (Chicago: Chicago University Press, 1992), 25.

CHAPTER 5: *ONE NIGHT IN PARIS* (HILTON): WEALTH, CELEBRITY, AND THE POLITICS OF HUMILIATION

1. Nancy Jo Sales, "Hip-Hop Debs," *Vanity Fair* (September 2000): 378.

2. Sales, "Hip-Hop Debs," 381.

3. Leo Braudy, *The Frenzy of Renown: Fame and Its History* (New York: Oxford University Press, 1986), 9.

4. P. David Marshall, *Celebrity and Power: Fame in Contemporary Culture* (Minneapolis: University of Minnesota Press, 1997), 246.

5. Paris Hilton and Merle Ginsberg, *Confessions of an Heiress: A Tongue-in-Chic Peek Behind the Pose* (New York: Fireside Books, 2004), 6.

6. Reported in Sales, "Hip-Hop Debs," 352.

7. Braudy, *The Frenzy of Renown*, 5.

8. In many ways, Paris Hilton comes across as incapable of privacy—to such an extent that she has reportedly claimed to be so accustomed to being photographed that "she hears clicking noises even when there are no cameras." This quote comes from paparazzo photographer Ron Galella. See Krista Smith, "The Inescapable Paris," *Vanity Fair* (October 2005): 284.

9. It is also worth mentioning that almost all of the bodies in the photograph are fragmented in some way or another; the image is cropped to remove the heads of three of the men, to show only the leg and hip of another man at the far right, and to cut off the bottom part of Paris's right leg. Each of the surfers also shares the same basic shape and build, and the two male faces that are visible have strikingly similar features (dark eyes as well as dark, shoulder-length hair). These details—particularly the group of indistinguishable men whose partial bodies suggest that there are more of them staring at her off camera—imply a desire for Paris Hilton that is infinitely reproducible.

10. Sales, "Hip-Hop Debs," 378.

11. Marshall, *Celebrity and Power*, 246.

12. Jared Bernstein, Elizabeth McNichol, and Karen Lyons, "Pulling Apart: A State-by-State Analysis of Income," *Economic Policy Institute* (January 2006): 4, http://www.epinet.org/content.cfm?id=2246.

13. Bernstein, McNichol, and Lyons, "Pulling Apart," 11.

14. Founder and former president of the Economic Policy Institute, Jeff Faux spoke at this conference and warned of impending "political unrest." For more on this, see Andrew Leonard, "Class Warfare, Anyone?" Salon.com, http://www.salon.com/tech/htww/2006/01/24/faux/index.html/. Steven Pearlstein of *The Washington Post* sees the need for "fundamental tax reform" (including "a reasonable inheritance tax") as a far cry from "class warfare." See Steven Pearlstein, "Solving Inequality Problem Won't Take Class Warfare," *The Washington Post,* March 15 2006, D01. And for a critical response to the Economic Policy Institute's report, see Tim Kane, "Income Relativism," *National Review Online,* January 30, 2006, http://article.nationalreview.com/?q=ZmVjZmlzZDI2OTY4ZTdiYTEwOWViNDViYzdiYzY0OTc=.

15. Kevin Phillips, *Wealth and Democracy* (New York: Broadway Books, 2002), 124.

16. Ibid., 392.

17. Marshall, *Celebrity and Power*, 243.

18. Benjamin Franklin, *The Autobiography of Benjamin Franklin* (New York: Dover, 1996 [written between 1771–1790]), 1.

19. Franklin, *The Autobiography of Benjamin Franklin,* 50.

20. John Kasson, *Rudeness and Civility: Manners in Nineteenth-Century Urban American* (New York: Hill and Wang, 1990), 30.

21. Hilton and Ginsberg, *Confessions of an Heiress,* 4.

22. Ibid.

23. Quoted in Smith, "The Inescapable Paris," 288.

24. Braudy, *The Frenzy of Renown,* 7.

25. Hilton and Ginsberg, *Confessions of an Heiress,* 6.

26. Ibid., 9.

27. Ibid., 11.

28. Ibid., 13.

29. Ibid., 10.

30. See Maureen Callahan, "How to Be an Heir-Head: Paris Hilton Dishes Bad Advice in New Book," *The New York Post,* September 8, 2004, 73. Elizabeth Barr's "A Little Paris Is Still Way Too Much" (*The Buffalo News,* October 24, 2004, G7) begins with the following statement: "We all knew this ubiquitous amoral party whore had suspected depth." And Pia Catton's review for *The New York Sun* criticizes the self-conscious celebration of the self in *Confessions* in comparison with Gloria Vanderbilt's autobiography. See Pia Catton, "Not All Heiresses Are Created Equal," *The New York Sun,* September 22, 2004, 15.

31. This review was posted on September 26, 2004 by isala "Isabel and Lars" (Fairbanks, Alaska, US).

32. This was posted by Tim C. (Vatican City) on January 10, 2006.

33. Quoted in Smith, "The Inescapable Paris," 280.

34. This doesn't mean that urban biases about the South are not part of the show. Most notably, the unseen narrator (James DuMont) is either imitating a Southern accent poorly or exaggerating one for absurd dramatic effect. Nevertheless, the Leding family is not set up as a cliché, in part, because the focus of the show is on the humiliating adventures of Hilton and Richie.

35. *The Simple Life,* "Ro-Day-O vs. Ro-Dee-O," episode 1, Fox 2003.

36. In a recent interview on *Live with Regis and Kelly,* Paris Hilton claims that her "stupid" comments on *The Simple Life* are intentional and that she finds it amusing when people take her seriously. Whether or not this is true, these self-serving remarks don't change the message that this kind of moment sends to the viewing public (particularly when the show first aired). See Paris Hilton, interview by Regis Philbin and Kelly Ripa, *Live with Regis and Kelly,* ABC, June 13, 2006.

37. James Friedman, "Introduction," in *Reality Squared: Televisual Discourse on the Real,* ed. James Friedman (New Brunswick, NJ: Rutgers University Press, 2002), 8.

38. Anita Biressi and Heather Nunn, *Reality T.V.: Realism and Revelation* (London: Wallflower Press, 2005), 147.

39. Annette Hill, *"Big Brother:* The Real Audience," *Television & New Media* 3.3 (Summer 2002): 324.

40. *The Simple Life,* "Ro-Day-O vs. Ro-Dee-O," episode 1, Fox 2003.

41. Michel Foucault, *The History of Sexuality: Volume 1* (trans. Robert Hurley; New York: Pantheon, 1978), 61–62.

42. Ibid., 62.

43. Ibid., 61.

44. *The Simple Life,* "Good-bye and Good Luck," episode 7, Fox 2003.

45. *The Simple Life,* "Ro-Day-O vs. Ro-Dee-O," episode 1, Fox 2003.

46. *The Simple Life,* "Good-bye and Good Luck," episode 7, Fox 2003.

47. Hilton and Ginsberg, *Confessions of an Heiress,* 5.

48. *The Simple Life,* "Boy Crazy," episode 6, Fox 2003.

49. *The Simple Life,* "Good-bye and Good Luck," episode 7, Fox 2003.

50. *Cool Hand Luke,* DVD, directed by Stuart Rosenberg (1967; Los Angeles, CA: Warner Home Video, 1997).

51. Smith, "The Inescapable Paris," 288.

52. In September 2004, another sex tape featuring Hilton started circulating on the internet. This video featured Hilton "with Nick Carter, a former member of the band Backstreet Boys, and Jason Shaw, a Tommy Hilfiger model." See Ariel Levy,

Female Chauvinist Pigs: Women and the Rise of Raunch Culture (New York: Free Press, 2005), 28.

53. To see these comments, visit the PTC website at: http://www.parentstv.org/ptc/advertisers/campaign.asp.

54. I am borrowing this phrase from Ariel Levy's *Female Chauvinist Pigs: Women and the Rise of Raunch Culture*, which I discuss later in the essay.

55. Walter Kendrick, *The Secret Museum: Pornography in Modern Culture* (New York: Viking Press, 1987), 95.

56. Rick Kushman, "Paris Hilton and the Future of Advertising," *Sacramento Bee*. June 7, 2005, Entertainment.

57. Kendrick, *The Secret Museum*, 281.

58. This number does not include the version sold via the internet by Rick Solomon, the co-star, prior to his deal with Red Light. According to *The New York Times*, this video also received an award from "a porn industry trade group for Top Selling Title of the Year in 2005." See Lola Ogunnaike, "Sex, Lawsuits, and Celebrities Caught on Tape," *The New York Times*, March 19, 2006, sec 9: 1.

59. Minette Hillyer, "Sex in the Suburban: Porn, Home Movies, and the Live Action Performance of Love in *Pam and Tommy Lee: Hardcore and Uncensored,*" in *Porn Studies*, ed. Linda Williams (Durham: Duke University Press, 2004), 53.

60. For more on this, see the first chapter of Linda Williams, *Hard Core: Power, Pleasure, and the "Frenzy of the Visible"* (Berkeley: University of California Press, 1989).

61. Chuck Kleinhans, "Pamela Anderson on the Slippery Slope," in *The End of Cinema As We Know It: American Films in the Nineties*, ed. Jon Lewis (New York: New York University Press, 2001), 297.

62. As Minette Hillyer's "Sex in the Suburban: Porn, Home Movies, and the Live Action Performance of Love in *Pam and Tommy Lee: Hardcore and Uncensored*" reminds us, "while the footage per se shows little evidence of planning, or even coherence beyond the strictly circumstantial, what is at stake here is not the documenting of reality, but the creation of a product, bound as much by conventions as by circumstances." See Hillyer, "Sex in the Suburban," 69.

63. Rick Salomon was married to actress Shannen Doherty during the filming of this tape. Their marriage was annulled in 2003, and this adds another dimension to the scandalous celebrity draw for the tape.

64. Not surprisingly, this moment will be repeated at the end of the night-vision sequence, operating both as a frame device for the first part of the tape and as a marker that divides the night-vision segment from the footage filmed in color. It is a frame that blurs the line between Paris Hilton's private and public life, suggesting that in both spheres she is preoccupied with presenting herself for public consumption.

65. Levy, *Female Chauvinist Pigs*, 30.

66. Williams, *Hard Core*, 22.

67. This customer review, "Cum for Paris, Stay for Porn," was posted on June 14, 2004 by Master Tang.

68. Quoted in Smith, "The Inescapable Paris," 288.

69. Salomon was married to Shannen Doherty briefly between 2002–2003.

70. See Ogunnaike, "Sex, Lawsuits and Celebrities Caught on Tape," *The New York Times*, March 19, 2006, sec 9.

71. In January 2005, Paris Hilton was so upset about the video that she reportedly stole a copy from a street vendor in Hollywood. See "Paris Hilton Cleans Up Smut Shop," *UPI*, February 2, 2005.

CHAPTER 6: *FEAR FACTOR*: PORNOGRAPHY, REALITY TELEVISION, AND RED STATE AMERICA

1. Part of the problem when discussing reality is disagreement over the term itself. This problem is only exacerbated by the seeming oxymoron of "reality television." For a detailed overview of the problems of terminology, see Su Holmes and Deborah Jermyn's "Introduction" to their collection *Understanding Reality Television* (London: Routledge, 2004).

2. Quoting Viereck from Tom Reiss, "The First Conservative," profile of Peter Viereck, *New Yorker*, 24 October 2005, 47.

3. Walter Kendrick, *The Secret Museum: Pornography in Modern Culture* (New York: Penguin, 1988), xiii.

4. Kendrick, xiii.

5. Quoting Warhol from Victoria Mappleback, "Money Shot," in Dolan Cummings et al, eds., *Reality TV: How Real is Real?* (London: Hodder and Stoughton, 2002), 17.

6. Ara Osterweil, "Andy Warhol's Blow Job: Toward the Recognition of a Pornographic Avant-garde," in Linda Williams, ed., *Porn Studies* (Durham: Duke UP, 2004), 437.

7. Jean Baudrillard, *Ecstasy of Communication*, trans. Bernard and Caroline Schutze (New York: Semiotext[e], 1988), 21.

8. Linda Williams, *Hard Core: Power, Pleasure, and the "Frenzy of the Visible"* (Berkeley: U of California P, 1989), 304.

9. Steven Johnson, *Everything Bad is Good for You: How Today's Popular Culture Is Actually Making Us Smarter* (New York: Riverhead, 2005), 97–98.

10. Frank Rich, "Operation Iraqi Infoganda," *New York Times*, 28 March 2004, Sec. 2. Lexis Nexis. (accessed 7 October 2005).

11. Jean Baudrillard, *Selected Writings* (Stanford: Stanford UP, 2001), 157.

12. Williams, *Hard Core*, 303.

13. Williams, *Hard Core*, 126.

14. Williams, *Hard Core*, 126–127.

15. "*Fear Factor*." http://www.nbc.com/Fear_Factor (accessed October 7, 2005). A more recent visit to the website—January 22, 2007—however, informs the reader that "Casting and open calls have ended." Fortunately, many of these episodes have by now aired, so they can be found under "Rewind Archives": athttp://www.nbc.com/Fear_Factor/rewind/619_2.shtml. As a promotional website, <http://www.nbc.com/Fear_Factor> is updated frequently and thus makes citations of it less than reliable (accessed January 22, 2007).

16. Williams, *Hard Core*, 303.

17. Daniel Bernardi, "Cyborgs in Cyberspace: White Pride, Pedophilic Pornography, and Donna Harraway's Manifesto," in James Friedman, ed., *Reality Squared: Televisual Discourse in the Real* (New Brunswick: Rutgers UP, 2002), 168.

18. "*Fear Factor*." http://www.nbc.com/Fear_Factor/gross/index.shtml (accessed October 7, 2005).

19. These brutal descriptions comprise the majority of the introduction to the second edition; see all of xiii–xxvii and xxviii–xl *passim*. Andrea Dworkin, *Pornography: Men Possessing Women* (New York: Plume, 1989).

20. Quoted in Nichols Fox, "Gawk Shows," 1991, in Santi V. Buscemi and Charlotte Smith, eds., *75 Readings*, 9th ed. (New York: McGraw-Hill, 2004), 247.

21. "Fear Factor." http://www.nbcuniversalstore.com/index.php?&spid=&v=nbunb cnowffrall&pagemax=all (accessed October 7, 2005).

22. "Fear Factor." http://www.nbc.com/Fear_Factor/rewind/619_2.shtml (accessed October 7, 2005).

23. Jean Baudrillard, *Selected Writings*, 173.

24. Ron Suskind, "Without a Doubt," *New York Times*, 17 October 2004 Sect. 6: 44. Lexis Nexis (accessed October 7, 2005).

25. Henry Giroux, *Beyond the Spectacle of Terrorism: Global Uncertainty and the Challenge of the New Media* (Boulder: Paradigm, 2006), 3.

26. "Fear factor." *Wikipedia, The Free Encyclopedia*. http://en.wikipedia.org/w/index.php?title=Fear_factor&oldid=20950603 (accessed November 11, 2005).

27. Dworkin, *Pornography*, xxi.

CHAPTER 7: FREAK SHOWS IN JESUS LAND: HOWARD STERN AND GEORGE BUSH'S AMERICA

1. James Howard Gibbons. "Even Vulgar Programs Ought to Have a Spark of Wit," *Houston Chronicle*, July 26, 2004, 9.

2. Mike Thomas. "In Defense of Howard Stern: The Shock Jock Sells Sex, But his Skills as a Truth-Telling Observer and Interviewer Get Lost in the Shuffle," *Chicago Sun-Times*, July 31, 2004, 39.

3. Susan J. Douglas. *Listening In: Radio and the American Imagination, from Amos 'n' Andy and Edward R. Murrow to Wolfman Jack and Howard Stern* (New York: Random House, 1999), 7.

4. Douglas, 8.

5. Douglas, 285.

6. Howard Stern. *Miss America* (New York: Harper Collins, 1995), 354.

7. Bill Moyers. "Bigger and Bigger Media," *Moyers on America,* http://www.pbs.org/moyers/moyersonamerica/net/bigger.html (accessed January 5, 2007).

8. Howard Stern. "If FCC Fines Me, Why Does Oprah Get a Pass?" *Chicago Sun-Times*, November 2, 2004, 39.

9. Thomas, Mike.

10. Howard Stern quoted in Josh Wolk, "Stalking Stern," *Entertainment Weekly*, 4/07/06, 22–24.

11. Bob Barr, "Indecency Obsession Amounts to Overkill," *Atlanta Journal-Constitution* (April 13, 2005): 13A.

12. Thomas, Mike.

13. Howard Stern, *Private Parts* (New York: Simon and Schuster, 1993), 38.

14. Howard Stern, *Miss America* (New York: Harper Collins, 1995), 3–50.

15. Sharon Zechowski, "Howard Stern and the Women who Love Him: Working-Class Subjectivity and the Discourse of Male Talk." *Dissertation*. Ohio University. 2002.

16. Lynn Hall. Personal Discussion. June 2004.

17. Michel Foucault, *The History of Sexuality. Vol. 1. An Introduction,* Trans. Robert Hurley (New York: Vintage, 1980), 106.

18. Foucault, 3.

19. Foucault, 85.

20. For more examples, see Stern's *Miss America,* 275–409.

21. Stern, *Miss America,* 397.

22. Max Blumenthal, "Generation Chickenhawk," *The Nation (Online Only).* http://www.thenation.com/doc/20050711/blumenthal (date accessed June 11, 2005).

23. Steven Thomma, "Stern Helping Kerry's Cause: Radio Talker's Bush Bashing is Swaying Listeners, Poll Finds," *Milwaukee Journal-Sentinel,* June 12, 2004, 6B.

24. Howard Stern, Interview with Jaques Steinberg, "Howard Stern Prepares for Life Without Limits," *New York Times,* October 20, 2005, E1.

CHAPTER 8: TOYS ARE US: CONTEMPORARY FEMINISMS AND THE CONSUMPTION OF SEXUALITY

1. Brian McManus, "Good Vibrations: Haunted by Dildos, the Nightfly Buzzes through a Home Sex Toy Sales Party," *Houston Press,* May 5, 2005.

2. Alison Lara, "In the Drugstore Aisle: Pleasure Products: Sex Toys for Women Finding More Retail Shelf Space," *Chicago Tribune,* December 21, 2005, Women's News section; Jack Neff, "Foreplay in Aisle Seven: Sexcessories Get Boost," *Advertising Age,* June 13, 2005, 6; Gail Rosenblum, "Women's Pleasure Products Sizzle on the Shelves," *Minneapolis Star Tribune,* June 25, 2006.

3. Feona Attwood, "Fashion and Passion: Marketing Sex to Women," *Sexualities* 8, no.4 (2005): 397.

4. Jean Kilbourne, *Killing Us Softly III,* dir. Sut Jhally. Media Education Foundation, Northampton, Mass. 2000, videocassette.

5. Attwood, "Fashion and Passion," 403.

6. Rachel Vennings, interview by Angie Han, "Short Answers," *Advocate,* August 16, 2005, 86; Claire Cavanah, interview by D. Parvaz, "Be 'Sex Positive' and Fear No Pleasure," *Seattle Post-Intelligencer,* November 21, 2003.

7. Jessica Giordani, interview by Tristan Taormino, "The Sweet Spot," *Print* 58, no. 4 (2004): 54–59.

8. June Juffer, *At Home With Pornography: Women, Sex and Everyday Life* (New York: New York University Press, 1998), 73–74.

9. Juffer, *At Home With Pornography,* 82.

10. Attwood, "Fashion and Passion," 396.

11. Juffer, *At Home With Pornography,* 72.

12. Dennis Hall, "Good Vibrations: Eros and Instrumental Knowledge," *Journal of Popular Culture* 34, no.1 (2000): 3.

13. "Founders," smittenkittenonline.com, http://www.smittenkittenonline.com/pages/founders.cfm (accessed November 29, 2006).

14. "Babeland Parties," babeland.com, http://www.babeland.com/ aboutbabeland-party-details/ (accessed December 13, 2006).

15. Hall, "Good Vibrations," 7.

16. John Berger, *Ways of Seeing* (London: Penguin, 1977).

17. Adela C. Licona, "(B)orderlands' Rhetorics and Representations: The Trans-

formative Potential of Feminist Third-Space Scholarship and Zines," *NWSA Journal* 17, no. 2 (2005): 104–129.

18. Mary Celeste Kearney, *Girls Make Media* (New York: Taylor and Francis, 2006), 157–61.

19. Ibid., 162.

20. Ibid., 162.

21. Ibid., 164.

22. Jennifer Pritchett, interview by Candace Furniss, "Sex Toys and the Revolution," *Confluence* 12, no. 2 (August 2006), http://www.stlconfluence.org/article (accessed December 13, 2006).

23. Anne Marie Todd, "The Aesthetic Turn in Green Marketing: Environmental Consumer Ethics of National Personal Care Products." *Ethics and Environment* 9, no. 2 (2004): 90, 98–99.

24. Jennifer Pritchett, interview by Emily Gertz, "Naughty by Nature," *Grist. Environmental News and Commentary*, December 6, 2005, http://www.grist.org/news/main dish/2005/12/06/gertz/index.html (accessed December 13, 2006).

25. Jennifer Pritchett, interview by Candace Furniss, "Sex Toys and the Revolution," *Confluence* 12, no. 2 (August 2006), http://www.stlconfluence.org/article (accessed December 13, 2006).

26. "Founders," smittenkittenonline.com.

27. Joseph Heath, and Andrew Potter, *Nation of Rebels: Why Counterculture Became Consumer Culture* (New York: Harper Business, 2004), 199–200.

28. Ibid.

29. "Press Kit," babeland.com, http://www.babeland.com/about/presskit/ (accessed December 13, 2006).

30. "Babeland Story," babeland.com, http://www.babeland.com/about/presskit/about/presskit/history (accessed December 13, 2006).

31. Hall, "Good Vibrations," 1.

32. Susan Bordo, *Unbearable Weight: Feminism, Western Culture and the Body* (Berkeley: University of California Press, 1993).

33. Ibid.

34. Laura Kipnis, "(Male) Desire and (Female) Disgust: Reading Hustler," in *Cultural Studies*, ed. Lawrence Grossberg, Cary Nelson and Paula Treichler (New York: Routledge, 1992), 373–91.

35. Bordo, *Unbearable Weight*.

36. Attwood, "Fashion and Passion," 394; Hall, "Good Vibrations," 1–2.

37. "About Us," smittenkittenonline.com, http://www.smittenkittenonline.com/pages/aboutus.cfm (accessed November 29, 2006).

38. "Dildos," babeland.com, http://www.babeland.com/shoppingadvice/dildoadvice (accessed November 22, 2006).

39. Pierre Bourdieu, *Distinction: A Social Critique of the Judgment of Taste*, trans. Richard Nice (Cambridge, MA: Harvard University Press, 1984).

40. D. Parvaz, "Be 'Sex Positive' and Fear No Pleasure," *Seattle Post-Intelligencer*, November 21, 2003.

41. Rachel Venning, interview by Tristan Taormino, "The Sweet Spot," *Print.* 58, no. 4 (2004): 54–59.

42. "Education," smittenkittenonline.com, http://www.smittenkittenonline.com/pages/Education.cfm (accessed November 29, 2006).

43. Juffer, *At Home With Pornography*, 83.

44. Barbara Ehrenreich and Diedre English, *Complaints and Disorders: The Sexual Politics of Sickness* (Old Westbury, NY: Feminist Press, 1973).

45. "Education," smittenkittenonline.com.

46. Attwood, "Fashion and Passion," 393.

47. Ibid., 400.

48. "Babeland Parties," babeland.com.

49. Katherine-Lee H. Weille, "The Psychodynamics of Consensual Sadomasochistic and Dominant-Submissive Sexual Games," *Studies in Gender and Sexuality* 3, no. 2 (2002): 131–60.

50. Amber Kinser, "Negotiating Spaces For/Through Third Wave Feminism," *NWSA Journal* 16, no. 3 (2004): 144.

51. Heath and Potter, *Nation of Rebels*, 129.

52. Ibid., 200.

53. Kinser, "Negotiating Spaces," 144.

54. Hall, "Good Vibrations," 7.

55. Kinser, "Negotiating Spaces,"144; Susan Archer Mann and Douglas J. Huffman, "The Decentering of Second Wave Feminism and the Rise of the Third Wave," *Science and Society* 69, no.1 (2005): 74.

56. Juffer, *At Home With Pornography*, 35–68.

CHAPTER 9: CLEAN PORN: THE VISUAL AESTHETICS OF HYGIENE, HOT SEX, AND HAIR REMOVAL

1. See Sara Bodnar, "Beyond the Brazilian Wax," *Cosmopolitan* 240.5 (May 2006): 232. In addition, the Web site for the e-book *Hot Pink: The Girls' Guide to Primping, Passion, and Pubic Fashion*, lists "flattering, fun pubic hair styles for you and a lover," including "Power puff (or magic muff), Fan [. . .] Rain cloud, Soul patch, Pubic sculpture (think topiary!)," and more. See Deborah Driggs and Karen Risch, *Hot Pink: The Girls' Guide to Primping, Passion, and Pubic Fashion* (2004), http://www.hotpink book.com.

2. Cary Tennis, "Since You Asked: All the Guys I'm Dating Want Me to Shave Down There," Salon.com, http://www.salon.com/mwt/col/tenn/2006/08/08/shaving/. Readers' letters in response: http://letters.salon.com/mwt/col/tenn/2006/08/08/shaving/view/?show=ec.

3. Bodnar, "Beyond the Brazilian Wax," 232.

4. John Berger, *Ways of Seeing* (New York: Penguin, 1977; first appearance 1972 as BBC television show), 55.

5. Pauline Réage, *The Story of O* (trans. Sabine d'Estrées; New York: Ballantine, 1965), 161.

6. In a feature called "Lesbian Pubic Hair," the Web site Lesbian Life, for example, features a letter from someone just coming out, wondering how lesbians prefer their partner's pubic hair. The advice columnist tells the writer to do as she likes and that "Most of the lesbians I spoke to preferred a natural bush." See http://lesbianlife.about.com/od/lesbiansex/a/Lesbian Bush.htm.

7. Hannah McCouch, "What Your Bikini Waxer Really Thinks: A woman who spends her days doing Brazilian-style hair removal breaks her code of silence (True Confession.)" *Cosmopolitan* 232.1 (January 2002): 93.

8. Berger, *Ways of Seeing*, 54.

9. Another example from literary erotica is found in the story "The Basque and Bijou," written by Anaïs Nin for a private collector around 1940. In it the man known as the Basque has three of his friends hold the prostitute Bijou (who is also his lover) down on his bed so he can shave her with a straight razor and demonstrate that her bare vulva looks like "the paintings by that woman" (presumably Georgia O'Keefe). Once he has made her into an artwork this way, he stimulates her until she seems to be taking too much pleasure in his activity; he stops so that his friends won't see her climax. See Anaïs Nin, "The Basque and Bijou," in *Delta of Venus: Erotica* (New York: Bantam 1969, 1977 [stories written 1940–1941]), 154–201.

10. Slavoj Zizek, *The Plague of Fantasies* (London: Verso 1997), 5–6.

11. Driggs and Risch, *Hot Pink*, http://www.hotpinkbook.com.

12. McCouch, "What Your Bikini Waxer Really Thinks," 93.

13. See, for example, Philip Rawson's *Erotic Art of India* (New York: Gallery Books, 1977) or Crescent Books's *The Perfect Union* (New York, 1974).

14. Irma Kurtz (pseudonym), "Agony," *Cosmopolitan* 226.3 (March 1999): 74.

15. Paula Szuchman, "The History of Bikini Waxing: Hairstyles Come and Go—Even Down Below (Your Body)," *Cosmopolitan* 237.21 (Summer–Fall, 2004): 90.

16. Ibid.

17. Szuchman, "The History of Bikini Waxing," 90.

18. Quoted in Gay Daly, *Pre-Raphaelites in Love* (New York: Ticknor & Fields, 1989), 163.

19. See Daly, 139. Things ended well for poor Effie, however: After a trial and a humiliating physical examination to prove her virginity, she obtained her annulment and an apparently happy marriage to the painter John Everett Millais.

20. Terri Kapsalis might disagree; on page 82 of *Public Privates: Performing Gynecology from Both Ends of the Speculum* (Durham: Duke University Press 1997), she writes, "there is often only a tenuous distinction between the categories of art and pornography."

21. M. H. Dunlop describes child pornography sold "behind green curtains at the rear of photograph shops"—and even featured in the *New York Herald*, with adolescent girls photographed with the clothes sliding off their bodies. See M. H. Dunlop, *Gilded City: Scandal and Sensation in Turn-of-the-Century New York* (New York: Perennial, 2000), 156.

22. Dunlop, *Gilded City*, 52.

23. For a brief history of the painting's ownership, see Peter J. Gärtner, *Musée d'Orsay* (Cologne: Könemann Verlagsgesellschaft, 2001), 96–99.

24. Pamela Paul, *Pornified: How Pornography Is Transforming Our Lives, Our Relationships, and Our Families* (New York: Times Books/Henry Holt, 2005), 4.

25. Ibid, 15, 116.

26. Linda Williams, *Hard Core: Power, Pleasure, and the "Frenzy of the Visible"* (Berkeley: University of California Press, 1989, 1999), 36.

27. Ibid.

28. Ibid, 48–49.

29. Quoted by Michael Castleman, "Porn-Star Secrets: Going Naked in Front of the Camera Necessitates Lots of Hair-Removal Tricks," on Salon.com (September 6, 2006), http://archive.salon.com/sex/feature/2000/09/06/hair_removal/rpint.html.

30. Legs McNeil and Jennifer Osborne, with Peter Pavia, *The Other Hollywood: The*

Uncensored Oral History of the Porn Film Industry (New York: ReganBooks, 2005), 368.

31. Of course, earlier actresses were concerned about their pubic grooming, if not shaving. Sharon Mitchell, a star of the mid-1970s, says she traded pubic beauty sessions for lessons in fellatio: "Then I got into pussy hair coiffing. So I would exchange these cock-sucking lessons in exchange [sic] for coiffing Vanessa's pussy hair." See McNeil and Osborne, *The Other Hollywood*, 144.

32. Ibid, 370.

33. Horace Newcomb, *TV: The Most Popular Art* (New York: Anchor Books, 1974), 243–64.

34. Perhaps because of increased demand for intimacy, and for sheer volume of movies produced, some benefits came to women in video. VHS, however unexpectedly, empowered porn actresses, who now outearn their male counterparts. Ginger Lynn, a popular actress of the 1980s, says that when she began her career around 1983, she demanded, "I want script and cast approval, and I want a thousand dollars per scene . . . these are the things I need in order for me to feel good about what I'm doing." Director Henri Pachard says, "Women didn't discover their power until video came along. Until then the power belonged to the director." See McNeil and Osborne, *The Other Hollywood*, p. 366. This phenomenon is all the more interesting because the women are, as just about anyone would agree, objectified so strongly. Theorist Dennis Giles points out that men are not the "heroes" of pornographic films; their characters are much less developed than the women's. Giles describes the viewer gazing at the vulva in a process of "projective identification," by which the male viewer projects some of his own rejected sexual urges, such as passivity, onto the actress. As he watches the male actor possess her, he can identify with both figures onscreen. See Dennis Giles, "Pornographic Space: The Other Place," *The 1977 Film Studies Annual: Part 2* (Pleasantville, NY: Redgrave, 1977), 55–57. Pornography may be the one industry in which this objectification pays off: A Brazilian wax could mean a bigger paycheck.

35. McNeil and Osborne, *The Other Hollywood*, 10.

36. Paul, *Pornified*, 10.

37. Marco Tosa, *Barbie: Four Decades of Fashion, Fantasy, and Fun* (New York: Abrams 1997, 27–29.

38. See, for example, Paul, *Pornified*, 120.

39. Paul, *Pornified*, 92.

40. Ibid, 2.

41. Kurtz, "Agony," 74.

42. Ariel Levy, *Female Chauvinist Pigs: Women and the Rise of Raunch Culture* (New York: Free Press, 2005), 3–4 (emphasis in the original).

43. Ibid, 196 (emphasis in the original).

44. *Sex and the City*, "Sex and Another City," episode 44 (directed by John David Coles, written by Jenny Bicks: HBO, 2001).

45. *Sex and the City*, "The One," episode 86 (directed by David Frankel, written by Michael Patrick King, HBO. 2004).

46. "100% Amateurs" (advertisement), *Penthouse*, August 2001: 153.

47. "Extreme Hardcore Videos" (advertisement), *Penthouse*, July 2001: 163.

48. Even Americans recognize this as a typically American obsession. Suellen Hoy, author of *Chasing Dirt*, writes of the first time she saw "a woman in a beautiful bathing suit who didn't shave at all!": the people around her "said the woman was 'foreign,' and shaving legs and underarms was an 'American' custom" (xiii).

49. Mary Douglas, *Purity and Danger: An Analysis of the Concepts of Pollution and Taboo* (London: Routledge, 1984), 4.

50. Quoted in Levy, *Female Chauvanist Pig*, 58.

51. Ibid.

52. *Emannuelle in America* (directed by Joe d'Amato, screenplay by Maria Pisa Fusco), 1976.

53. Suellen Hoy, *Chasing Dirt: The American Pursuit of Cleanliness* (New York: Oxford University Press, 1995), 3.

54. Quoted in Hoy, *Chasing Dirt*, 4.

55. For a complete discussion of woman's role, see Hoy, *Chasing Dirt*, 7 and 15–25.

56. See, for example, Michel Foucault, *The History of Sexuality, Volume 3: The Care of the Self* (translated by Robert Hurley; New York: Vintage, 1986), especially 31–34.

57. Elizabeth Goodman, "Bare Down There?", *Cosmopolitan* 226.4 (April 1999): 118.

58. Julia Califano, "'My Guy Wants Me to Try a Bikini Wax that Leaves Me Totally Bare. Is That Safe?' (His & Hers)," *Cosmopolitan* 235.1 (July 2003): 106.

59. Ginny Graves, "What's Up Down There (Vagina Examination)," *Cosmopolitan* 231.3 (September 2001): 332.

60. Szuchman, "The History of Bikini Waxing," 90.

61. *Cathouse* (TV series, documentary, produced and directed by Patti Kaplan), HBO, 2005.

62. Michel Foucault might suggest that this transformation of visual investment in hairlessness into a concern with cleanliness has to do with the hygienic role assigned to sexuality with the advent of Freud and other like-minded doctors. The new sexual science, he writes, "set itself up as the supreme authority in matters of hygienic necessity . . . ; it claimed to ensure the physical vigor and moral cleanliness of the social body." See *The History of Sexuality, Volume 1: An Introduction* (translated by Robert Hurley; New York: Vintage 1978, 1990), 54.

63. Goodman, "Bare Down There?," 118.

64. Joan Walsh, "From Happy Trails to Landing Strips, a Bikini-Waxer Muses on the Fine Line Between Pleasure and Pain (Mothers Who Think)," Salon.com (June 12, 1998), http://www.salon.com/mwt/time/1998/06/12time.html.

65. University of Iowa Student Health Service, "Health Iowa," http://uistudenthealth.com.

66. This part of hygienic ideology may be driven as much by the personal care industry's desire to make a buck as by the porn industry's. Hoy demonstrates that many body-care necessities came out of the soap industry's marketing departments. For example, she says, Francis Countway, the president of Lever Brothers in the 1920s, was "the individual most responsible for the 'discovery' of body odors"; he essentially invented b.o. so his company would have a market for its wares. Listerine did the same thing for halitosis (147). See also Elizabeth Shove's *Comfort, Cleanliness, and Convenience: The Social Organization of Normality* (Oxford: Berg 2003), 89.

CHAPTER 10: YOUR PRIVACY'S SHOWING: PORNOGRAPHY AT YOUR LOCAL LIBRARY

1. United States Census Bureau, *2007 Statistical Abstract: The National Databook*, http://www.census.gov/compendia/statab/information_communications/ internet_access_and_usage/ (accessed January 27, 2007).

2. Bill and Melinda Gates Foundation, *Toward Equality of Access: the Role of Public Libraries in Addressing the Digital Divide* (2004), http://www.gatesfoundation. org/ nr/ Downloads/libraries/uslibraries/reports/TowardEqualityofAccess.pdf. (accessed January 27, 2007).

3. New York Public Library, NYPL Policy on Public Use of the Internet, 2004, *http://www.nypl.org/pr/pubuse.cfm* (accessed January 27, 2007).

4. Florida State University, *Public Libraries and the Internet 2004: Survey Results and Findings*, 2004, http://www.ii.fsu.edu/projectFiles/plinternet/2004.plinternet.study. pdf (accessed January 27, 2007).

5. Joseph W. Slade, *Pornography in America: A Reference Handbook* (ABC-CLIO, 2000).

6. Al Cooper, Dana E. Putnam, et al., "Online Sexual Compulsivity: Getting Tangled in the Net," *Sexual Addiction and Compulsivity* 6 (1999): 79–104.

7. Michael W. Ross, "Typing, Doing and Being: Sexuality and the Internet," *Journal of Sex Research* 42, no. 4 (2005): 342–352.

8. William A. Fisher and Azy Barak, "Internet Pornography: A Social Psychological Perspective on Internet Sexuality," *Journal of Sex Research* 38, no. 4 (2001): 312–323.

9. David E. Smith, "How Safe Are Our Kids in Public Libraries? Chicago's CBS-2 Investigative Report." Illinois Family Institute, *http://www.illinoisfamily.org/news/* contentview.asp?c=33136 (accessed January 27, 2007).

10. Al Cooper, David L. Delmonico, et al., "Online Sexual Activity: An Examination of Potentially Problematic Behaviors," *Sexual Addiction and Compulsivity* 11 (2004): 129–143.

11. American Library Association, "Library Bill of Rights," 53.1, http://www. ala.org/ala/ourassociation/governingdocs/policymanual/intellectual.htm (accessed January 27, 2007).

12. Katrien Jacobs, "Pornography in Small Places and Other Spaces," *Cultural Studies* 18, no. 1 (2004): 67–83.

13. Mark S. Adams, Jessica Oye, et al., "Sexuality of Older Adults and the Internet: From Sex Education to Cybersex," *Sexual and Relationship Therapy* 13, no. 3 (2003): 405–415.

14. Sylvain C. Boies, Al Cooper, et al., "Variations in Internet-Related Problems and Psychosocial Functioning in Online Sexual Activities: Implications for Social and Sexual Development of Young Adults," *CyberPsychology and Behavior* 7, no. 2 (2004): 207–30.

15. American Library Association, 53.1.14.

16. Bill and Melinda Gates Foundation.

17. American Library Association, 52.4

18. Al Cooper, David L. Delmonico, 129–43.

19. George M. Eberhart, "Security Officers Overstep in Maryland Library Incident," *American Libraries* 37, no. 4 (2006): 12.

20. News Fronts, "Sex Offender Banned from Oregon Library," *American Libraries* 34, no. 10 (2003): 22.

21. Markkula Center for Applied Ethics, "Access, Internet and Public Libraries: A Report to Santa Clara Public Libraries," 1997, http://www.scu.edu/ethics/practicing/ focusareas/technology/libraryaccess/homepage.html (accessed January 27, 2007).

22. Wendy Adamson, "Sex in the City: What Happened at the Minneapolis Public Library," *Off Our Backs,* September–October 2003: 28–31.

23. Gary Dean, "Public Libraries, Pornography, and the Damage Done: A Case Study," *Library Administration and Management* 18, no. 1 (2004): 8–13.

Index

About the Editors and Contributors

THE EDITORS

Ann C. Hall is a professor of English at Ohio Dominican University. She has published several books including *A Kind of Alaska: Women in the Plays of O'Neill, Pinter, and Shepard,* and *Delights, Desires, and Dilemmas: Essays on Women in the Media* (editor), numerous articles on theatre, film, feminism, and pop culture. She is currently at work on a collection of short stories about Old Spice.

Mardia J. Bishop had presented and published on contemporary theatre, popular culture, the fabrication of the female body, and body image. She currently teaches theatre and communication courses at Shorter College and directs performance events in the Atlanta area. She holds a Ph.D. in theatre from The Ohio State University.

THE CONTRIBUTORS

Sue Banks holds a Masters of Library and Information Science from Kent State University. She has worked as a director, administrator, and reference librarian in public libraries across Ohio and Kentucky since 1997. She is a member of the American Library Association, the Public Libraries Association, and the Library Administration and Management Association.

Susann Cokal is the author of novels *Mirabilis* and *Breath and Bones,* as well as scholarly articles on authors such as Jeannete Winterson, Georges Bataille, and F. Scott Fitzgerald. She is an Assistant Professor of English and Creative Writing at Virginia Commonwealth University. She holds Ph.D.s from Berkeley and SUNY Binghamton.

Thomas Fahy is the Director of the American Studies Program and an Assistant Professor of English at Long Island University, C. W. Post. He has published eight books, including *Freak Shows and the Modern American Imagination* (2006), *Gabriel García Márquez's* Love in the Time of Cholera: *A Reader's Guide* (2003), a novel, *Night Visions* (2004), and several edited collections— *Considering David Chase* (2007), *Considering Alan Ball* (2006), *Considering Aaron Sorkin* (2005), *Captive Audience: Prison and Captivity in Contemporary Theater* (2003), and *Peering Behind the Curtain: Disability, Illness, and the Extraordinary Body in Contemporary Theater* (2002).

Hannah B. Harvey is an Assistant Professor of Performance Studies at Kennesaw State University. She recently earned her doctorate from The University of North Carolina at Chapel Hill, where her dissertation was directed by Dr. D. Soyini Madison. She is an award-winning actor and adaptor, and her research has been published in *Storytelling, Self, Society*. Hannah teaches courses in performance ethnography, oral traditions, and the adaptation and performance of literature. She is currently completing a book on the politics of Appalachian identity to be titled *Out of the Dark: A Performance Ethnography of Appalachian Coal Mining*.

Dawn Heinecken is an Associate Professor of Women's and Gender Studies at the University of Louisville and is the author of *The Warrior Women of Television: A Feminist Cultural Analysis of the New Female Body in Popular Media* (2004). Along with Vickie Rutledge Shields, she has co-authored *Measuring Up: How Advertising Affects Self-Image* (2002), which was awarded the 2004 National Communication Association's "Excellence in Visual Communication Research Award." She has published articles on such topics as Christian garage bands, professional wrestling, as well as *Buffy the Vampire Slayer*.

Jesse Kavadlo teaches English, humanities, and writing at Maryville University of St. Louis. He received his Ph.D. in English from Fordham University and is the author of *Don DeLillo: Balance at the Edge of Belief* (2004) as well as numerous essays about American fiction, popular culture, and pedagogy.

Katherine N. Kinnick is Director of the Pre-College Programs and Associate Professor of Communication at Kennesaw State University. She developed the Gender, Race, and Media course at KSU and is the author of numerous publications and presentations on topics related to media portrayals of women. She is the recipient of the University's Distinguished Teaching Award, was a Governor's Training Fellow, and served as president of the Georgia Communications Association. She holds a Ph.D. in Mass Communication from the University of Georgia.

Karen Robinson is an Associate Professor of Theatre and Performance Studies at Kennesaw State University. She is also an Associate Artist with the Georgia Shakespeare Festival and has directed numerous productions that range from Shakespeare and other classical authors to world premieres of new plays. She holds an MFA in directing from New York University.

Judith Roof is the author of five books, most recently *The Poetics of DNA* (Minnesota, 2007). She is a founding member of SteinSemble Performance Group.